VISCERAL BUKOWSKI
INSIDE THE SNIPER LANDSCAPE OF L.A. WRITERS

VISCERAL BUKOWSKI
INSIDE THE SNIPER LANDSCAPE OF L.A. WRITERS

BEN PLEASANTS

FOREWORD BY DIGBY DIEHL

2004 SUN DOG PRESS   NORTHVILLE, MICHIGAN

Visceral Bukowski
Inside the Sniper Landscape of L.A. Writers

Copyright © 2004 by Ben Pleasants

Foreword copyright © 2004 by Digby Diehl

Cover design by Grey Christian
Cover photograph copyright © 2004 by Lawrence Robbin

Designed by Judy Berlinski

Many of the photographs and art in this book appear courtesy of Ben Pleasants. Other art appears courtesy of the publisher.

All rights reserved. No part of this book may be reproduced in any form without written permission from the publisher, unless by reviewers who wish to quote brief passages.

The following material has previously been published:
  "Shoot Out At Scandia" (*L.A. MAG*)
  "Bukowski At The Races" (*Reader*)
  "When Bukowski Was a Nazi" & "How To Write a Short Story"
    (*Hollywood Investigator*)

Published by Sun Dog Press
22058 Cumberland Dr.
Northville, MI 48167
sundogpr@voyager.net

Library of Congress Cataloging-in-Publication Data
Pleasants, Ben, 1940-
   Visceral Bukowski : inside the sniper landscape of L.A. writers / Ben Pleasants ; foreword by Digby Diehl.— 1st ed.
      p. cm.
   Includes bibliographical references.
   ISBN 0-941543-38-2 (pbk. : alk. paper)
   1. Bukowski, Charles. 2. Authors, American—Homes and haunts—California—Los Angeles. 3. Pleasants, Ben, 1940—Friends and associates. 4. Authors, American—20th century—Biography. 5. Los Angeles (Calif.)—Intellectual life. 6. Los Angeles (Calif.)—Biography. 7. Beat generation—Biography—Biography. I. Title.

PS3552.U4Z78 2004
811'.54—dc22

2004056531

Manufactured in the United States of America   First Edition

*To Paula, my loving wife,
who brought me back from the dead.*

CONTENTS

ix	FOREWORD BY DIGBY DIEHL
xii	PREFACE
xvii	ACKNOWLEDGMENTS
19	Shoot Out At Scandia!
29	Walt Whitman and the Long Island Railroad
35	UCLA in the Sixties
40	Westwood @ Night: 1964-67
50	Night Shift @ The L.A. Times
57	Bukowski @ the Typer: 1967
64	Steve Richmond, Made of Lizard Skin
82	William "Baldy" Mullinax
95	Harold Mortenson: The Facts of Fiction
116	When Bukowski was a Nazi
140	LACC
146	Wormwood
154	A Day at the Races
160	William Wantling and the Meat School of Poetry
164	Friends
169	Andernach: 1977
187	Nights at the Post Office
200	Sharks & Vegetables
212	How to Write a Short Story
226	CODA

Bukowski on Carlton Way with Butch the cat.

FOREWORD
by Digby Diehl

Ben Pleasants and I both came to UCLA in the fall of 1964—he, two years out of Hofstra in New York; I, two years out of Rutgers in New Jersey. As young men who shared a passion for writing and the arts, we met through the campus newspaper's arts section, *Intro*. Established six years earlier, the weekly supplement was a remarkable hotbed of talent, which included writers Laurence Goldstein, Larry Dietz, Burt Prelutsky, Joel Siegel, Norman Hartweg, Harry Shearer, Lewis Segal, and artist Hank Hinton. Ben and I shared many parallels in our careers: we both were involved with UCLA campus publications that caused censorship scandals; we both wrote theater reviews as stringers for the *Los Angeles Times*; we both were energetic contributors to the *Los Angeles Free Press*; and, although our careers have diverged, we both have continued to write throughout our lives.

In this volume, Ben begins by evoking memories of Los Angeles in the 1960s with a vividness and joyous abandon that sweeps me back into an era I recall with considerable happiness. His descriptions of Westwood, the political energy, the libraries, the *Daily Bruin*, and the campus in general are wonderfully evocative, as are his delightfully candid memories of youthful love affairs. When we began as stringers for the *Times*, it was very much a writer's newspaper, and the freedom allowed even to young non-staff contributors was considerable. Under publisher Otis Chandler's watchful eye, the *Times* nurtured good writing, and some true giants of journalism—including Jack Smith, Jim Murray, Robert Kirsch, and Charles Champlin—taught by example in every edition.

Ben generously credits me with being the first book editor to run his reviews of Charles Bukowski, and I am sure he is correct, if only because I know that my predecessor and mentor at the *Times*, Robert Kirsch, disliked Bukowski's writing. What Ben may not have known until he read these words is that I shared Kirsch's view. My support of Ben and of his Bukowski reviews did not emerge from any liberal sentiments or spirit of friendship. They emerged from two precepts I developed early in my editorship. First, as I regularly read reviews from publications all over the country, I was appalled to see that then—as now—the great majority of book editors and book reviewers focused almost exclusively on that great mecca of book publishing, New York City. In those days, the *Los Angeles Times* was the most important journalistic voice of the West and I determined that its book section should be a voice for the literature of the West. It seemed only reasonable that local authors could expect a review (not necessarily a positive review) in their hometown newspaper. Second, I learned from some of my own *Times* editors—including Jim Bellows, Jean Sharley Taylor, and Charles Champlin—that an editor does not have to agree with all of his or her writers. An editor has to have confidence in a writer's ability to argue the merits of a point-of-view with skill and intelligence. I had confidence in Ben, and he never disappointed me.

This remarkable dual memoir does not disappoint either. The "Beverly Hills Anarchist" (Ben) and the "Dirty Old Man" (Buk) both come to life through a series of rambling conversations, comic adventures, and stories that are insightful and entertaining. Ben decided to be Bukowski's official biographer early in their friendship, and Bukowski opened up his life to Ben with typical raucous candor. With equal openness, Ben reports their long nights of smoking cigars, drinking and trading stories about writers for stories about women. Despite numerous comical refusals from Bukowski's ex-wives, old girlfriends, and former companions, Ben persisted in locating people who knew Buk in most phases of his life. Here is Ben's description: "…. Whenever he sent me to interview a friend it always ended up the same way—either he owed them money or he'd smashed up all their furniture or he'd peed on their sofa, or he slept with the wife or girlfriend." I was fascinated by Ben's techniques of interviewing people Bukowski had offended and by his tenacity in pursuing every possible biographical lead. The sexism, Nazism, the drunkenness, the cruelties—it is all here, unflinchingly described—but always with sympathy for the man. As their unlikely friendship unfolds in these pages, Ben is frank about why he is attracted to Buk's sense of freedom, his reckless audacity, his refusal to take the safe or easy route. You may be shocked or disgusted by some passages, but you definitely come away knowing Bukowski, in all his glory.

On the other hand, Ben has always had a professorial look, a gentlemanly manner that makes the radicalism of his thinking particularly amazing. He portrays himself in this book with the same forthright assessments as he portrays his biographical subject. Perhaps all biographers should be this open, because his admiration for Buk is infectious. In the end, Ben has done more than a Boswellian job. He has told the intertwined stories of two different men's lives effectively and engagingly. Moreover, he has made Bukowski and Bukowski's bizarre philosophy of life come alive so vividly that these revelations may illuminate the man's work. If, after finishing this book, each reader is prepared—as I am—to re-read Bukowski's work with a fresh understanding, then Ben, Buk's friend and literary biographer, has done his job well.

PREFACE

This is a memoir of two friends; Charles Bukowski and myself. We were close for more than twenty years, from 1965 to 1985, Bukowski's most creative period. During all those years we never argued, we never fought and we never attacked each other in print. Bukowski dubbed me his Beverly Hills Anarchist and that name stuck long after I had moved from Beverly Hills.

In the Seventies, I suggested becoming his biographer and Bukowski was enthusiastic.

As I began researching his life in the early Seventies, Bukowski explained "My existence has been pretty boring. I worked shit jobs and wrote when I wasn't working. Except for *Story Magazine*, all my works were published in little magazines, things no one of importance ever read. I fought with women, did time in jail, went to the races, got thrown out of crappy apartments, quit or was fired from a hundred jobs and drank. That's about it. I'll never win a Nobel Prize."

On the surface that was all true, but what was important was the level of reality he experienced and wrote about. And he made me promise, if I really wanted to tell his story, I should leave out nothing. Tell it all: the rotten childhood and his brutal father; his great love of all things German, including the Nazis; the friends along the way who one by one betrayed him; and all the women and jobs. He gave me a few leads. He called his ex-wife. She didn't want to talk. He gave me the phone number of an uncle in Palm Springs. When I called him, he said Bukowski owed him seven thousand dollars for his mother's medical bills.

We discussed his three best friends: Haddox, Mortenson and Mullinax. One was dead, one missing, one alive. In one way or another I got to all of them.

But what Bukowski told me about each of them was often completely at odds with what they said.

It wouldn't be easy. He thought he had an uncle in Andernach, the place in Germany where Bukowski was born. Uncle Heinrich Fett. I found him a year before Bukowski arrived in Europe, but much of what he told me, Bukowski didn't want in print.

And then there were the women from Jane Cooney Baker to the two Lindas and all the wreckage in-between. Over two decades, he introduced me to several and I got them down on tape, puttering around in the kitchen or seated on broken furniture in Bukowski's latest place of residence as we talked together about everything. Especially writers.

There were the ones he read and admired: Pound, Jeffers, Celine, Nietzsche, Schopenhauer, Richmond, Hamsun and John Fante. The Fante of *Ask the Dust*. The Fante who opened all the doors for him when he was still a teenager. John Fante, the novelist. I'd never heard of him. All his books were stolen from the downtown public library.

But Bukowski kept me on it till I found the real John Fante in the flesh and did an article for the *L.A. Times* that turned a corner for all three of us. Hours and hours of tapes you'll never hear, banned from public usage, banned forever by the Fante family. But that's another book. My next. The real John Fante at home, a blind man without legs who the world had flushed down the toilet. Bringing him back from that. Bukowski and I shared that together.

We sat together at John Fante's funeral in Malibu when his reputation had just begun to build in Europe.

Writers, writers, writers. Bukowski was even funnier on tape talking about the ones he hated. Scott Fitzgerald was too soft for him. He told me he never read *The Great Gatsby*. Thomas Mann was too boring. Too polished. He didn't have the short chapter snap of a John Fante. Steinbeck he thought was weak. There were the poets; the ones who lived off family money or the sweat and salaries of wives or lovers.

And then there were the jobs of his life.

All the early tapes came before *Ham on Rye* or *Women* or *Factotum*. There is a whole tape on jobs! A whole tape on women! A whole tape on childhood. Bukowski later thanked me for sticking with one subject at a time, forcing his thoughts and memories back to specific places he had happily forgotten. The method worked for both of us.

He could reel off the name of every job he ever worked at from his first employment in the railroad yards of Los Angeles through his final days at the post office. Everything.

He drove me around in his beat up blue VW, through the streets of his childhood, the racetracks of L.A., to the Olympic Auditorium for a prize fight. We must have gone to the races together fifty times or more. He said I was good company. I knew how to keep quiet. We'd talk in the car on the way in and on the way back; but the track was a place of business for Bukowski, where he used his skills with numbers and averages to beat the world of suckers.

We walked through the streets of his city, past boyhood memories, the library at LACC, the Grand Central Market, the steps where Arturo Bandini climbed out the window when he left Camilla on Bunker Hill. We drank in the bars on Alvarado, stopped at the house in Pasadena where his grandfather lived when Bukowski met him as a boy. He took me everywhere. His parent's last house in Temple City. An apartment near downtown where he lived with Jane. The place Baldy Mullinax recalled many years later. Everywhere but his parents' graves.

He gave me it all. I was a part of it. He wanted me to get it right. After all, I was the first writer to critically review Bukowski's books in the *L.A. Times*. Before Black Sparrow and City Lights! We later worked together at the *Free Press*. I championed his right to exist as a writer. He defended my right to publish on forbidden subjects.

Once, when I suggested in a poem that Palestinians were actually human beings with a legitimate right to be heard, Bukowski chided a coeditor at *Laugh Literary and Man the Humping Guns* for suppressing a poem I wrote on the subject. "If you can't get it into *Laugh Literary* when I'm an editor," he said "think how rough it will be in the real world, where the writing is printed on newsprint, not toilet paper." He bet me on the spot that I would never get anything printed in mainstream presses that said anything positive about Arabs. Many years later, I won the bet.

As a pair Bukowski and I were well matched emotionally: we were not exactly successful with women, had spent most of our lives struggling from paycheck to paycheck, were both able to laugh at ourselves, wrote with humor and powerful vulgarity, smoked and drank among the beautiful people, and attacked with fervor the synthetic truths of American television, American newspapers, American movies and American popular music.

Bukowski once called Hollywood "A hemorrhoid on the asshole of art."

But there was one problem for a Bukowski biographer, one big problem for a person like me who knew him well: the difference between fact and fiction. We talked about anyone and everything over shared bottles of whiskey, cigars and fatty sandwiches at the various apartments, parties, racetracks, restaurants and newspaper offices in L.A. As I got it down on tape, on the phone, in my journals and notebooks and in various letters, post cards, shirt cardboards and race programs, I found there were three levels of Bukowski truths.

One was what Bukowski told me. Another was what the people I interviewed said. The third was the way he used the people he knew in very autobiographical novels. There was the real Baldy Mullinax I met and interviewed. The Baldy in the novel *Ham on Rye* and in various stories and poems. And the Baldy I had on my notes before Bukowski wrote *Ham on Rye*. And then there was the argument between them when they were confronted with what each had said about the other. Three levels of truth.

The women in *Women* are even more of a problem. Bukowski gave me the entire Liza Williams suicide scene on tape before he wrote the novel. On page 54 he describes Liza as Dee Dee, a Jewish mare to Bukowski's German stallion for which he seeks forgiveness of the Fatherland. On page six he writes "This novel is a work of fiction and no character is intended to portray any person or combination of persons living or dead." That was a problem for me. Many years before writing *Women* Bukowski had described for me the exact events that occurred on page sixty-one, where Dee Dee takes pills and Chinaski pulls her false teeth out. The only problem with Bukowski's narrative on tape is the fact that Dee Dee is Liza Williams. This was true of Harold Mortenson, who he called Abe Mortenson in *Ham on Rye*.

I found Harold in 2002. We compared what Bukowski wrote to what really happened. Harold was mostly amused. He had dined at Bukowski's house several times. Met Bukowski's parents. Collided with Bukowski at a sand lot baseball game. "But the facts were all twisted," said Harold. "How did he get so full of hate?"

There is an advantage in knowing the subject you are writing about: you have the subject alive and glowing in his place in time. But for a writer like Charles Bukowski, who used almost everyone he ever knew as material for poems, stories, novels and plays, most of what he wrote as fiction is transfigured and transmogrified fact.

The characters in more than half of Bukowski's novels are real people, served up steaming hot with a vengeance from the author. Heinrich Fett, his German uncle, for instance, gave me an entirely different view of Bukowski's father. One Bukowski rejected out of hand, even when it was backed up by letters written back and forth between Henry Bukowski Senior, Katharina Fett Bukowski and Heinrich Fett. There are a hundred more examples.

All this was perplexing to me. The idea of a biography faded.

I decided to take the easy way out and write a memoir. That's what this is.

It's not balanced. It's not safe and restrained and reasonable and fair. It's the Bukowski I knew: Bukowski the writer, the man, Bukowski the clown and Bukowski the devil. It's what I heard and saw and recorded at a specific place in time.

It's *Visceral Bukowski*. Under the skin, confessional. Through my eyes without apologies. It's about: the women, the poets, the family, the friends and enemies who came and went through both our lives at that moment in time.

As for myself, in the Taoist sense, I am nothing at all. But before I bore you with my own little life and what led up to my first meeting with America's master poet Charles Bukowski, let me throw you head first into the madness and delight of a typical Bukowski session as we sat together in late night rooms and in freeway traffic in the non-Hollywood L.A., spitting into the eyes of God, two discarded gutter poets, watching the Sixties squeal to a halt. Some of it's funny, some of it's angry, some of it's sad, some of it's crazy; but it was real, all trapped on tape, the memoir of two friends sharing the ordinary moments of our only too ordinary lives.

—Ben Pleasants

ACKNOWLEDGMENTS

Major thanks to Al Berlinski, who fought for this book and made it happen. Huge thanks to Judy Berlinski, who is the most patient, thorough and intelligent editor I've ever worked with. Thanks also to Rodger Claire at *Los Angles Magazine*; Jim Davis, UCLA rare bookman; Rolf Degan in Andernach before Bukowski got there; Digby Diehl who created the *L.A. Times Book Review*; Dan Fante for his passion and courage; Lawrence Ferlinghetti for the many interviews; Larry Flynt for taking on the U.S. government; Charlotte Gusay for her love of poetry; Penny Grenoble as the witty editor of the *Free Press*; Ken Hyer, book detective; Neville Johnson for his legal genius; Jan Riddling, historian, the 100th Bomber Squadron; Samuel Edward Konkin III for composition of text; Bob and Marilyn Ladendorff for refuge; Marcy Mendelson for her sensual photography; Michael Montfort for a final look; Harold Mortenson for his memory and friendship; William "Baldy" Mullinax for his gentle humor; Jane Louie and Danielle for Grenoble; Steve Richmond for being Steve Richmond, the American Rimbaud; Lory Robbin for brilliant covers; Samantha Scully for keeping the light on; Frances Smith for her ferocity; Mark Sullivan for saving the negatives; Tom Thompson for taking on the system; James Vowell at the *Reader* for keeping his sense of humor; George Whitman at Shakespeare & Co. for killing the bed bugs; and Clay Wofford at Bleeding Hearts for keeping art alive.

Special thanks to Alexandra Pleasants Costa who lived it and survived, and the three Costa boys: Greg, Martin and Victor.

A special thanks to Joyce and John Fante who let me see what true creation is.

Lastly, to Charles, Marina and Linda Bukowski, I am profoundly grateful. I learned from Buk that "Fame is an elevator ride up the asshole of time." My line, not his.

"The drinks came in huge balloon glasses, one size smaller than a goldfish bowl. We drank to 'Charles Bukowski, poet.'"

Shoot Out At Scandia!

"He was bored, and he ordered the waiter to bring me another glass of red wine. That was his signal. That was my chance to dance on the table of death, juggling life's silverware. And I did just that."

It was a train ride at Scandia
with L.A.'s dark poet as the
drunken engineer, rolling glass by
glass toward oblivion . . .

One sugar-sticky hot afternoon, my phone rang. My apartment on Doheny had just been ransacked, and I was sifting through an armload of slashed cowboy shirts. I was in my Waylon Jennings period. Take my money and my great-grandfather's pocket watch (which they did), but don't mess with my western shirts.

Through my irritation came a taut, sexy voice. "Mr. Pleasants?"

"Yes."

"Mr. Ben Pleasants?"

"That's me."

"The man who writes less than factual articles about Charles Bukowski, our poet laureate of the street?"

"Well . . ." I felt my guard immediately go up, as it always did when Bukowski was involved.

"Just kidding," she laughed. It was one of those empty cine noir laughs, a slip on the trigger of a submachine gun. *Ha-ha-ha-ha*. I was cautious.

"I'm calling from Chrysalis Records. We're giving a little party for Mr. Bukowski—he made a poetry record for us."

She popped her gum four times. *Ping, pang, poom, poom.* "It's going to be at Scandia next Tuesday—you know, on Sunset. We'd like you to be there, Mr. Pleasants. Come to the office first."

She read me an address. I could hear Blondie booming her big single in the background: "CALL ME."

"Well, are you going to come?" she asked.

"Are *you*?"

I could envision her getting into James Dean's 1950 Mercury: tight black skirt, too much lipstick, hair swept into a blond ponytail. Like the girl in the Popov ad. Papa loves Popov.

"Count on it." With that, she let off four more blasts on her chewing gum—*ping, pang, poom, poom*—then hung up.

This was going to be sheer heaven, even without my western shirts. Just me and Blondie and a big-bucks record company dining at Scandia. For some reason, I'd forgotten about Bukowski and his retinue.

At noon on Tuesday, I drove up Doheny in my 1965 Cadillac. The shocks were sagging, the seat covers were cut in three places, and the muffler was hanging low. I reached into my pocket, got out my Bic lighter and torched a Muriel wood tip. I had the feeling history was going to be made that afternoon. I wasn't far off.

I found the record company in a high-rise just off Sunset. I drove into the cool vault of the underground garage and handed my keys to the valet. He gave my sagging Caddy the once-over. "A classic," I said before he could make a comment.

"*Si, mon. Pinche cabrón.*" I didn't tell him I knew what that meant. The elevator whisked me to the 10th floor. I looked around for the sexy voice from the telephone, but no one seemed to fit it. I was the first of the Bukowski party to arrive. How crazy that sounded. How long had it been since I'd picked him up drunk, with a wheel falling off his Volkswagen?

In a few minutes, Bukowski came into the office with his wife, Linda. "Ben," he said. He looked puzzled. We hadn't spoken for more than six months. His beard had been trimmed and his hair cropped. He had on a new suede jacket, black pants, an ill-fitting green shirt and no tie. He looked like a demented U-boat captain who had surfaced in a port like Philadelphia five years after the end of World War II. We shook hands. We smiled. Linda smiled.

A record exec in a $500 suit showed me the cover of Bukowski's new record. It was one of his automatic paintings done with an open tube of oil paint splattered on canvas, as though it were toothpaste. When I looked at it, I laughed, and then Bukowski laughed. And I was brought back into the spirit of who he was: a writer who took on life directly, trimming away the crud with a straight razor and a sense of humor.

Linda wore a low-cut dress that showed everything above the waist. Jesus, she sure took her vitamins. I tried not to look.

Bukowski posed for pictures. Then Linda and Bukowski both posed for pictures. *Click. Click. Click.* Everybody was given a record. The title was something like *Bukowski Reads Bukowski*. One of the execs said it was going to be a winner. "Better be," said the other. We followed them into the elevator, out of the building and across Sunset to Scandia. I forgot about the Popov girl with the sexy voice who popped her gum. I was back at my old job—literary investigator. Wasn't I the guy who relocated John Fante? And how about Kathryn Forbes, the author of *Mama's Bank Account*? True, she was dead when I got there.

We made our way up the little hill, a jaunty procession of Los Angeles notables—the two record execs, Bukowski and his wife, a reporter from a college paper, his photographer, a French translator of Bukowski's book, and me. The director Barbet Schroeder, who'd been friends with Bukowski when he was in Paris, would join us at the restaurant.

The maître d' ushered us in with dignity. Someone in a tux was playing Schubert on an apricot piano. The young reporter who entered without a jacket was tugged ceremoniously into a coatroom. He reentered in a gray cutaway that covered his torn Levi's.

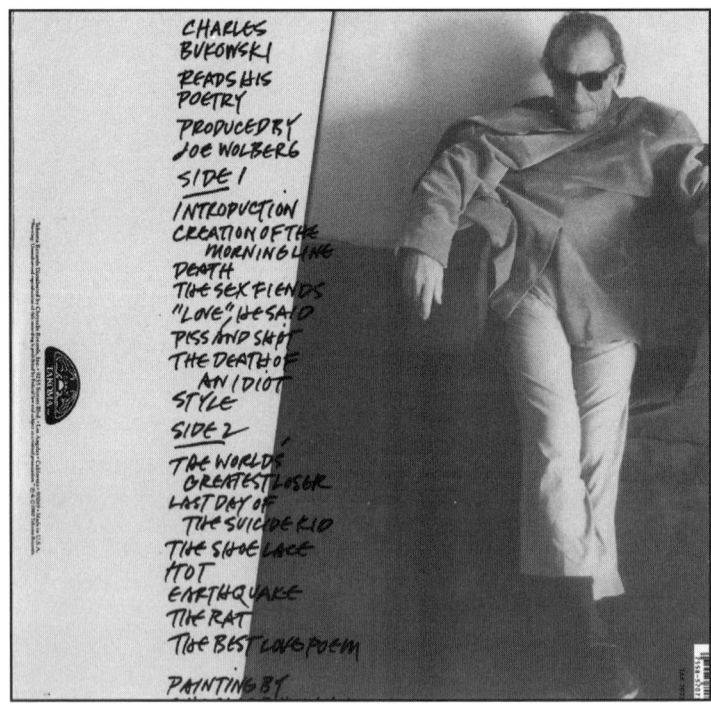

It was Scandia in the late '70s—the Jimmy Carter years. There was money in the air. We lined up at the bar. Everyone ordered everything: frappés, boilermakers, Xanadu flips. I had a Salty Dog. It was marvelous. The drinks came in great cubes of glass, flashing ice and whiskey. The glasses had heft to them. There was something very solid about the drinks at Scandia. The maître d' said our table would be ready in 10 minutes. No one was in a hurry. We were in one of the finest joints in the city.

We settled in with a little manly chatter about horses and literature—just nervous talk. Then Linda started in about Barbet. "When will Barbet get here? He's so much fun. When we were all in Paris, Barbet went around and set fires in all the trash cans in the Luxembourg Gardens. It was splendid. Wouldn't it be absolutely terrible if Barbet didn't show up? Wouldn't it be an absolute bore?"

Bukowski didn't seem to think so. Neither did the French translator. I just sipped my Salty Dog. They had the salt spread around the glass just right. I thought about old Barbet. Middle-aged Barbet. I'd met him twice before at Bukowski's place in San Pedro. He was dating Kathleen Tynan, the widow of noted British literary critic Kenneth Tynan. He'd come along after Bukowski's Hollywood years, after his life on Carlton Way in the shadow of the Time Motel, where they charged by the hour, where blue spiders crawled up the moon and Bukowski had done much of his best work.

Barbet was a French aristocrat polished from head to foot: big dogs, soccer scarves, floppy cable-stitched sweaters. He was tall and handsome and suave. He'd done that amusing film on Idi Amin and another on a talented gorilla.

He was a lot of fun. He once told me how he went about seducing French women. He liked them middle class and Catholic. He'd meet them right outside Notre Dame after confession and engage them in innocent conversation. Then he'd take them to a bar for a drink and get them home to bed before his girlfriend came back. But that was just the beginning. Sex was one thing, but the real test came when he showed them his diamond stickpin. Or was it a hat pin? This he

Left: From the album cover of Bukowski Reads His Poetry.

would plunge into the plumpest part of the young woman's breast until a teardrop of deep, red blood ran down her nipple onto her soft belly. If she was pregnant, that would be even more delicious, he said.

Yes, it really would be terrible if Barbet didn't show up.

The maître d' returned and showed us to our table. It was large and round, with a pure white linen cloth, huge silver implements and sparkling crystal. The luncheon was to begin with a toast. Bukowski ordered white wine. Linda ordered white wine. The two record execs ordered white wine. The college reporter and his photographer ordered white wine. I ordered a good Bordeaux. The drinks came in huge balloon glasses, one size smaller than a goldfish bowl. We drank to "Charles Bukowski, poet." When the glasses were drained, Bukowski pointed at me and warned the waiter, "Watch out for Ben when he drinks red wine."

It was a portent of things to come.

The waiter poured a second round—seven white and one red. Barbet was nowhere in sight. Bukowski and his French translator were having a few words—it was over his translation. Bukowski had been told it was no good. The slang was wrong. That's why he wasn't making as much money in France as he was in Germany. Barbet had told him.

There was that name again. A drop of red wine slid down onto my chin. The French translator whimpered like a puppy.

The meal came on flashing silver trays. Bukowski had the cracked crab. I had the veal. The execs had lamb or roast beef or shark. Linda had a salad. The French translator by this time was near tears. Course after course arrived in stylish pageantry: shrimp cocktail, cold soups, hot breads, little potatoes in gravy. The waiters marched about like picadors in the air-conditioned afternoon.

And then Barbet arrived. He was stone sober and dapper and powdered and cool, while each of us had consumed five balloon glasses of red or white wine. Thirty-five white and five red. Barbet was charming as usual—but he was sober and we were not. We were on a train ride, with Charles Bukowski as the drunken engineer, rolling glass by glass further toward oblivion. Barbet had gotten on at the last stop.

He saw immediately what was going on and ordered a quick white wine to catch up, but we were going 50 miles an hour and he had to start from a walk.

I was shouting about Vanessa Redgrave's right to make movies in America. Barbet didn't care for the topic. No one seemed to. Barbet and Bukowski had just finished a screenplay for *Barfly*. Barbet wanted to talk about that. I wanted to talk about Vanessa and the JDL, who had just blown up a theater down the block from me. The record execs wanted to talk about the record. The French translator wasn't talking.

When I used the word *bomb*, it brought raised eyebrows from every corner of the room. It was a subject as popular at Scandia as slum housing or sweatshops in East L.A. Still, I continued to present my opinion, to press Vanessa's case, until Bukowski ordered the waiter to cut off my supply.

"He's had enough," he said. *He* was one to talk—the man who once told me alcoholics rarely need Ex-Lax. After all those six-packs. And now, thanks to Linda, his fridge was filled with vitamins from A to zinc, and beet greens and carrot tops.

Barbet prevailed on the topic of the agenda and began to speak about "our film." They were in preproduction for "our film." The money was coming—the *big* money. (Though none of us knew it then, they would take eight more years to get *Barfly* off the ground.) It was the American film business. It killed Fitzgerald and a hundred others, but it was the big parade toward fame and fortune. We'd all heard it before, and it sounded stale even with a French accent. Besides, most of us were staggering around looking for the men's room.

When we returned, Barbet, with his charming grin, was still talking about "our film." Bukowski was becoming morose. He was bored, and he ordered the waiter to bring me another glass of red wine. That was his signal. That was my chance to dance on the table of death, juggling life's silverware. And I did just that. It was now past 4, and all the businessmen had left. I picked up a little boiled potato and flung it at one of the waiters. I tossed it like a grenade, so he didn't know where it was coming from. He looked at Bukowski, who by now was laughing. Then I accidentally smashed two wine glasses to bits, spilling the dark red burgundy all over the white linen cloth. Bukowski was disappointed. He wanted more.

"That's nothing, Ben. Anyone can smash a wineglass. Why don't you throw one at that painting?"

Bukowski pointed to a blue-and-white blur somewhere in the vicinity of the pastry cart. Now he was the demented U-boat captain again, giving orders to his men as he attacked the ports of Baltimore. I let fly with a half-filled glass of white wine, and it hit the painting smack in the middle with a shattering crash. For the first time in two years, I saw on Bukowski's face a look that approached enlightenment. He could have been the Buddha. He turned to Barbet.

"He missed it, right?"

"Direct hit," said Barbet. "Right in the middle."

With wine all over the place, I set out for the men's room. Before I reached the bar, someone had launched a chocolate mousse at the maître d'. There was raucous laughter and oaths in three languages. All we needed was an orchestra.

But when I returned from the men's room, the mood had changed entirely. The record execs were grim. The college reporter and his photographer had fled. Barbet was no longer smiling, and Bukowski wasn't laughing. Linda sat between the two, and her face was strained. Bukowski was talking about Barbet and Linda. It was hard talk. The-man-who-took-my-woman talk. I'd heard it before with the other Linda—Linda King, Bukowski's old girlfriend. The staff was cleaning the chocolate mousse off the wall, and the waiter was washing paprika off his collar. Now everyone in the room was serious except me. The translator had found his moment and was cursing and shouting at Barbet in French. A waiter was cursing in Spanish. I was busy eating my cantaloupe, happy as a clam.

The Barbet-Bukowski discourse continued unabated. "I didn't like the way you hugged her in the living room," Bukowski said. Good old Barbet—the man who would capture the essentials of Claus Von Bulow on film. Nominated for an Academy Award. And yet, to me he will always be the man who sticks diamond stickpins or hat pins into the breasts of plump young Catholic matrons.

Finally, to the relief of the two execs and the entire restaurant staff, we found ourselves outside in the bright Los Angeles sun, squinting as though it were Algiers. We tried to negotiate the subtle downslope of Sunset as it plunged toward the Beverly Hills line, but it wasn't easy. Barbet did a matador's dance, flicking his blazer at a red sports car. I had seen this done one night in Nice with tragic results both for the matador and the sports car, but this time the driver pulled to a stop and put a wrist on her horn. Only fraternity studs performed stunts like that in broad daylight, but the problem was Barbet was still stone sober. He was out of sync.

When I reached the other side of the street, I was in a festive mood. I decided to hitch a ride on a mail cart that was passing by at the time. I rode it halfway down the hill, ending up in a pile of manila envelopes. Someone pulled me to my feet—aided by my tie—and cursed me out very rapidly in a Slavic tongue. "Ben gets crazy when he's like this," Bukowski howled. He seemed genuinely concerned. "Somebody better take him home."

I'd done the same for him many times. But in the lateness of the afternoon, the record execs had added up the tab, and they'd had enough.

"Ben's okay," said one of them. "He'll find his way home fine. Alone."

Alone—the word rang in my head, as an elevator shot the load of them out of the record-company-building lobby into the skies of Beverly Hills: Linda, Bukowski, Barbet and the two execs. I don't know where the translator had gone. Probably back to France.

I went in the opposite direction, plunging into the Hades of the subgarage, where I wandered about looking for my Cadillac. I never found it, thank God, slipping on pools of oil, falling and wounding my knee. To this day, I don't know how I reached the outside world. When I got home to the slashed cowboy shirts, I fell into an unmade bed and slept for two days.

A week later, I saw Bukowski at Santa Anita. He looked much better. He was alone with his program, doping the horses. He thanked me for my Scandia performance, then went to place a bet. I was happy for him. He had Linda, and he had Barbet. He had Hollywood—the real Hollywood, not the Time Motel. He didn't need me any more.

Six months later, I was invited to a Sunday brunch at Scandia. The maître d' remembered me. He was cordial. "You're the writer, Ben Pleasants?"

"Yes. You remember that day?"

"It still brings a smile," he said. I looked for the waiter I hit with the boiled potato, but he was not there.

"He's off today," the maître d' said, anticipating. I sat with my middle-class friends as the sun flooded in from the garden. I ordered champagne and strawberries. When the waiter brought the large glass, he said quietly, "I think you should only have one, sir."

I agreed. The "sir" was a nice touch.

Besides, it was a quiet Sunday, and Charles Bukowski wasn't there.

Walt Whitman and The Long Island Railroad

I've always believed fate decides a writer's destiny, but often in a comic way. For me, growing up on Long Island in the 1950s, deliverance arrived in the form of a Long Island Railroad express train headed for Riverhead on October 5, 1962. The newspaper accounts differ slightly, but they would agree with Walt Whitman when he said:

"One is never entirely without the instinct of looking around."

Long Island Press, October 6, 1962:

Youth Risks Life To Save Dog

Arthur Pleasants is a dog lover. He proved that yesterday when he gambled with his life to save a stray dog. Suffolk police gave this account:

Arthur, 22, of 150 Secatogue Avenue, Farmingdale, was near the Long Island Railroad tracks on Pineaire Drive, Brentwood, about 3:25 p.m. when he saw a dog scamper between the rails. In the distance, Arthur heard the sound of a train whistle. It was an eastbound train that had just left the Brentwood station. He ran to the tracks, grabbed the dog and dashed off, but not before the train brushed him and threw him to the siding.

Arthur suffered a broken arm and possible internal injuries. He is reported in satisfactory condition today at Southside Hospital,

Bay Shore. Police say the dog scampered off in the excitement and could not be found.

Newsday, with a circulation of more than one million readers, was more to the point:

Saves Dog But Not Self

Edgewood—A Brentwood Junior High School teacher suffered a broken right arm when struck by a train near the Pineaire station of the Long Island Rail Road yesterday afternoon. And all for a dog.

The instructor, Arthur Pleasants, 22, of 150 Secatogue Avenue, Farmingdale, was waiting for a westbound train at the station at 5:25 p.m. when he saw the dog wandering on the eastbound track unaware of an oncoming train. He successfully shooed the animal but was unable to jump entirely clear himself. The train was going an estimated 50 MPH at the time. Pleasants, married and father-to-be, was in satisfactory condition at Southside Hospital, Bay Shore.

Later, the ASPCA awarded me their Medal of Honor, the only real medal I ever received.

I'd been reading Walt Whitman's "Oh Pioneers" that day. After missing my train, I walked along the railroad tracks looking westward, tired of the comfortable suburban flatland that stretched from Montauk and Orient Points to Queens. I wanted high mountains and rushing rivers. I wanted the West.

A few years ago I wrote the following about my life on Long Island in the 1950s and what lay ahead for me there if I'd remained:

Long Island flops about in the mid-Atlantic region between the Great South Bay and the Long Island Sound like a giant flounder swimming haplessly into the miasma of midtown Manhattan. Or it could be described as a giant bottle with New York City as the cork.

What residents refer to as The Island does not include the fish face of Brooklyn and Queens, but only the flatland torso and legs that stretch from Glen Cove and the Rockaways eastward, trailing spits of sand on both shores into the choppy surf as far as Montauk and Orient Points.

Technically, the two legs of the fish make The Island somewhat of a Darwinian cross between a land mammal and a cold-blooded aquatic creature, rather a mermaid in reverse, with a fish head at one end and two very proper legs at the other. If you include Shelter Island between the two legs, The Island takes on a masculine aspect. I fully expect one day to see those shapely legs plant themselves deep in the Atlantic Ocean and rise up to their full height of one hundred ten miles, knocking over the Statue of Liberty and snapping the Brooklyn Bridge forever from Manhattan.

But to the residents of Long Island those two struts of land, filled with fishermen and farmers on the northern end, and writers, dress designers, painters, bankers, and film stars on the southern, loom like distant castles cut off by a drawbridge of wealth or time, ever beyond the reach of the struggling middle class.

Mythical figures lived out there like P.G. Wodehouse and Fairfield Porter and Jackson Pollock and John Steinbeck! Commuter trains don't reach that far into dreamland. No. The Island I refer to is that endless flatland where small houses and little towns crowd together into one another linked only by a conveyor belt to Manhattan called The Long Island Railroad, a sordid little toy train that carries bleary-eyed residents from their beds to their desks five days a week until illness or death intervene.

In my worst nightmares names of those treadmill towns haunted my sleep: Hicksville, Bethpage, Garden City, Hempstead, Islip, Patchogue, Plainview, Seaford, and Levittown. This is the land of Amy Fisher and Joey Buttafucco, where love springs eternal in the body shop of life and the high point of land, Mays Hill, is forty feet above sea level. Long Islanders live out their lives caught between the Atlantic Ocean to the East and Manhattan to the West. They live and die there and never go anywhere, chasing dirty little trains on weekdays and smoking lawn mowers on weekends, cut off forever from the mighty mountains of Colorado and the canyons of Arizona.

My greatest dread as a child was to be condemned forever to the flatland treadmill of the Long Island Railroad. But Walt Whitman intervened."

All my life, when things were going badly, I would always be saved by poets, by poetry.

My pocket paperback Whitman was hit dead on by the train and ground to mulch, but poetry—especially his poetry and what little I had written of my own—was what I longed to write. Even though I knew a poet on his own, without an academy to pay the way, would struggle with poverty and madness like Hart Crane, I was drawn to it like a drunk to cheap wine.

The Long Island Railroad had told me something that day: Life is short; live it! Don't throw it away riding the 6:15 from Manhassett or New Haven or Montclair; seek out the high mountains and the rushing rivers I read of in Whitman and John Muir; leave behind the flatland of Long Island. The Long Island Railroad, striking my right arm at 50 MPH, had given me an epiphany on that day in October, a great burst of light. That's what a poet needs—the direct interference of the gods. It was not the last time that would happen to me.

So, in July of 1963, after finishing my first year of teaching, I moved to San Diego with my young wife, Pamela, and my infant daughter, Alexandra. The mountains weren't so high and the rivers were dry, but the bluffs of La Jolla, where the Pacific Ocean crashed into caves filled with seals and pelicans, made me feel free to write poems and read the new poets as they came to my work station at the circulation desk of the University of California San Diego Library.

The University of California San Diego in 1963 consisted of two large buildings and a master plan. Set on a bluff above La Jolla and the Pacific, in less than a decade UCSD would grow from a few hundred students to 25,000. Already the faculty included two Nobel Prize winners, including Harold Urey, the brilliant chemist who isolated heavy water and discovered deuterium. His son, Eric, a graduate student at Scripps, worked with me in the library at the circulation desk. Most of our staff, male and female, were married.

My wife, daughter, and I lived in a snug one-bedroom apartment in Mission Beach, a twenty blocks long and four blocks wide community, divided by Mission Bay on the East and the Pacific Ocean on the West. During the week my hours were from 2:00 p.m. to 10:00 p.m., allowing me time to write poems and walk on the beach in the morning. The rest of the day I sat at the circulation desk, checking out books and talking with staff and students; or when there was an overload I sat in the back room with paint brush and paste bottle, processing and labeling new acquisitions.

The library was building for the future, and its budget seemed unlimited. Along with massive mountains of technical journals like *Acta Mathematica* and *Polaski Physcii*, there arrived Black Sun editions of James Joyce, rare volumes of William Blake's poems with etchings, bound leather sets of *Punch*, rare Hebrew Bibles and texts, Chinese literature with ivory clasps and all the modern poetry books and journals I could read.

At night, when students vanished into the rising sea fog and I was left by myself, I'd study the latest poetry of Robert Creeley or read Cid Corman's magazine *Origin* with its wondrous Japanese illustrations or leaf through the latest eccentricities from the avant-garde. That's where I first saw *The Outsider* published in New Orleans by *Loujon Press*. I remember clearly the day I discovered Charles Bukowski's lush volume *It Catches My Heart In Its Hands*, published by *Loujon* in a letterpress edition, bound in boards, and divided in sections by colored tissue paper. I pointed out to my friend, Wayne Rouse, who worked nights and was studying Russian, that great poets like Robert Frost or Richard Wilbur would probably never have a publication of their work in so fine an edition; and here was an unknown poet with limited talent who wrote complaints about his stomach, and the editors were bragging that the paper would last a thousand years. "And," I pointed out, "he wrote about Los Angeles." San Diegans spoke of Los Angeles the way New Yorkers mentioned New Jersey.

From The Outsider, issue 3, 1962.

A few months later I found myself accompanying the library truck driver, a guy who started his mornings with malt liquor, on a delivery run to UCLA. The librarian's secretary, Alvina Robertson, asked me to go along just to make sure he made it. It was a rough trip on a cloudy day, and the load of books in the back of the truck shifted several times. After unpacking our load at the University Research Library and watching the driver knock back two more malt liquors, I bailed out right in the middle of the UCLA campus and fate intervened again.

Here was a real university with thousands of students all walking about in purposeful disarray. They were arguing about art and politics and sex. They seemed happy. I had been out of college only two years with a B.A. in English from Hofstra. I longed to return and before I found my way downtown to catch the return Greyhound to San Diego I picked up entrance applications for myself and my wife.

Two months later we were both accepted: me as a graduate student in English and my wife as an undergraduate in music. We'd lived in San Diego for only a year, just long enough to adjust to the climate. I never looked back.

UCLA in the Sixties

Ghosts of UCLA

From the cover of Reader, 1981.

"When the little known bird of the inner ear, memory, begins to act up, I am troubled by what Edmund Husserl called the phenomenology of internal time consciousness, defined more specifically by me as ghosts."

UCLA in the fall of 1964 was a land of ghosts. There was the ghost of JFK, assassinated ten months before under circumstances that left the entire academic world suspicious about government and the military. There was the ghost of Arnold Schoenberg, who died in 1951, after teaching music theory and composition at UCLA for more than a decade. His name graced the ugliest building on campus, Schoenberg Hall, where my wife Pamela was taking classes in voice and music composition. Atonal Arnold. Schoenberg the scholar, largely self-taught. At night you could almost hear his crazy, sad "Gurrelieder," written for choral voices, ten horns, and iron chains straining through the high towers of Royce Hall and the College Library, clanking against the flagstaff in the center of the quad as the wind still blew the smell of jasmine through the warm night air. I once saw Rudolph Carnap, a living ghost, professor emeritus of philosophy at UCLA and author of *The Logical Syntax of Language*,

35

striding into the College Library at night, looking for a book in German. The reference librarian treated him with the respect one might give Thomas Mann; they might have been neighbors in the Palisades.

If UCLA was an island of serene ghosts in 1964, the city of Los Angeles was not. Unemployment was high, police violence and racial tension filled the newspapers, and the air was unbreathable. What you drove was what you were. In September of 1964 the 1957 Olds '88 I bought for $300 was giving out and I needed a job. We took a one-bedroom at 948 Fourteenth Street, Apartment G, in Santa Monica and counted our pennies. I tried the California Department of Employment in Santa Monica, but they told me on September 5th that the only position I was qualified for at night was a bellhop's job. "This is no San Diego," I wrote in my journal. "This is a mean motherfucker of a city." Even with a full load of classes in grad school, I knew I'd have to work forty hours a week at night to pay the rent.

But if the city of Los Angeles was cold and hard and racist, UCLA was not. My wife, Pamela, took her music classes in the morning, leaving me time for reading and caring for my daughter, Alexandra, who was one. All I cared about was poetry and literature; if only I could find a job doing what I loved.

Again, the fates intervened. On September 17th Jim Davis, head reference librarian at the College Library, hired me as a reference assistant. My hours were from 5:00 to 10:00 p.m., five days a week and eight hours on weekends. Two of the librarians, Sylvia Mortimer and Karen Augerson, both young, vivacious, and intelligent women, taught me the reference collection in a few weeks. On breaks upstairs in the reserve book room I was thrown in with a whole new set of friends: Blacks, Hispanics, Greeks, Koreans, Jews, Armenians, Japanese, South Africans, Tunisians, French—everything.

In early September I saw an ad in *The Daily Bruin*: "Writers wanted for Intro Section to write about poetry." I took up the challenge and pounded out a piece on modern poetry attacking the influence of Walt Whitman, defending Emily Dickinson as our greatest poet. The article was titled: "A Time for Carving." It appeared on September 30th and stirred up quite a noise.

The article prompted several replies on October 7th, the next week, including a long letter from a T.A. in the English department named Michael Gregory. It was titled: "Carving Mr. Pleasants," and in it Gregory criticized my attack on Whitman, claiming: ". . . a floundering masterpiece—even a masterful failure—is worth more poetically than the most exquisite and well-turned miniature. Emily Dickinson, sweet lady that she was, could not rank with Dante, Pound, Whitman . . ."

To my amazement, several of my professors and many of the women in my English classes took my view. I had no idea why. Professor Dembo, my advisor, and author of *The Sanscrit Charge*, a book on Hart Crane, suggested I should answer Mr. Gregory. When I returned to the *Daily Bruin* office with a response to Gregory's letter, Larry Goldstein, the intro editor, was delighted. "I never thought poetry could be so controversial." My reply was hard and wounding; it shut him up and ended the controversy, but it brought me full force into the most important revolution going on in the sixties—the Sexual Revolution.

Gregory wrote me a note and asked if I'd meet him at his office. I got there an hour late and knocked on the door, which seemed to be stuck. I forced it open; on the desk was a redheaded graduate with her dress up and panties down, with a T.A. on top, enjoying an afternoon repast. It was not Michael Gregory. I backed out of the room before the T.A. could turn around, but the woman saw me and smiled.

I discussed what I'd seen with one of my friends at the College Library. He said the T.A. was just doing what he'd learned from his mentors; he mentioned one particular professor who was famous for his many seductions. He told me his specialty was neoclassicism. "It's all around you," he said. "You just need to look for it. Sex!"

After a few months my wife grew worried about our finances and dropped out of UCLA. She took a job in a bank in Santa Monica, and we hired a baby sitter to take care of my daughter when neither of us could be at home. Strains were beginning to show in our marriage. I went to parties with my friends from the College Library, and I was invited to sit on the board of *Westwind*, the UCLA literary magazine. The editor, Linda Wetherbee, was organizing a poetry reading of *Westwind* poets, myself included, for November 18, 1964. At the last minute she told me she had a cold and asked me to MC. "You're Mr. Poetry around here."

That event completely changed my life.

It was advertised in the *Daily Bruin* on that Wednesday in the following manner:

> WESTWIND
>
> Meeting at 2 p.m. in SU Women's Lounge. Westwind poetry reading. Jazz and coffee for all interested persons.

Copies of the magazine would go on sale for fifty cents each.

I was nervous and I banged the microphone. I'd never been in the women's lounge in the student union before, but the jazz musicians were set to go and there was fairly decent coffee. Larry Goldstein read his prize-winning poem, "Night at Sodom." There was partisan applause. The musicians, especially the sax player, were really getting into it. I introduced Melody Brennon who read her poem, "To H.B." It was sensual and sexual. The sax player loved it. Then I introduced a poet named Steve Richmond who was finishing up his last year in law school. The poem used black dialect the way writers like Octavus Roy Cohen did, including the words "mother fucker." He was not wildly applauded and one old woman called his work "blatantly racist."

I looked around for the woman who had written sensual Sappho-like elegies. I read her name, but she did not appear. Then I read my poem, "The Boys Who Make The Noise," delighting in the way the sax player followed my lines.

After the final poet read, a coughing Linda Wetherbee stood up and thanked the audience to great applause. I was glad it was over and I put down the mike, but then a skinny, short-haired fellow in the back of the room stood up and asked if he could read his poems. I gave him the mike. He read two poems copied onto notepaper in blue ballpoint. The sax tried to follow him but he read too softly, and the poems didn't seem to make much sense. Later, I found out from Steve Richmond, it was Jim Morrison, founder of The Doors. The next time I saw him he was performing on the Sunset Strip.

As we were having our coffee, selling copies of *Westwind*, Linda Wetherbee informed us that the current issue had been seized by the UCLA administration. I couldn't believe it. I thought that only happened in countries like Spain under Franco or the USSR under Stalin, not at UCLA under Franklin Murphy.

I asked Wetherbee to explain their action:

"Richmond's poem. They didn't like his 'mother fucker' line."

So we were in the vanguard of what became the free speech movement; we were just a little ahead of our time. By 1965, politically, UCLA had come alive. Draft boards were knocking on the door of the university, and the students answered with teach-ins, protests, and sit-ins. That summer the city exploded into rioting following a disturbance in Watts. On campus, students were radicalized: Frank Zappa switched from classical music to rock; Jim Morrison moved over to the Sunset Strip; Francis Ford Coppola had taken the Goldwyn Prize at UCLA and was out writing scripts; and Steve Richmond opened a book store in Santa Monica for underground poets. A colleague who worked in the College Library as a guard told me to look up a friend he knew at the *L.A. Times*. He was Meyer Rosen. "He'll make you a copy boy," he told me. "At night."

Westwood @ Night: 1964-67

Cover from the Westwind *publication removed by administration officials.*

When the winter '64 issue of *Westwind* with the erotic Greek cover was seized by the administration, not a single professor raised a pinky to question the action; none of them came to our defense. It made me question what I was doing in academia, but the next day I did meet the girl who wrote those short poems that sounded so much like Sappho or Martial. With medium-length black hair and whiskey brown eyes, tall and full-bodied, she looked like Anouk Aimee, only younger and more beautiful.

Early in November I began an ambitious two-part series on contemporary poets I admired called "Healing Songs: Poets of the sixties." The three poets I praised were Charles Reznikoff, an Objectivist, famous for his volume *By The Waters of Manhattan*; William Stafford's haunting work *Traveling Through The Dark*; and my personal favorite, Galway Kinnell's *What A Kingdom It Was*.

I was living for poetry: to read it, to write it, to write about it. I hardly went to class, between babysitting, working, parties, and writing articles.

By the end of the term my marriage was falling apart, and most of my classes were running incompletes. My wife was entertaining the next-door neighbor, a British gentleman who stayed at home while his wife worked at the nearby country club. My advisor, Lawrence Dembo, and my friends in the College Library advised me to "wash out the semester. Don't let your grades go to F's."

I followed their advice, added twelve more hours to my workweek, shelving books at the Santa Monica Library and prepared for the worst.

Instead, a funny thing happened. First I received two letters from Galway Kinnell thanking me for my review; and then I fell in love. With Anouk Aimee.

Later in the spring term, she came running up to me in the quad. "He's here. Today. Galway Kinnell. Reading in the Humanities building this afternoon. I heard it in my French class. Just thought you'd like to know." She smiled the way Anouk Aimee would smile a year or two later in her greatest film, *A Man And A Woman*.

On a Friday afternoon, we went together to hear the poet Galway Kinnell, almost holding hands. The reading had been arranged by the chair of the UCLA French department to celebrate Kinnell's translation of the poetry of Francois Villon by New American Library.

Tall, youthful, intelligent and energetic, in a starched white shirt and blue tie, with piercing eyes, straight hair, broad shoulders and a thin smile, he was everything Charles Bukowski despised in a poet. After an introduction by the chair of the French department, Kinnell asked the five hundred people seated in Humanities 1200 one question: "I wonder if anyone out there knows a man by the name of Ben Pleasants?" I stood up and waved. Anouk Aimee took my hand. And then he read, brilliantly, with great passion and feeling to prolonged applause. He was modest and sensitive and gentle—a humanist, my idea of what a poet should be in 1965.

When the reading was finished I was invited to the reception to meet the poet. After the professors had paid their respects and Anouk Aimee had returned to her dorm, Kinnell took me aside and we spoke for a few minutes. He told me he was constantly traveling, city to city, university to university. He said it was hard on him and hard on his wife. Up close he looked tired, frazzled, the stubble of a beard already forming on his chin. I asked him about his poem, "For William Carlos Williams," in which he wrote, "You hung around inside the rimmed / Circles of your heavy glasses and smiled and / So passed a lonely evening." I'd printed the poem in its entirety in my article. It was one of my personal favorites. Kinnell laughed and said it was true for Williams and it was true for him. If I wanted to be a poet and survive, that's what I had to look forward to. He asked if I could put him up for the evening; I told him I was having trouble at home. He understood.

Years later, when we met in New York, Kinnell recalled the reading at UCLA and mentioned his translation of Villon which, he said, had passed before the public almost unnoticed. He spoke with a sense of irony, without sadness or anger or bitterness, as a Spaniard might speak, with stoicism.

After the Kinnell reading Anouk Aimee became my close friend. We had coffee together several times a week, and I walked her home through the night-blooming jasmine almost every evening. She told me a little about her "dates." She hinted, and I could see it in her poetry, that she was sexually active. I made no effort to tell her I was married. By then the wife of the British gentleman had found out about her husband's indiscretions. We moved to Westwood—Veteran Avenue just South of Montana. It was a short walk to UCLA.

My wife was now working at Rand Corporation. My daughter was in a preschool. I should have felt guilty, but I didn't.

I was in love with Anouk Aimee; I always will be.

She borrowed my Keats, the Oxford edition with scribbled notes from high school. Then I lent her my library card so she could use the URL. Only grad students could get in there at the time. She worked nearby at Franz Hall in the Ed. Psych Library, so I got in the habit of walking her back to Reiber Hall where she lived with a roommate. On the nights she didn't work, I'd phone her from the desk at Reiber, and she'd come down from her room on the third floor. The roommate, wise beyond her years, was always looking out for her; she was tough and protective and cautious about the men who pursued her best friend. She knew she was brilliant and radiantly beautiful. She knew she was Anouk Aimee!

We held hands a few times and I kissed her on the cheek like a sister, but she gave me no reason to go further. We spoke mostly about

Healing Songs: Poets of the Sixties

by Ben Pleasants

PART ONE

Israel is like a bird
That a creeping weasel has wounded in the head
Or a man knocked against a wall—
The cattle have trampled it
But it still flutters.

—Charles Reznikoff

For a long time Europe bled—bled like Israel—and the wounds were very open, and the crying was in public. The aristocracy at the turn of the century crouched like some crumpled hat on a scattered bed of nightmares, under a winter of howling sirens and oncoming war; and all that came and all that passed. It was a fulfillment of the dream of mass production, mass education, mass duende; the end of the prophecy of Oswald Spengler. But as the Greek in Alexandria, Constantino Cavafy, remarked,

"It is night and the barbarians have not come. And some men have arrived from the frontiers And they say there are no barbarians any longer."

And indeed, here in this decade the heavy snows of Spengler's winter have not fallen, art and exerpession have not perished, and because, or in spite of, impending atomic disasters some peoples of the world have begun to shoulder their burdens of responsibility to the poor, the uneducated, the overworked, and the sick. The sun shines over Yevtushenkov's Siberian taiga for the first time ever. Great cities rise from the tin-shack towns of Africa, plannned and built by the black man's hand. China feeds her millions without Russian help. These are not fearful signs, nor do they indicate the superiority of one system over the other; they merely indicate that the world is growing up, solving its own problems, bit by bit, nation by nation. Why then should the art of our civilization point toward the last gasp of a humanity that is not dying?

In Europe the bleeding has stopped but the crying continues. "Where were the French in 1936 and 1937 when Spain was breathing its bloody last?" asks Sarte in his Troubled Sleep. "Where was the Pope, Pius the XII, when Facism set its plague upon the house of Israel," writes Rolf Hochhuth in The Deputy, and "Isn't this all a joke?" chortles that Irishman who lives in France in Waiting for Godot. "This is madness," states Artaud. "This is life, we'll flee together through the hole in the bathroom wall," says Natalie Sarrute in Portrait of a Man Unknown, "This is beautiful," laughs Genet.

Sure the English who don't fight much anyway, or not until their time comes, hitch their garters high enough to do battle with the Buttery Book, the factory owner's wife, and Mrs. Grundy's daughter. but the rest of Europe, like some ball-less bull cries out for her loss of love and feeling.

Why pretend that we have suffered what they have suffered? American poets are tired of crying tears that are not their own, and are fed up with laughter that springs from affectation rather than feeling. If Karl Shapiro wants to tell us about his war experiences, we don't want to listen, and if Kenneth Rexroth wants to babble on about the plight of all great poets in the modern world, we could care less. Leave the slush for pay T.V. We're tired of freaks and clusters of college poets — we're looking for mountains with snow on them.

GALWAY KINNELL

"I can support it no longer.
Laughing ruefully at myself
For all I claim to have suffered
I get up. Damned nightmarer!
It is New Hampshire out there,
It is nearly the dawn.
The song of the whippoorwill stops
And the dimension of depth seizes everything."

Galway Kinnell has published two volumes of very fine American poetry. The first, What A Kingdom It Was, Houghton, Mifflin Press, $3.75 (83 pp.) caused a mild stir when it appeared in 1960 and the book is still in print. The second, Flower Herding on Mount Monadnock, same publisher,

GALWAY KINNELL
Away from European Sickness, Into Self

$3.00 (58 pp.) made its appearance this year and caused almost no stir at all. Kinnell, a teacher by profession, but by no means academic in his poetry, sets forth a zesty work of sharp phrases and fresh images — a happy blending of common sense and control, the result of a deliberate and ordered life. Although his poems bite and damn at times, they are tightly hatched and affirmative. His shorter poems often pounce on the living dead men of our time, but more by way of pathos than by sardony.

"In a parlor containing a table
And three chairs, three men confided
Their inmost thoughts to one another.
I, said the first, am miserable.
I am miserable, the second said.

I think that for me the correct word
Is miserable, asserted the third.
Well, they said at last, It's quarter to two.
Good night. Cheer up. Sleep well.
You too. You too. You too."

Although today he mocks today's frauds "with equal strength and fine impartiality" it is the quiet mocking of subtlety, and therefore renders itself well to effect the difficult task of satire.

For William Carlos Williams

"When you came and you talked and you read with your
Private zest from the varicose marble
Of the podium, the lovers of literature
Paid you the tribute of their almost total
Inattention, although someone when you spoke of a pig
Did squirm, and it is only fair to report another giggled. But you didn't even care. You seemed
Above remarking we were not your friends.
You hung around inside the rimmed
Circles of your heavy glasses and smiled and
So passed a lonely evening."

None of Galway Kinnell's shorter poems is especially brilliant, although they seem new and imaginative. Where he excels, and where he is most needed, is in the longer, more sustained poems — 100 lines plus — those works which American poets since Rexroth (The Phoenix and The Tortoise) have consistently failed to produce. "The Avenue Bearing the Initial of Christ Into the New World," a poem concerned with the sounds of Avenue C in New York City, is probably as good a poem as anything written since Hart Crane's The Bridge, and a much more useful bit of work than that masterpiece. Kinnell captures the life blood of slum New York, it sighsand sounds and ghettoed romance, its constant vitality and constant death existing simultaneously with "Gold's Junkhouse," "perambulator skeletons," "a roof leak wucking in a pail," and "Nathan Kugler Chicken Store Fresh Killed Daily." He sees the sickness and the dying, the despair; but above that the beauty of life, fired layer upon layer, and all the rising and all the falling and all the inbetween undulations of a city of thorn and tissue and flesh.

"We scattered over the lonely seaways,
Over the lonely deserts did we run,
In dark lanes and alleys we did hide ourselves . . .
The lungs put out the light of the world as they
The heart beats without windows in its night,
Heave and collapse, the brain turns and rattles
In its own black axelgrease—In the nighttime
Of the blood they are laughing and saving,
Our little tane, what a kingdom it was!
oi weih, oi weih.

Galway Kinnell has plunged into the midst of a supposed world of despair and grief, battled life in the slums of Hoboken and New York, quite aware of the consequences of such a fight, and comes away with a singing head of warm thoughts. He is a resolute, honest, and affirmative writer, unable to bleed for an overfed nation, unable to bawl for what is not tragic.

Ed. Note:
Part two will appear next week in Intro.

From Intro *magazine, November, 1964.*

poets. I was trying to recall a line by T.S. Eliot that rattled around in my head, but I couldn't find the poem it came from. I told her I remembered it as "In the spring came Christ the tiger."

She wasn't Christian but all the boys she dated were and she'd read Eliot. She told me she loved the resonances of his poems, the musical repetitions and his unexpected swings into comedy and irony:

"In the rooms the women come and go, talking of Michelangelo."

When I mentioned I liked the painter Rouault, that in some strange way he reminded me of Eliot, she brought me a large poster of "The Old King."

I supposed it was the softness of her voice that caught me. She had very large breasts, and wore her dark hair shortish so that a wisp of it covered her right eye. "My private eye," she called it. She had a smile that would come and go in a second; you had to look for it, and she had that quality in a woman that makes men devotees for life: she was humble and did not seek fame. She turned her face away from the camera. Her elegiac poems were as exquisite as Catullus and she wrote on the same subjects: love and betrayal.

I treasured the time I spent with her. I thought she wanted me as a confidant, so I never mentioned I was married. She was twenty; I was twenty-five. Like all poets who are intoxicated with love, I wrote poems to her but never showed them, and dreamt of her in my sleep.

Then one winter evening in the College Library, working with my friend Sylvia Mortimer, I received a little note. It said, "Juvenescence." That was all.

I asked my friend Sylvia what it meant.

"There was a young woman here about an hour ago. She said she wanted to talk to you about T.S. Eliot."

I jumped up. "I'm sure she's gone by now. Sorry." Sylvia was perhaps trying to be protective; she knew I was married and had a young daughter. I looked around in the stacks, first on the first floor, then on the second, finally on the third.

"They told me you'd be here at six," she said. It was 7:30. She was standing in the Z section, bibliography, those dark almond eyes, only one visible under her hair. My heart was pounding.

"I found your quote," she said. "The word isn't *spring,* it's *juvenescence.* 'In the juvenescence of the year came Christ the tiger.'" Then she pulled out the familiar *T.S. Eliot: Complete Poems and Plays* and opened the book to "Gerontion." She read it aloud: "'Signs are taken for wonders. We would see a sign. The word within a word, unable to speak a word.'" She looked up into my eyes. I was hardly breathing. "'Swaddled with darkness. In the juvenescence of the year / came Christ the tiger.'"

Before she could finish I kissed her on the mouth right there in the stacks, unable to control myself. After a moment, her eyes still closed, she pushed me away.

"I just wanted you to see the quote." I held on to her. She kissed me on the cheek.

"Not here," she said.

"How about if we meet tomorrow. After dinner." I agreed. "I'll wait for you where?"

"Why not here?"

"No. They looked at me funny." They knew I was married.

"How about by the flagpole?"

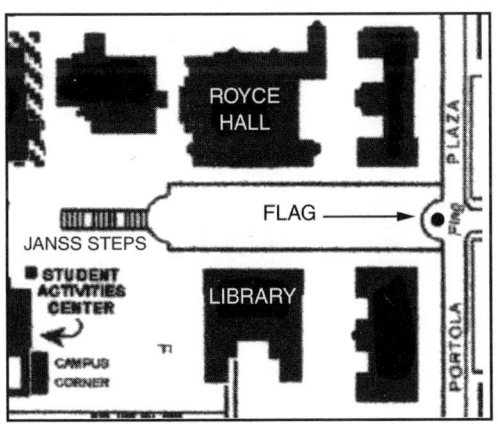

"Okay." We made a time. Seven o'clock. I took off work the next evening; it must have been Friday. I thought about her all day.

If you know the UCLA campus, walk up Janss Steps toward the quad and you'll see the flagpole shooting up eighty feet into the air between Royce Hall and the College Library. There's a small island there that protects the flagpole from automobiles, a circle of concrete, now cracked and broken at the base, but then it was fully circular and whole.

I arrived at six thirty-eight, rehearsing what I should tell her if she asked me about a girlfriend or a wife. I've never been very good at lying.

I wanted to be there early so I could think out what I was getting into, but when I arrived, she was standing there on the concrete island studying the plaque. It read:

> THIS FLAGSTAFF
> IS THE GIFT OF
> MR. JAKE GIMBEL
> 1929

She smiled that quick smile and we stood briefly together on the base of the flagpole. I kissed her eye, the one I could find. She had on a loden-colored car coat that made her complexion look even more dusky than it was. It was cold and she was wearing black leather gloves. I could see her breath; her breathing was rapid.

"Did you want dinner?" I asked.

"Had dinner. Could we just walk into Westwood? Alone?"

First we talked about New York. She told me she came from Westchester and her father was a successful salesman. She said she really knew her father; that he stayed home when business was slow and loved to be with his two girls. She told me she had a sister whose husband worked for Lucille Ball. Her sister was prettier than she. I didn't think that was possible. She said she was studying to be a teacher.

I told her I grew up on Long Island, that my parents were always fighting, and I moved as far away as I could the minute I got out of college.

I told her I'd worked at Macy's on 34th Street and I recognized the Gimbel brass logo at the base of the flagstaff because I'd put aside a small part of my tiny salary every week to buy foreign stamps at Gimbels. Macy's didn't have a stamp department. She laughed about New York, how crazy it was.

We descended the hill past Kirkhoff, lit up with *Daily Bruin* staffers who worked all night. We stood outside the window where the *Westwind* office was. She laughed and told me how she'd written a poem to a former boyfriend, and her roommate had suggested submitting it.

"It was a very private poem," she said. "About milk."

"Private like your eye?"

I could tell from her tone of voice that she was very sexual, very honest, but there was a bit of sadness mixed in. She asked if I had a favorite relative. I told her my grandmother, who lived on the Hudson River Palisades overlooking Hoboken, New Jersey and the Todd Shipyards, just beyond was the entire Manhattan skyline. I told her my grandmother was Jewish.

"So am I," she laughed. "Does that matter?"

For me, being part Jewish had been a problem. I had Jewish friends in Boy Scouts and Jewish relatives, but most of the neighborhood kids I grew up with, part of the middle-middle class, did not know Jews and didn't like them. They were all Republicans who were stunned when Dewey lost to Truman. They weren't fond of Catholics either. As time wore on and my father did better at work, I moved away from that kind of thinking; but try as I will, my feelings about being part Jewish are always with me.

"Your Jewishness doesn't bother me," I told her, but I knew it was more complicated than that. Besides, as she told me, her current boyfriend was Catholic. His name was Murphy and he had a motorcycle. I was five years older than she; I had a dying Buick '56 and a wife and daughter.

The night was stinging cold. We walked down Westwood Boulevard past Campbell's bookstore, talking about poets. I did most of the talking; she did most of the listening. I mentioned the *Westwind* reading. She told me she was impressed: how the saxophone player could sketch in the colors of poems without knowing the text. I extemporized a few poems. "Poets could do that, too," I said. I suggested we stop at Will Wright's for ice cream. The air was freezing. She thought that would be delightful. I told her about their Nestlerode Buhla, an exotic flavor that sounded Middle-Eastern. Maybe Turkish. To me she looked Turkish, like Anouk Aimee.

We ate a few spoonfuls of ice cream and stared at the newly-constructed but as yet unopened building across the street. One of

Westwood's first high-rises. As we reached the cold air again it began to snow. Just a few light flakes, but snow is rare in L.A. There was a guard outside the unopened building. I was feeling very merry and extemporaneous. I asked him what the view was like from the top floor. Looking at the beautiful face of Anouk Aimee, he said, "Go see. There's no heat in the building, but it's warmer up there than it is out here."

We took the elevator up and walked to the southeast corner, to what would become Monte's Steak House. Looking out the window down Wilshire, we could see the low apartments and two-story hotels that led to the Los Angeles Country Club (no Jews allowed) and Beverly Hills (mostly Jewish). Then Anouk Aimee, taking charge of the situation, took off her gloves and traced a finger across the frosted window, just one rising stroke against the cold.

I kissed her full on the mouth. She took off her coat and stroked my cheek and kissed my eyes that were now wet with tears. Tears of joy. I unbuttoned her blouse and kissed her shoulders. The large room filled with wiring, uninstalled drywall, and boxes of material that may have contained furniture and fixtures, was chilly and only partly lit. She was shivering. I asked if she wanted me to stop. She nodded no. I removed her blouse and pulled away her bra. She had lovely breasts, large and well-formed, with tiny nipples. After I removed her skirt and her panties she put her coat back on. "Do you have something to put on?" The era before birth control pills.

I didn't. I was not prepared. I thought we would just go for coffee. She asked if we could go to my place. I kissed her belly, her breasts, her shoulders, catching the scent of her as the few snowflakes outside turned to rain. "I'm married," I told her. She continued to hold me. I could hear her heart beating.

"I thought that might be so," she said finally, after she put her clothes back on. "So I'll just have to be your friend." We took the elevator down to the bottom floor. The guard at the door was smiling. "How did you like it?" he asked. "The view, I mean." I don't remember what I said. I walked her back up Westwood Boulevard, past the Chatham and Hamburger Hamlet, over to Gayley and up the hill to Reiber Hall.

When I tried to say something, she kissed me again and told me not to speak. She was my muse, my . . . my . . . Anouk Aimee, and I held her there in the cold rain knowing I could never love her fully, without bounds or limits in the traditional way as fiancée or wife, as mother to my children. That's the way life is. Poets don't get the whole package.

"I still want to be your friend," she said. "And I'll watch out for you. I'll love you in my own way."

As my marriage continued to disintegrate, only the little girl who clung to me as daddy, and the muse I'm calling Anouk Aimee, had any real meaning. We had our moment. As the poet Galway Kinnell had said in one of his earliest poems, "nonparallel lines meet once, then part."

Night Shift @ The L.A. Times

> "For me, my years at the L.A. Times opened doors that never closed. Cecil Smith taught me patience; from Art Seidenbaum I learned the value of a sense of humor; and from Charles Champlin, the ultimate Hollywood insider always on his way to Cannes, I learned that Hollywood seduces and kills writers."
>
> —Ben Pleasants

In the summer of 1967, I began my career as a newspaperman at the *L.A. Times*. My job was to work the wire desk and slice off copy from the AP and UPI wire services. At twenty-six I was a glorified copy boy, but it got me inside.

Bill Smith was Sunday editor, the last of a dying generation who spat into a brass spittoon. *Ppttt-ding.* Just like in the movies. He'd still yell "BOY" when he needed copy from the wire desk; but like most of the old ones, he was pretty tame. Chet Euell was the makeup editor, and every night I'd watch him trim the end of thirty cigars, smoking one every sixteen minutes as, page by page, he assembled the newspaper from back to front. The talk was intensely masculine, laced with profanity, whiskey and tobacco of every variety. Morgue photos were a continual source of entertainment. When I began we had one black writer who covered black issues and one woman who worked in Metro; they called her "their girl."

Politically incorrect in the style of H.L. Mencken, was our night city editor, Glenn Binford, who had nicknames for all the brass and all the copyboys and all reporters. Evening after evening I'd recall his howls as the inebriated weather reporter was still finishing up his copy ten minutes before deadline. "Dick," he'd yell, "we give you the easiest job there is and you still can't raise that head over your typewriter."

I told myself in the first two weeks that night city editor was the one place I was not going to end up at the *L.A. Times.* Another was cub reporter at the LAPD. It's true, they could fix your traffic tickets, but I heard enough nasty stuff from the beat reporter at the *Herald* to know that was a dead end too.

What I wanted was to write about poetry and theater. In a month I got my wish. First Robert Kirsch, the *Times Book Review* editor, gave me a few forgettable books of poetry to review. Then Cecil Smith, the drama critic, sent me out to review some plays. The first was *A Streetcar Named Desire,* a work I'd even labored on in summer stock on Long Island, playing the part of the paper boy; just a few lines, but I got to kiss Blanche Dubois. Smith was a gruff Texan with a crew cut who looked more like a master sergeant in the Marine Corps than a drama critic; but he liked my work and I liked his sense of humor. He was one of the old-time newspaper boys who'd come up the hard way, not from the Ivy League.

Each Friday afternoon I'd wedge myself into Cecil's tiny office in the critic's wing of the third floor. My pay was $25 an article plus gas. I kept my night job as a copy boy. If my car was running right, I'd agree to drive as far east as Pomona for a performance of director Andrew Doe's *House of Atreus,* or as far South as Costa Mesa for the latest English import from the South Coast Repertory Theatre. Smith even gave me a shot at reviewing Bill Ball's American Conservatory Theatre in San Francisco including: *Thieves' Carnival* by Jean Anouilh and Brandon Thomas' delightful old war horse *Charlie's Aunt.* With a salary of $200 a week including gas money, my greatest dread was arriving at the theater to discover the play had been canceled; that meant no pay. And then there were nights when the play did open, but there was no audience.

---

16 Los Angeles Times
Part I—SAT., AUG. 19, 1967

'Streetcar' Adequately Performed

Tennessee Williams' durable play, "A Streetcar Named Desire," first performed in 1949, remains today the playwright's most substantial and compelling work. Amateur groups have battered it, eccentric directors have synthesized and methodized it and yet the play survives.

A new production by the Company of Angels, which opened Thursday night on Vine and Waring, is generally successful. Director Alan Factor, who has confined his recent work to television, presents a conservative, but sensible rendering of the play.

Factor's Stanley Kowalski, as played by Michael Pataki, is forceful and primitive, although at times, especially when his feelings are hurt, Pataki slips to a Stanley Stanislavsky.

Happily Resigned

Stella is pert, lively and sympathetic. Nancy Burnett, who takes the role, succeeds in creating a Southern belle happily resigned to a physical existence in the sensual slums of New Orleans' French Quarter.

But the strength of the play must rest upon Blanche Du Bois, Stella's sister. It is the lithe but fragile figure of Blanche, symbol of an old and ordered South, that moves across the stage in an attempt to check Stanley, who represents the modern man, devoid of ethics, in a world governed by desire.

Tracy Carter handles the role exceedingly well. She completely carries the central portion of the play, which contains some of Williams' most beautiful lines. Her love scene with Mitch, played by Mill Kogan, is especially memorable.

51

My second assignment as theater reviewer for the *Times* was Samuel Beckett's *Happy Days* at Hoskins Memorial Park in Pasadena. The play was outdoors and the sky was threatening. When I arrived, the audience consisted of a woman in a blanket who lived in the park, the director who was waiting for the *Times* reviewer to arrive before starting the play, two old people with hearing aids, and a drunk who would occasionally appear from behind a bush, startled that a play was going on outside his living quarters.

The performance, directed by William Wanrooy, was one of the finest renderings of Beckett I'd ever seen and I've seen many, and the whole evening proved to be an adventure in the absurd. The two older people with hearing aids kept yelling, "What did he say?" "Did you get that?" "Was that supposed to be funny?" and "Where can I find the bathroom." The rains came and went and the lights sparked and sizzled. The woman in the blanket took it off and walked out into the rain stark naked. People wandered in front of the stage walking their dogs. Lovers sat down for a few minutes and made out in the back row. It was the kind of audience Samuel Beckett would have adored!

When I returned to my typewriter after midnight, Chet Euell had smoked his last cigar and put the paper to bed. The street edition was already roaring through the presses bound for distribution, but I sat there at the typewriter I shared with Wyn Blevins and pounded out my review, making it look like *Happy Days* had been cheered on by an audience of hundreds. Such was my power and I learned to use it well.

The job as reviewer was full of surprises. Once, when my car wouldn't start, I arrived fifteen minutes late for a performance of *The Bacchae* by Sophocles. Hoping to crawl into a back seat and eke out my living anonymously, I discovered they'd delayed the play waiting for the *Times* reviewer. "You're the man from the *Times*?" asked the director. They had me. I was led to the front row and stuck in the center seat while a Hollywood type who'd been kept waiting whispered loudly to his mistress, "Is that the schmuck who kept us waiting? Who does he think he is, Orson Welles?"

And sometimes the results were even more trying. When David Sheehan was owner of the Century City Playhouse, I arrived on time to review Edward Albee's *Fam and Yam*, a satire on Tennessee

Williams' life and lifestyle. Outside at the ticket booth a young sleek-haired coed warned me the show was still in previews and not to be reviewed. Creative director and major-domo Sheehan had neglected to inform the *Times*. "You can't go in," she told me. "No press pack, no press." There went one-half of my week's salary plus gas money. But there's something to say about being a newspaperman; it's a profession that demands a double spine and balls of brass. I convinced the young lady in the ticket booth that I'd driven miles to see *Fam and Yam*. She let me in with the comps and told me to sit in the back row, "Where Mr. Sheehan can't see you."

I found *Fam and Yam* delightful, especially singling out an actor named Wadsworth Taylor for his portrayal of Williams in the role of Fam. What the hell, since I loved the play what would it matter if I reviewed it? The next evening, working at the wire desk, I got a call from David Sheehan. He was not nice. He did not care if I liked the play, and he told me he'd fired the girl who worked at the ticket booth.

Later, I received a letter from Wadsworth Taylor thanking me for my review. He'd been wondering if all that money he'd spent on acting lessons had been worth it. Maybe it had. I was touched.

By that time I'd grown quite close to Cecil Smith. He had become a friend and a mentor. He told me to forget about David Sheehan. "Concentrate on the writers and the actors," he told me. "Any time you discover new talent in those two areas you're doing the world a favor. Whatever is backstage, leave backstage!"

I began to have fun with the job. Occasionally, I'd allow myself a little drollery. Once, while reviewing a terrible production of Shaw's *Androcles and the Lion*, where the actors seemed to be in three different plays, I concentrated most of my review on the actor who played the lion. True, he had no lines, but he clearly knew what Shaw wanted and his mime was delicious; the actor wrote back with a warm reply.

But after a few years I found myself reviewing the same Pinter one-acts for the fourth time. In a cocky mood, I even told Smith I refused to do musicals "because it doesn't make any sense for a guy to stop talking and suddenly sing." Worst of all, I got on Charles Champlin's nerves. He was the entertainment editor of the *L.A. Times* and Cecil Smith's boss.

Then one night, polishing my work at 2:00 a.m. after a drive from Costa Mesa, I asked myself the inevitable question: What gives me the right to review plays when I've never had a play performed?

After writing reviews for about a year, I gave up the wire desk and my meetings with Cecil Smith were held in the cafeteria on the Tenth Floor, away from Charles Champlin. When I asked Smith the question about reviewing plays when I'd never had one produced, Smith laughed and told me I had a lot to learn. He asked if I'd ever written one. I told him I had a one-act I'd completed at UCLA while slogging it out in the Intro section with fledgling reviewers like Digby Diehl and Joel Siegel. "Send it on to New Theatre for Now," he told me. That was the playwright division of the Center Theatre Group. I figured they would never even read it and forgot all about it after I'd licked the stamp. One week later I got a call from the New Theatre for Now reader Dyanne Simon. "I want to do your play," she said.

"The New Theatre For Now wants to do my play?"

"No," she said. "They hate it. I want to do it for Company of Angels. Is that okay?"

I told her I was delighted but at work I kept it quiet. The last thing I wanted, working with a bunch of critics, was to mention I had a play in production, even if it was a one act.

Company of Angels was a showcase theater for actors located on Vine in Hollywood. The play featured three Long Island farmers who got paid twice a month and spent all their wages on food. It was titled "The Gluttons." The food bills for one night were about ten dollars and the actors had to ingest so much food on stage they stopped eating before noon each day in order to perform in the evening.

For the first time in my life I got to see theater from backstage in the role of playwright; it was a position I thoroughly enjoyed. The play ran for a week and the Company of Angels passed on producing "The Gluttons," but I went back to work as a reviewer with a completely different point of view: writing plays was more fun that writing about them.

After Cecil Smith was bumped from theater to television, I moved over to the Book Review to write about writers. Art Seidenbaum, the *Times'* book editor and a delightful wit, gave me a chance to do profiles on writers like John Fante; Budd Schulberg; Lawrence Ferlinghetti; James Laughlin, editor of *New Directions*; Kate Braverman, the rising young star on the Los Angeles poetry scene; and Charles Bukowski. The poets I reviewed at the *Times* included John Ashbery, W.H. Auden, Elizabeth Bishop, Phillip Booth, John Brockman, Bernie Casey, Robert Creeley, Babette Deutsch, J.L. Davis, Lawrence Ferlinghetti, Allen Ginsberg, Arthur Gregor, Richard Hugo, Rolfe Humphries, Galway Kinnell, Kenneth Koch, Philip Lamantia, Jack Marshall, Michael McClure, Pablo Neruda, Harold Norse, Pablo Picasso (he did write poetry), Marge Piercy, Ezra Pound, Jerome Rothenberg, May Sarton, James Schuyler, Gary Snyder, Anne Waldman, Richard Watts, and Richard Wilbur. There were others I've forgotten. The *Free Press*, the *L.A. Vanguard*, *Books West* and *The Herald Examiner* also asked for poetry reviews and interviews.

Bukowski, for one, was impressed. "Don't forget to send a copy [of *Post Office*] to Ben Pleasants" he wrote to his publisher, John Martin.

"There's a possibility he may review it in the *Times*; though we have no way of knowing. He has tried to push my stuff before, but they often cut it back." Though I met Charles Bukowski in 1965, it wasn't until 1969 that I reviewed *The Days Run Away Like Wild Horses Over The Hills*, along with *Dirty Old Man* and the *Penguin Modern Poets 13* but, as I told Bukowski at the time, the books were assigned by Digby Diehl, the creator of the *L.A. Times Book Review*.

I left the *L.A. Times* for good in 1984. Of the friends I'd known as a copy boy, Gary Mayfield, who used to answer the nut phone with the reply, "Tell it to Jesus," was shot to death by the outraged son of a divorced woman as they lay in bed consummating their relationship. Poor Gary made the front page and was later featured in Gay Talese's history of the sexual revolution, *Thy Neighbor's Wife*. A second, Charlie Boesch, one of the most honest people I ever knew, went on to become the *L.A. Times* editorial auditor and accountant and was arrested in the late nineties for embezzling three-quarters of a million dollars. A third, Michael Rudd, managed to put the whole thing behind him, first working for the Nixon administration as an environmentalist, and then taking over his father's construction company. Rudd became a lifelong friend.

For me, my years at the *L.A. Times* opened doors that never closed. Cecil Smith taught me patience; from Art Seidenbaum I learned the value of a sense of humor; and from Charles Champlin, the ultimate Hollywood insider always on his way to Cannes, I learned that Hollywood seduces and kills writers. He himself could have been a great one, but he chose to waste his time blabbing away on bad films and bad actors and bad directors. It was easier than sweating out a novel.

Bukowski @ the Typer: 1967

"Everything was covered with dust, beer bottles and dirty underwear except his typewriter."

When I first met Charles Bukowski he was living in a studio apartment on De Longpre and working at the post office downtown—the Terminal Annex—or, as Bukowski called it, The Terminal Anus. The part of Hollywood he lived in had been out of fashion since World War II: court apartments with a kitchen and a living room and bedroom combination. Everything was covered with dust, beer bottles and dirty underwear except his typewriter.

The one I remember was an old Underwood that sat on his desk under a post office sorting case he'd taken from work. He called it his typer, noun and active verb together. The sorting case had various compartments arranged in alphabetical order, like the one he had at work where he "stuck mail," only this one was for little magazines who were printing his poetry and stories.

In those days he worked the night shift, sorting mail late into the evening and writing during the day. On the weekends he'd drink and write and entertain. I was writing theater reviews for Cecil Smith at the *Los Angeles Times*; occasionally the book editor, Robert Kirsch, would hand me a poetry book to review. Not Charles Bukowski. James Schuyler, Babette Deutsch, Elizabeth Bishop, Gary Snyder, Pablo Neruda, Mark van Doren, Robert Creeley, Kenneth Koch, Richard

Hugo, and Ezra Pound to mention a few. It was great fun. I was the defacto poetry editor of the *Los Angeles Times*. Everyone sent me books to review, but I explained to all of them that the books had to be assigned. That applied to Bukowski, too, and at that time his books were not assigned for review at the *Los Angeles Times*.

That would come later.

When I sat and drank with Bukowski then, on those long ago Saturday nights in Hollywood, my wife had gone back to New York and Bukowski didn't have a date or he'd fought with his latest girlfriend or had no money for a restaurant. I wanted to talk about writers, but he always would change the subject to women. Women were "THE FEMALE" to Bukowski. They were mysterious, not quite human, and for the commander in chief of the Meat School of Poetry, they were not men. That was the thing. Think with your cock, not with your heart. That was the essence of the Meat School. Bukowski never considered me a member. He was right; I thought with my heart and it always got me in trouble. But I did remember Bukowski's first rule of etiquette for Meat School poets: always bring Bukowski two six packs of Pabst Blue Ribbon beer in bottles. He hated cans.

On this occasion, since we planned on drinking till the sun came up, I took along ten cigars of the cheap variety, rum-soaked Swishers, and Prince Edward Panatellas, and two good cigars I had to cut with my Swiss Army Knife, Cuesta Rey #25. Bukowski put on a pot of coffee for the morning. It boiled up on his stove all night and turned into a black soup.

First he talked about cunts. He liked to do that to shock people. The color of them, the smell of them, what the dark parts inside looked like, and what they tasted like. He wanted to know all I could tell him about cunts. At that point, I didn't know too much. Then he told me his long history of fucking, sucking and sniffing. He liked to talk about the smells of women; not the usual smells you read in romance novels, but the smell of the female animal. I told him about a woman who farted in my face as I made her come with my tongue. He said that had happened to him and he gave me several instances. Then he got into a subject that kept him going all his life: women who scabbed on their men; women who'd drag you into their closet or bedroom when the breadwinner was in the kitchen getting a beer. That, I knew a lot about. But I knew if I told him more than a little, it would be in his next set of poems, his anarchist friend from Beverly Hills.

I tried to get him to talk about writers. He wasn't interested in talking about writers—not even Jeffers.

Sooner or later we'd get down to money. "You actually get paid for writing about poetry?" he asked. I was living in Beverly Hills then, trying out teaching at South Gate Jr. High School, during the day and working at the *L.A. Times* at night. The fact that I worked for a living like he did without sponging off my family like most poets did, impressed him. I got paid for my writing, even if it was just from a newspaper. He hated writers who begged or lived off university creative writing programs or government grants.

All night we drank and smoked our cigars and talked about women. Finally, without asking him, Bukowski started in on the writers he most admired: Hamson and Hemingway and John Fante. I told him I'd never heard of John Fante.

"I think Hollywood swallowed him up," Bukowski told me. He said there was one book Fante had written that had changed his whole idea about writing. He told me to find it. It was titled *Ask the Dust*. It took me ten years before I found it.

He showed me some poems he'd written. They were single-spaced with a few typos. I asked if he'd ever had a typist. He told me no; that the experience of sitting at that machine and banging out his poems and stories was something he wanted to share with no one. "There's an editor I send all my stuff to—Marvin Malone. He cleans up the typos and sends back the bad stuff. That's all I need."

I asked him about Hemingway's story, "A Clean, Well-Lighted Place." Was that what writers needed? He laughed. His place was littered with dirty underwear, old newspapers covered in grease, and piles of old racing forms.

"So tell me about Anna."

I'd met Anna. Anna Purcell. She was Steve Richmond's girlfriend. She was a painter and she did the cover for Steve Richmond's first book, *Poems*. She was very beautiful, into food, and Bukowski was hot for her. I told him she wasn't seeing Richmond any more; she was seeing a jazz musician. Later, she married Taj Mahal and Bukowski laughed at the name. "What do we call her? Mrs. Mahal?"

He asked if I was tired of talking about women and writers. I told him I needed some fresh air, and besides he was all out of matches.

Outside at 3:00 a.m. and listing from liquor, we took a walk through Bukowski's Hollywood: past closed pool halls with hustlers standing outside in bell-bottoms. We were nuzzled by streetwalkers in mini skirts and approached by drug dealers hyping LSD or heroin or speed. One of them knew Bukowski and gave him matches.

When we returned and opened another Pabst Blue Ribbon, the apartment stank from stale food, beer, and vomit, but his typer, sitting on the table with a fresh pile of newly typed poems, was shiny and clean, as though it were one of Hemingway's hunting rifles, a lethal weapon Charles Bukowski used for blood sport because, as he told me then, on that long ago night in Hollywood, his life had always been fucked up and it always would be; but the typer allowed him to breathe. "It helps me survive," he said. "It allows me to get out the poison."

A decade later, when we both were working at the *Los Angeles Free Press*, Bukowski was writing his "Notes of a Dirty Old Man" column; I was editing the arts pages. After he quit the post office, living on a small salary from John Martin, an occasional story for Larry Flynt's *Hustler Magazine*, and his fifty dollars a week from *FREEP* as we called it, Buk had all day to write. I was working full time as a teacher of handicapped children at Shriners Hospital, spending half my time teaching in Spanish and really enjoying my life. Not talking about writers.

On my days off or on the weekend we'd head out to the track together, either Hollywood Park or Santa Anita, whichever had the current meet. Bukowski preferred Santa Anita to all the other racetracks in Los Angeles because, as he said, "It has more history. It don't look like a track that was built by Hollywood." Not the Hollywood he lived in: the land of junkies, whores, and winos, but the Hollywood of Louis B. Mayer and Marilyn Monroe and William Morris. His favorite track in all the world was Del Mar, but I never went there with him. He reserved that track for women when he had money.

It was during that time I first watched him working at his machine. We were colleagues on the *Free Press*; fellow newspaper hacks. One day he was finishing up his column, "Notes of A Dirty Old Man," written on deadline. I got there with my copy of the *Pasadena Star News* which we both bought for doping out the horses. The screen door was open and he was sitting by the window at his battered table, clacking that typer as though he were Chopin sitting at the piano composing an etude.

"Ben, just give me ten minutes. Sit in the other room while I get this goddam thing down on paper. There's plenty to read."

The sun was streaming in on his face and shoulders as I watched him from the bed, always unmade. I picked up an article he'd written for a newspaper in Amsterdam and looked at the pictures of women in their fifties showing their vulvas to young sailors, but he knew I was watching him work.

He'd pick up a new sheet and wind it into his machine, eyes half shut, no beer in sight. This was the life he'd dreamed of: writing for a living, writing on deadline, like Hemingway or Dostoevsky. He read parts of it aloud, laughing, grinding his teeth: "Penny's gonna kill me if I don't get it in today." Then he'd pull out the sheet he was working on, scratch a few lines with a pencil, screw in a fresh paper and start again. Penny was Penny Grenoble, editor of the *Free Press*, buffer between the owners of the newspaper and the old guy who'd show up stinking drunk with his finally finished column.

I got to see him working at his machine. It was a sacred thing to him. Buk and his typer. The only clean item in his apartment was his Underwood. The only clean item in his life.

That was the first time. Once, in the middle of a taping we were doing, he started writing thoughts on a shirt cardboard, and then he excused himself and wrote out a poem on his machine. It happened

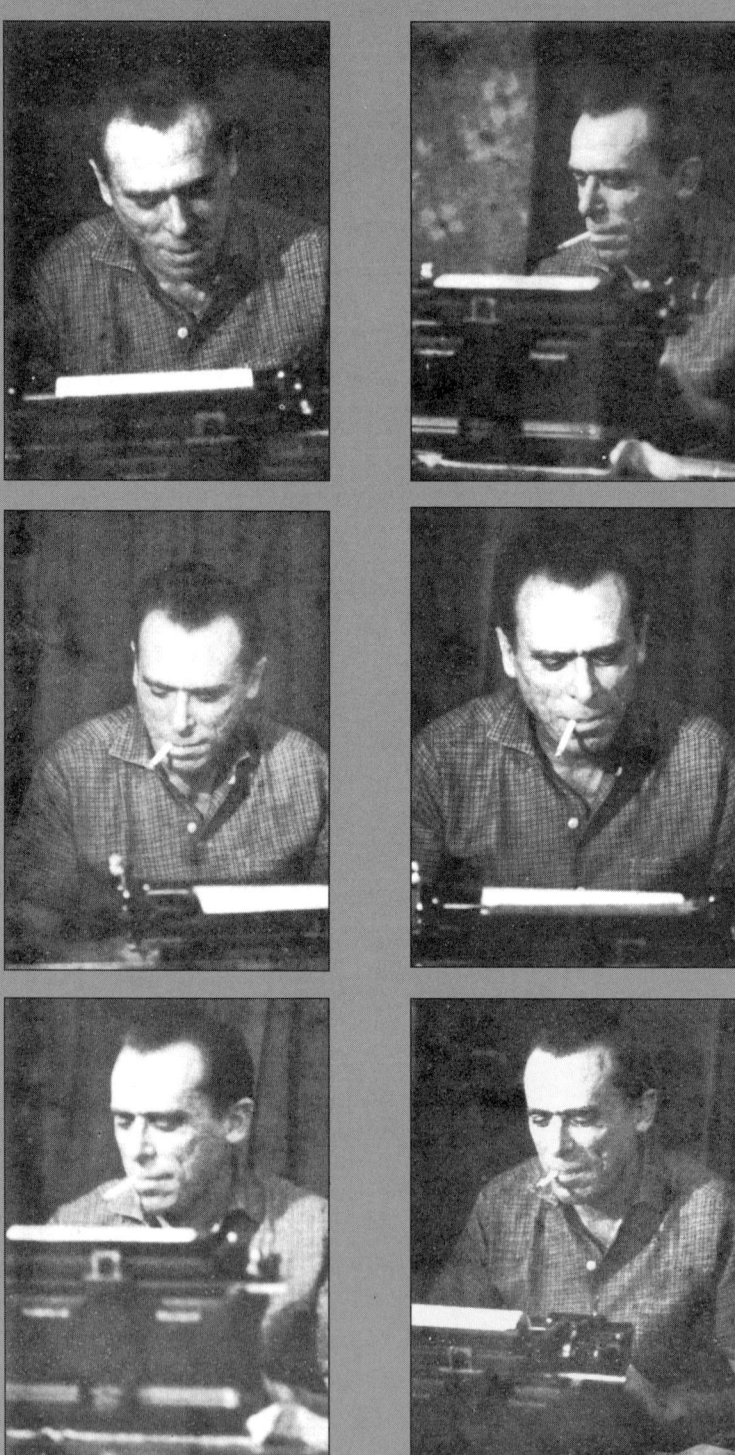

a third time after he drove me back from Hollywood Park in his blue VW. Working at that machine was a holy thing to Charles Bukowski.

When I showed him a book I'd reviewed on Henry Miller and Miller mentioned that Anais Nin was typing his manuscript, Bukowski balked. How could he let her do that? For Bukowski the time spent with his typer was personal, sexual, whether it was creating a poem or revising a novel or just writing letters.

Years later, when he bought his house on in San Pedro, he took me upstairs at night to the small room at the top of the house where he did his writing. There was a chair, the same battered table he had on Carlton Way, a dictionary, and his typer. Outside, in the dark, you could see the whole harbor of San Pedro lit up, but what impressed me most was that typer of his, gleaming by itself in the semi-darkness; not the Underwood he'd had in Hollywood. Linda King, his battling girlfriend, demolished that one after a fight they had while he was still living in Hollywood on Carlton Way. She'd thrown it out into the street, destroying the carriage, rendering it inoperable. It lay there dead beside his clothes and paintings and a few of his books.

I carried it back inside and put it on the table. He'd written *Post Office*, his first novel, on that machine, all his columns for the *Free Press* and *Open City* and a thousand poems. He'd changed the ribbon fifty times. "John Martin will want it for his museum," he told me that night long ago in Hollywood. It was like losing a part of himself. His typer. The machine he poured his life into.

Later, he switched to a computer.

STEVE RICHMOND, Made of Lizard Skin

© Laurence Robbin

I first met Steve Richmond at UCLA in the fall of 1964. I was writing long articles about poetry in the *Intro* section of the *UCLA Daily Bruin*. "There's this guy out there who wants to meet you," said arts editor, Larry Goldstein. "I think he's a law student. He has a new book of poetry out." He handed me a beautifully crafted little volume titled *Poems*, by Steve Richmond. I read the book and found it impressive. There was a poem about a leg that got up and ran off after Thelonius Monk. There was a poem about Richmond's masturbating sister. There was a two-word poem, "soft rain," that filled an otherwise blank page. And then there was the poem that defined him for what he was: It was about the fraternity slut who had fucked everyone else, but was refusing him, Steve Richmond. Steve stuck with it. The war between men and women. The Meat School mantra. Men over women. He jolted the girl with the names of all the brothers she'd slept with. He cried out in his maleness. He whined and begged and put his case to her: Was he not deserving? Was he not handsome? Where was justice if brother Steve was not worthy of pumping the vulva of the fraternity slut when everyone else had? In the end she relented. For Brother Steve. For the good of the frat, the submissive female bedding down with the Alpha Male.

It was a brilliant poem and went to the core of who Steve Richmond was: a hedonist who did what he wanted, got what he wanted, and took no prisoners.

A few days later Richmond showed up at the *Daily Bruin*. He was dynamic and full of projects. He bought me a cup of coffee in the Student Union and reeled off his plans. He was in the last year of law school. His old man, Abraham Richmond, had his whole life mapped out for him: LAWYER, LAWYER, LAWYER. One son a doctor; one son a lawyer. Steve humored the old man. He was finishing his courses in law, but what he really wanted was to be a poet and he had some very sound ideas about how to get there. His book *Poems* was published by a master printer named Donald Mishell. Donald had set up offices in Hollywood and was looking for a project to show off his work. Richmond, who'd known him from high school, offered his manuscript as the launching project of Tasmania Press.

And Steve Richmond had other ideas; he wanted to open a poetry store in Santa Monica. He told me his family had property there. He invited me down to tour the lands of the Berlin Trust, his family's' principality. I drove down in my faltering '57 Olds. He showed me his small house on Hollister, one block from the beach with a partial view of the Pacific. It was a simple cottage with one large open room, a bedroom in the back, a small kitchen and one bathroom. He told me it was owned by the trust and they owned the house next door, the one with a full view of the ocean. That one was rented out.

Richmond had a good setup. I was envious: I was working forty-four hours a week in two libraries while taking a full load in graduate school. I hardly had a few hours to sleep, while Steve Richmond had time to dream, listen to music, play basketball with the other princes, take drugs, collect the rents for the trust, and fuck.

As we sipped instant coffee, girls came to his door. Pretty girls. Young girls. He sent them away. "Come back later," he commanded. He offered me grass. He called it his stash. I'd had some before in San Diego and it did nothing for me. I refused. I told him it scratched my throat. I smoked my pipe instead. That bothered Steve. Steve distrusted nonusers, especially when he was giving it away. He had that proprietary thing going. The man behind the counter. Whether it was drugs or books or poems or women, he had to be the owner. The Padrone.

But he was interesting. As he smoked grass, he filled me in on what I was missing. Grass was nothing, he said. It was only the first step. LSD was where it was at, especially for poets. He showed me a blue tab and dared me to take a trip with him. It was the old game of jumping off the cliff together. I settled for a beer. That didn't please him either. Richmond didn't like drunks. Even though he only collected the rents, there was something of the landlord in him. Drunks and Blacks were considered bad for property.

Later that year, when we discussed the seizure of *Westwind* by the UCLA administration, I pointed out why they grabbed the issue: his poem was insulting to Blacks; it used dialogue out of Amos 'n Andy.

"Who cares," Richmond said. He was proud the issue was seized and proud it was his poem they singled out. He said he learned a lesson from that adventure: if you want to be noticed, write something so insulting it forces the authorities to act. What the hell, we were living in America. What could they do to us? It wasn't Stalin's Russia or Nazi Germany. We weren't Palestinians in Israel!

He was right. It was the perfect moment for literary revolt. Grove Press and Henry Miller had broken the back of the pornography laws with the publication of *Tropic of Cancer*. The doors had been thrown open for raw, masculine writing. No more Truman Capote. No more *To Kill a Mocking Bird*. Fuck the system. Fuck the New York publishers. We could do it on our own. Steve the lawyer was ready to jump off his father's lifetime plan wagon and emerge as Steve Richmond, Meat Poet.

He thought of himself as the new Blake. He was two-thirds through the mantra of the day: TUNE IN, TURN ON, DROP OUT!

He'd tuned in and turned on and now he was ready to drop out. Sorry Berlin Trust. Sorry Father Abraham. Fame was just around the corner. Steve had the money, Steve had the talent and Steve had all the pharmaceuticals.

When I told him I didn't take drugs, that literature was my only opiate, he was not impressed.

He was a sixties kind a guy. He thought I was soft.

We were different cats, I told him. Steve smoked cigarettes and I smoked a pipe. He had a house. I had an apartment. I had a wife and a kid; he was alone. He liked e.e. cummings; I liked Ezra Pound. I had been working since I was sixteen; he had never worked. He was a loner; I was a joiner.

He read me a poem about his ex-wife. He was already divorced. Marriage, he said, was not for him. He'd called her on the phone, the poem went, but "oh the relief, she wasn't there."

That was one thing he got right. Poets are better off alone. He wanted no wife and kids to come home to. He spoke of his father dragging two briefcases full of papers to work every day. The lawyer's rut. For what? A nice house and a fur coat for his mother? Money so Steve could go to law school? The middle class trap made him sick. He wanted out.

That made me laugh. I told him he was living off what he hated, living off relatives. He laughed that crazy Steve Richmond laugh and took me out on a tour of his kingdom, the domain of the Berlin Trust. They owned a hodgepodge of slum property: a late night market two blocks away, a mission that was some kind of thrift store, shops on the Venice Boardwalk, and a few houses, all bought by his mother's family during the Depression.

I doubt that a single building was to code. Lawrence Lipton, who I later met and who became my friend, described the area in his book *The Holy Barbarians* as "that slum by the sea."

Richmond's neighborhood was rightfully called P.O.P., Pacific Ocean Park. It was a faded, half-baked Coney Island. I'd seen it once in its glory days in an *Our Gang* comedy film from the 1930s. Then it was bright and shiny, filled with kids and rides; but when I got to it in person in the mid-sixties, it was rotting away building by building, rat-infested and almost deserted.

As Richmond and I sat by the seaside talking poetry, (what was good and what was bad according to Steve) he gave me his long, hard-on rant on art: Poetry must have muscle! No women, no queers. "Let the fags have San Francisco," he later wrote in one of his invective poems. Art, he said, would save us. Pleasants and Richmond. Art was the one thing *worth* saving. Life is short, art is long. It was a war and I was on the right track, he thought. Attacking Whitman. Poetry did not belong in the universities. Poetry did not belong to *Poetry Chicago*. Poetry did not belong to New York publishers. Poetry belonged in the record stores, out there on the street, as part of the popular culture. And he was right!

He mentioned Rilke. *Advice To A Young Poet*. Was there a point to all this?

There was.

He had met the progenitor raw meat artist Charles Bukowski. Bukowski, said Richmond, had Muscle. Bukowski stank of the streets. Bukowski wrote for the popular culture. Bukowski hated the universities with their safe little journals and safe little poets.

Bukowski, he said, was his mentor. And most of all, Bukowski was in an all-out war against the system.

I confessed to him that I'd read Bukowski in the *Outsider* while labeling books at UCSD and for me Bukowski was mostly a crybaby, whining about the toughness of his little life, the pains in his stomach, enraged at his failures, ever on the warpath against his mortal enemy, THE FEMALE.

I told Richmond he should think more about politics than poetry. He shrugged that off.

It was barely a year after the Kennedy assassination and the Vietnam War was just heating up. Richmond told me he hated politics. Art would demolish politics. Poetry would end war. We argued. Politics, I said, had a way of catching up with people who ignored it. Look what happened to the Jews. He thought I was trying to bait him. Test him. I wasn't. I didn't know he was Jewish, but I knew I'd hit a nerve.

I told him the strains of the Vietnam War had caused the U.S. military to draft single males right out of college. I was married. I had a kid. Richmond was the loner for art. He was vulnerable. He was single. War, I said, was the real meat school, the real macho thing, not poetry. War separated cowards from brave men. If that was what he was looking for, war had muscle! And if he hated it, he'd have to show up at the protest lines that were forming at lunch time outside the UCLA Student Union. Steve had other plans.

By 1965 the L.A. draft board was yanking friends of mine out of UCLA, dumping them on flights to Saigon right after Basic. Soon afterwards, Richmond got his draft notice.

That finally woke him up. Woke up the Meat Poet. He came forward with his canons of art. Without help from Donald Mishell and Tasmania Press, Richmond cranked out a mimeo-printed second book of poetry titled *Hitler Painted Roses*.

It was not exactly what Father Abraham or the Berlin Trust had in mind for him as a life plan, but *Hitler* was introduced by Charles Bukowski, the filet mignon of the Meat School.

Bukowski and Richmond, who had been communicating since March 24, 1965, were now comrades in art, linked together by a complex web of rage against women, hatred of academics and the *will* to crush fake art with the macho hammer of hard line poetry.

And it worked. Using Hitler as their mentor, Bukowski crowed in a March 2, 1966 letter to Richmond: "I am still excited about *Hitler Painted Roses* . . . I love the title. Why couldn't I have used that title? . . . *Hitler* is a perfect title."

In the time of Vietnam, it was glorious. *Hitler Painted Roses*. Ten years before Punk. Ten years before Joy Division and The Clash.

By 1965, Richmond had opened his bookstore in Santa Monica at 244 Ocean Park Boulevard. He called it Earth Books. It was located on a family property headed for demolition. Poet Richmond stocked it with mags like Ed Sanders' *Fuck You: A Magazine of the Arts*, *Ole*, Loujon's *The Outsider*, and *The Wormwood Review*. There you could find Celine, Artaud and all the Beat poets, along with Bukowski, D.A. Levy, Jack Micheline, William Wantling, Harold Norse and Steve Richmond behind the counter, in the flesh. Bukowski's *Crucifix in a Death Hand* was on its own stand and selling at cost.

Bukowski himself could be found there in person talking with a poet whose last name was Buckner, a writer Bukowski greatly admired. Harold Norse walked over from his mother's place in Venice. Anna Purcell's paintings were on the walls. It was the Meat Poet's moment in time! But even then there were problems. Bukowski volunteered to work in the store for free. He said he liked the neighborhood. It was nicer than Hollywood. Maybe Steve's family might have a place for him, Charles Bukowski, a place for the most important poet in America, according to Steve Richmond. A room and a bed for warrior Bukowski, commander of the Meat School of Poetry.

Richmond was happy to employ the maestro without pay as an assistant in his shop, but there was no room in the neighborhood for the muscle poet who drank and threw pork chops down on his kitchen floor. Richmond had been to his place on De Longpre. A pigsty. No deal: poetry was poetry and property was property!

Steve's poetry shop became a meeting place for poets and hangers-on. I first met Harold Norse at the shop, a bald little man in an ill-fitting wig. "He's a fag," said Richmond. I didn't much care about his sexuality, and I liked his poetry. Bukowski liked it too and he liked the fact that Norse had access to the big magazines and journals still denied Bukowski. His influence couldn't hurt, fag or no fag, Bukowski later told me.

It was at Steve Richmond's shop on Ocean that I first met Charles Bukowski. He was gray faced, yellow eyed, overweight, with that wry, monkey smile, broken shoes, protruding belly, a stubby beard. He looked just right in the neighborhood of Venice, hangout of the Beats. And he was just right for Steve Richmond in the mid-sixties. They were perfect for each other. Father and son.

When Richmond's draft notice arrived, Bukowski advised him.

"I hope the army doesn't get you. I'd suggest jail first, but I'm not your father." At Steve's house, when I was there, as an afterthought, Bukowski sketched in a bit of his own adventures with the draft board during World War Two. A few weeks in jail. Then freedom. He told him how he did it: ACT NUTS.

After a few sleepless nights, Richmond employed the same method: he ran a psycho-rant before his draft board peering crazily at his inquisitors, failing to respond to questions, twisting the intonations of their language, eyeing them with wild and weird expressions, interrupting in midsentence. His poem "4F and Flunked the Bar" has it down perfectly. In the end his draft board viewed Steve Richmond as emotionally unfit for service, same as Bukowski. No 4F. It was a Y category. Emotionally defective.

In his poem Richmond wails that he has been dropped by the hand of God, but in reality, in that time of war and rage Steve Richmond's prayers were answered. His life was spared from the dangers of war and the dull responsibilities of the law.

For Steve Richmond, 1965 was Graduation Day. He dropped out of the world of work and he never looked back. When I asked him why he had used 4F in his poem, he admitted the draft board had given him something else, but 4F sounded better in the poem.

In a way Charles Bukowski and Steve Richmond were much alike: Each hated what Bukowski called the "obvious and popular ideas about peace, war, govt., love, people, music, society. Everybody trying to show how good they are, how much they *know*, how much they *feel*, jeus, ju, jew, jesus christ . . . listen, kid, I am not anti-human, I am not pro-war, but listening to these, it is like eating a bucket of cake icing. Something is wrong. And what amuses me is that these are the same finks who were HOLLERING FOR WAR during and before world war II, running out to Spain, joining the Abraham Lincoln Brigade, fighting Franco."

Bukowski wrote that on June 20, 1966. People wrote crazy letters like that then. For many, it was an insane time.

For me it was heaven on earth. That same year I landed in the lap of the *L.A. Times*, right in the middle of the editorial department on third floor, a few steps away from the managing editor, Frank Haven's desk. It was the hub of the universe.

I was a twenty-five-year-old copyboy who worked the night shift, but almost immediately I ended up writing about theatre and poetry; just what I wanted. I was hardly Meat School. In fact, I was Old

School, but Richmond and Bukowski each asked me the same question: Could I could get their books reviewed in the *L.A. Times*?

FAME IS A FAT GUY ON SPEED, FAME IS AN ELEVATOR RIDE UP THE ASSHOLE OF TIME I wrote years later. Never mind Franco. Never mind jeus, ju, jew, jesus christ. It was all about tap-dancing out there in the center of the universe, keeping it interesting.

Why is Bukowski world famous today and Richmond unknown? I knew them both and I have the answer: Richmond was a narcissist, in love with his own visage, while Bukowski saw the horror and irony and craziness of life around every corner. Bukowski was a man on fire, Bukowski was an engaged writer, Bukowski heard the clear voice in the icebox that kept him up all night. Bukowski kept it interesting.

And he could read you in five minutes.

In an hour's talk the poet Bukowski could unravel the crooked core of any male writer's psyche; the crossed wires that would later lead to fame, suicide, madness or murder. He had it every time, when it came to men.

Of women he had no understanding at all.

Women were another species to Bukowski; he called them the FEMALE. But Bukowski liked the way Steve Richmond handled women, the way they walked five steps behind him and said nothing till they were summoned.

That was not me at all. Bukowski took less than twenty minutes to figure me out. With women, I was a nonstarter. I told him about the troubles with my wife.

I thought he'd mock me, laugh at me for staying with her. Instead he looked at me sadly and told me he'd been there himself. With Jane. Not Richmond. Steve, he said, commanded respect from women. Bukowski told me how Jane would come home night after night with the stink of other men's cum on her mouth and lips. I told him how I confronted the wife who worked at the country club with what was going on. He said that the pain women inflict on men was one of the great motivaters for poets. He said that writers needed exquisite agonies, pain that stayed with them forever and that was the one thing Steve Richmond was lacking. His life was too easy. Richmond would never have that to draw on. When I mentioned the word love, Bukowski threw it off with disdain. He said the German philosopher Schopenhauer who had written "The woman is by nature meant to obey." But not guys like us, said Bukowski. I knew what he meant The title he came up with years later, *Love Is A Dog From Hell*, best explains his world view of men and women.

Steve Richmond had chicks. Before the women's movement exploded on the scene, Steve had it right. Steve had women figured out. Steve's women did his typing for him, cooked his steaks, did his laundry. His house was always neat. Steve had chicks lined up at the door. They brought him grass and later heroin. They bought and sold for him. They fucked him when he needed fucking and they let him be when he wanted to be alone.

That's what Bukowski admired most in Steve Richmond.

"Steve knows how to make women jump," he told me. "Steve is good looking. Steve has the long green. He drives a nice car and has his own place to sleep. Property. Women can smell that on him."

Women weren't the problem with Steve Richmond. And money wasn't the problem either. Bukowski was a little envious. Richmond had what Bukowski wanted: He had money for sports cars and women and drugs; he had youth and strength: he worked out playing basketball, had a place to fish at June Lake in the High Sierra; women crawled all over him. And then there were all those holdings his family owned: apartment units and stores and little houses.

Steve Richmond's problem was Steve Richmond. Self-love always bothered Bukowski.

Richmond was cagey about the rental property his family owned. The Berlin Trust. Bukowski had always been a renter. He gloried in being poor. Richmond was rich. But while Bukowski got the shit beat out of him every night at the post office, he was looking for that soft core that would nail Steve Richmond to the wall. It took him a lot more than twenty minutes to find it, but he finally wrestled from Steve how he made his money. Rent collector for the Berlin Trust.

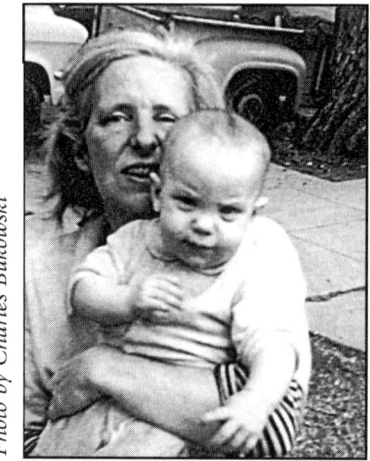

Photo by Charles Bukowski

Frances and Marina.

After asking for a little house by the ocean, if not for him, then for Frances and his kid Marina, Richmond blew him off. On the assault, Bukowski discovered Richmond's greatest vulnerability. Ego. Vanity. That's where Bukowski had him.

Every good poet has a core of craziness, said Bukowski. Steve Richmond's was his vanity but he had one fatal flaw: an inability to laugh at himself.

In the mid-sixties, Steve Richmond fired his second shot in the war against middle class art. *Hitler Painted Roses* had not sold well and was reviewed only by a few little mags like *Wormwood* and *Ole*. Richmond was in a hurry. He put out a newspaper in Santa Monica with the headlines screaming FUCK HATE. It was a slightly unbalanced manifesto on art. He stuck one in my mailbox when I lived on Veteran Avenue in Westwood. If he wanted attention, he got it. SMUT PEDDLER JAILED screamed back the *Santa Monica Evening Outlook*, his local paper.

But again there was nothing. No one came to Richmond's defense. There was no H.L. Mencken out there to scoop him up as he did for Dreiser or John Fante. Richmond got only laughter. Derisive laughter. Bukowski warned him of the repercussions. In a letter dated Sept. 8, 1966, he wrote:

> I don't know about the newspaper. It seems like a good way to get rid of some crankshafts and grease and orange peelings, but there is an elemental form and glazed ice fire type of thing lost in this project . . . what I mean is there's a tendency to relax too much and gargle something out of the side of the mouth.

Bukowski, Meat School Mentor, wanted writing with more fire, like *Hitler Painted Roses*, a title, he confessed, he would have been too timid to use. Indeed, he said, *Loujon* had taken *Crucifix in a Death Hand* from the title of a poem after rejecting several outrageous Bukowski proposals. In the balls category Steve Richmond was way

2/19

May put out a BUKOWSKI record again — this time all him. My calling may be a record producer under the EARTH ROSE LABEL. he sells, what the hell & U need $ lately. Poetry Records, shitty but right now beats anything else → candles, etc. & they won't buy ME now. How's this idea sound?

You will probably send me some horrendous but correct philosophical reason why I shouldn't do this (the Buk record) but hopefully by time U receive your letter the record will be out & selling a million. what a way to get rich, spread the word of a true poet god (BUK) & LIVE OFF the talent of other men.

Steve

ahead of Bukowski; art was a different story. Bukowski saw the FUCK HATE handout as an exercise in pure egotism.

Steve Richmond's egotism was legendary.

I'd experienced it several times during the course of our association over a period of twenty years, dating from 1964 to 1984.

It flared up first at a coffee house in Richmond's neighborhood called Venice West. Steve took me there to read poetry. He introduced me to the owner, who knew Steve and agreed to the reading. Steve read first, two poems from his book *Poems*. He had a dull monotone voice that never reached the audience. The poems made no sense to them at all. Then I read a few political poems, one on the Palestinians. They drew cheers. When I sat down at our table, the owner brought me over a piece of three-day-old lemon pie and a cup of coffee. "On the house." Steve got nothing. It made him angry. Out came frat brother Steve again. Were his poems not better than mine? Why did he not get a piece of pie? They made him pay for his coffee.

I told him I had a pair of shoes falling off me and he wore polished boots. The good Burghers of Venice knew him as a landlord's son. That was all. He shouldn't take it personally. He did. He always did.

Later, when I asked Bukowski if he ever read at the Venice West he told me no. It was a Beat place and he was not a Beat. Besides, they didn't pay.

Still, Steve Richmond had moves. Bukowski told him about the *Wormwood Review*, suggesting he submit there. When they took a batch of Steve's poems, he did the same for me. When my work got accepted in the next issue, Steve wrote a poem attacking one of the poems *Wormwood* had published. It was a Chinese style poem and Richmond mocked one of lines with "the pigpiss image of white geese flying north." It was his way of saying I'm the owner of the poetry store.

Later, in a poem, Steve described a late night drinking party at his house attended by Bukowski, Neeli Cherry, Richmond and myself. It was titled "The Tic and the Talker." Neeli was the Tic and I was the Talker. Richmond was the wise and silent disciple of Bukowski. When I read it, I sat back and laughed.

And then there was the fact that none of us were published in prestigious quarterlies.

Bukowski saw the comedy of printing poetry in mimeo format; Richmond did not. "Get it up there in 8 1/2 by 11 mimeo." Mimeo gave voice to very small poets. In a letter dated 7-25-68 Bukowski, when he was editing a poetry section for John Bryan's *Open City*, complained:

> . . . the boys don't like to be rejected. . . . this is the danger of these guys printing each other's work in their little mimeos and reading to each other before the lesbians and homos: they get deluded into thinking they are doing something.

Richmond decided to try something new. He played me a recording made of his Bar Mitzvah and made me sit through it as someone read, I think, from the "Song of Songs." He told me he was planning to make a record of a ninety minute tape he'd done of a drunken Charles Bukowski ranting on Steve's sofa. Later Steve sent me a hand scrawled note announcing the work was finished. He gave me a copy. It was titled *Ninety Minutes in Hell*. Bukowski was a little embarrassed, but he grew angry when Carl Weisner, his German translator, ordered a hundred copies paying for it by check and Steve pocketed the money without sending on the records. Instead he sent back a snotty letter proclaiming himself a poet, not an errand boy.

There was the frat brat again. All ego.

About that time John Martin entered the picture. In a letter dated November something, 1966, Bukowski told Richmond a John What's His Name had sold his library for $49,500 and wanted to publish a book of his poems. He'd already done a broadside, but Bukowski had promised his next book of poems to John Webb. He told Steve he'd write a novel for John What's His Name instead.

That was his first novel, *Post Office*. I got it reviewed in the *L.A. Times*. Prior to the that, the agreement between the Webbs and Bukowski had fallen through, and John Martin's first book by Bukowski was poetry. By that time, correspondence between Bukowski and Richmond had diminished.

I saw Bukowski more, Richmond saw him less. Bukowski's career was taking off. Not only was he a best-selling writer in Germany, the Webbs, who paid him nothing, were replaced by John Martin, who put Bukowski on an allowance. While Richmond's *Ninety Minutes In Hell*, with no distribution, languished in a closet somewhere, Apple Records came along to do some tapings.

It was common for all Bukowski's friends to seek his help on getting published by Black Sparrow Press, myself included. When Steve Richmond sent him a stack of three hundred poems, Bukowski, who was breaking away from the little mags, finally slapped down the frat boy poet with a stinging poem of his own titled "300 Poems." That was in early 1973. Richmond wrote back an anonymous note proclaiming his brilliance and calling his mentor "the knifer."

Bukowski, who was weary of the whole thing, fired back a reply, not sure if the note had been written by Harold Norse or Steve. He put it on the same paper.

"I'll have to presume it's you, Steven," he said. Bukowski said he'd sent on Norse poems and the Richmond poems with instructions to John Martin "to print you and Norse, feeling that you both deserve it. I am not out to get anybody. You guys are ridiculous," he concluded.

City Lights later published the Norse poems and I reviewed them in the *L.A. Times*. Richmond's work was done by Earth Books, a Richmond enterprise, but in fact it is an amazing book titled *Earth Rose*. Completely overlooked, except for the *Littles*, it sat on the shelf with no distribution. I never got to review it because it was never assigned, considered by the book editor a vanity project.

The seventies drove Steve Richmond and me in opposite directions. We only linked up seriously at the *Free Press* Symposium with Bukowski, Gerry Locklin and Ron Koertge, two *Wormwood* poets from the L.A. area. I saw Bukowski often during those days, but I rarely saw Steve Richmond. When I ran into him once in Venice, Steve showed me with pride the candle shop he'd opened on the boardwalk. The shop was called Steve's Sensuous Candles and was located in a family property behind a bikini shop. Bukowski and I spoke of Richmond from time to time, but for each of us he was becoming a distant memory.

For me the seventies was a time of political involvement.

As a member of the IWW (Industrial Workers of the World), I was exploring my anarchist roots. I lived on Doheny Drive in Beverly Hills and Bukowski referred to me as a Beverly Hills anarchist. One day Steve called me up. He said he wanted to discuss a few ideas. I told him I was in the middle of an IWW meeting. He didn't believe me. When Steve arrived, our group of seven, including Tom Thompson, former managing editor of the *Free Press* and then editor of *Vanguard*, were engaged in a furious argument about money missing from the treasury. Pure comic madness. Steve showed up on drugs, amazed that a meeting was going on, then dragged me back into my daughter's

bedroom to give me his plan. He wanted to blow up the Martin Cadillac dealership in Los Angeles. I told Steve he needed to get a grip. Find a life.

When I later told Bukowski about the incident, Bukowski laughed. He said Steve had the wrong Martin.

Later events were even funnier. A former girlfriend of Richmond's wrote a poem in the *Venice Beachhead* titled "Steve Richmond, Made of Lizard Skin." Her name was Melody Brennon and she brought symmetry to the entire Richmond story. Melody was one of the poets who read at the *Westwind* reading in 1965, along with Richmond and Jim Morrison. In her poem she let go with both feminist barrels, mocking Richmond in his male chauvinist pigdom. Richmond was furious. He wrote a letter to the newspaper denouncing the poem, the poet and the paper that printed her slanderous sentiments, calling the rag "the Venice Bullshit Head." Again Steve's actions were hilarious: a comic coda to Richmond's frat boy lifestyle. If only he could have laughed at himself said Bukowski. The Venice Bullshit Head became one of Bukowski's favorite Steve Richmond stories.

I went on with my life and became arts editor of the *L.A. Vanguard*.

When I sent Steve Richmond a copy of my interviews with Kenneth Rexroth and Marge Piercy, Piercy wrote me back complaining that an L.A. poet had called her a fascist. It was Steve Richmond. She went on to describe a trip she had taken to one of the Nazi death camps and said that the word Fascist should be used a lot more carefully.

I passed this on to Bukowski and later found it funny that two writers were calling each other Nazis when they were both Jews hiding behind Anglo names.

With Richmond it was always that way. He could never laugh at himself.

Looking back, I have mixed feelings about Steve Richmond. His poetry, especially the Gagaku poems, ranks as some of the most neglected important work done by an American poet since World War Two. Bukowski praised his poetry over and over in his letters, which Richmond photocopied for me before he sold them to John Martin for a reported $800.

Was there a promise made by the publisher of Black Sparrow to put out a volume like the Durrell/Miller letters? Steve was hopeful there was. Only small bits and pieces of Bukowski's letters to Richmond have appeared so far and I have never seen any of Richmond's letters to Bukowski in print by Black Sparrow or anyone else. That's a shame.

Their letters on both sides are some of the finest things Bukowski and Richmond ever wrote. They attest to an incredible friendship between the American Verlaine and his young Rimbaud, but poetry in America is a sinister business.

In time, as his work is read in Japan and France especially, Richmond will gain his place among the important poets of his day. He is an original, a writer who studies the self with a microscope. Bukowski had it right when he wrote Steve Richmond:

> A good first edition. you've done it: make a sound into the stucco-heart swamp stink of what's around us. Don't feel sad that the world is not jumping up and down and knocking at your door . . . you are a part of literary history now, even though that history is bad and full of snipers and traitors and fools and fakes . . . anything that works will kill itself or anything that looks for profit ($$$) under the cloak of art.

William "Baldy" Mullinax

Things never quite worked out for William "Baldy" Mullinax, Bukowski's closest childhood friend. In his high school yearbook he was known as Dr. Mull. His father had been a general practitioner in West Los Angeles with a thriving practice until unwise investments and The Great Depression ruined his career.

"My dad was forced to sell his house on Draper, near what's now Cheviot Hills, and move us into a smaller place on Washington Boulevard, near downtown," he told me.

When I interviewed Baldy in the late seventies, he was still living in the same neighborhood, a small, framed house at 5472 Third Street. "I was born in Nebraska on July 17, 1920. I'm older than Hank by a month," he said. "I met him in front of a popcorn stand when we were both starting out at Mount Vernon Junior High School. He had really bad skin and he was afraid of girls."

He told me friends started calling him Baldy in high school because his hair had thinned when he was fourteen. "Maybe it came from the chemicals they put in the swimming pool," he said.

He showed me around his little house, neat as a pin, everything in place.

"My wife works," he said. He was uncomfortable with a tape machine, so I turned it off. We sat on the sofa for a few minutes and he got me a glass of water.

He walked with a limp; his left leg seemed twisted. "I'm on disability," he told me.

He looked nervous. In a house that neat, I could understand why. It was a woman's house, his wife's house.

He asked if I'd like to take a drive, a little tour of the neighborhood? Hank's neighborhood? He struggled to get up. "Let me get my cane," he said. I could see he was in pain and he dragged his leg as he walked.

"I had a hip fusion in the late fifties that never quite took. Arthritis," he told me. Then he opened up a closet door and pulled out a wood-handled .22 pistol. I told him I'd turned off the tape machine. That I had a note pad.

He laughed. "Don't worry," he said. "I'll just take this with me in the car. Protection." Bukowski had warned me a little about "Baldy." The two of them weren't getting along too well at that juncture; there seemed to be a bit of a disagreement about who did what with Jane Cooney Baker. And Bukowski said "Baldy's" marriage was falling apart. And then there was the story Bukowski wrote about the homosexual incident between himself and Baldy.

But Baldy was friendly to me. As he turned and hobbled out the door, he said, "I can't run so well any more. It's pretty bad out there for white guys like me who can't run. The neighborhood turned ten years ago."

I hadn't heard that word since my last trip to Baltimore in the fifties.

Most of the students I taught were black or Hispanic. Bukowski looked down on Baldy Mullinax because he lived in a black neighborhood. It was like that in those days; besides, I was living in Beverly Hills.

I asked if he wanted me to drive.

"You write, I'll drive."

As he climbed into the car, Baldy told me he'd been mugged twice and robbed once.

"They wait till you open the car door, just as you're ready to crawl in, and then they get you. Pretty smart. You can't do anything. In this city, you can't survive without a car. There used to be street cars."

Then he reached over, put the .22 pistol in the glove compartment and started up the engine. We drove south on Third Avenue until we hit Seventeenth Street. "It curves around here," he said, pointing at white-framed houses with fresh paint and perfect lawns.

"When I was a kid, this whole area was all white. Now it's turned." I pointed out that the lawns were all trimmed and the houses were nicely painted. He nodded.

As we circled Mount Vernon Junior High School, he indicated various aspects of disrepair. "This used to be a rich kids' school," he told me. "Now they all live on the West Side."

It was at that point I told Baldy I was a teacher in the Los Angeles City Schools. Currently.

He seemed disappointed. "I thought you were a writer. Hank showed me some stuff you wrote in the *L.A. Times.*"

I told him I did that, too. That writers in Los Angeles, unless they wrote for TV or the movies or advertising, made little money.

"Like Hank," he said. "He still lives in a studio apartment." I could sense the tension that still existed between the two, the male competitive thing that little boys have.

"He's getting up there," I told him. "He makes a lot more than I do."

As we drove, Baldy asked me a few questions about his childhood friend. He wanted to know if I thought he was any good. I told him Bukowski was a one hundred percent American original with the kind of talent that would survive long after we were all dead. Baldy looked surprised and a little envious. And then he asked the obvious question:

"Why isn't he famous?"

I told him it had a lot to do with taste. Bukowski, I said, was published in *Hustler* and *Adam* and the *Free Press* and little magazines like *Wormwood*. He'd tried *The Atlantic, Harpers, The New Yorker,* and *Poetry Chicago,* but they'd all turned him down without comment.

"Even *Esquire?*"

I had to think about that, but I was pretty sure Bukowski had never been published in *Esquire*.

Then he asked me about my teaching. I told him I'd been at it since 1967; that I was teaching inpatients at Shriners Hospital through L.A.U.S.D.

"Patients? You mean sick kids?" That confused him even more.

He stopped the car and parked in front of Mount Vernon Junior High School.

"You know this school?"

I told him I'd substituted there for a few weeks when I first started teaching.

"Pretty rough, huh? It was all white when Hank and I went there. And a few Japs and Chinese." It was funny he said it that way. I asked if he'd been in the war, and he told me we'd talk about that later, after the tour. Then I asked if he'd heard the story Bukowski told about Asian women. He laughed. "You mean about how they had slanted . . . ?"

"Pussies?" I finished it for him. When it came to epithets, Baldy was a perfect gentleman.

"He thought because their eyes were slanty . . ."

It was early afternoon and as we watched a girl's hockey team compete on the grass, I told Baldy about my sub assignment at Mount Vernon Junior High. The students were about ninety percent black. They were well dressed and well behaved. On my first day the V.P. gave me one simple piece of advice. "Lock the room when you leave. These kids are okay. They'll do exactly what you ask them to do. Just remember to lock the door when you leave."

"You want to see Bukowski's house over on Longwood? It's pretty much the same."

I nodded yes. I wanted to see Bukowski's house through Baldy Mullinax's eyes.

As we drove west on Washington Boulevard, I told Baldy about my two weeks at Mount Vernon Junior High. My students were well behaved and did exactly what I asked them to do. They liked to talk about social issues and, since I was subbing in an American History class, I let them talk and argue and analyze issues. I told him they called the Watts Riots the Watts Rebellion. Baldy seemed interested.

"My wife and I are one of the last white couples to stay in the neighborhood," he said. He told me he had a daughter who lived elsewhere; I think he said San Diego.

Then he told me about the last mugging he'd received. "I hit the kid with my cane. Pretty hard. Now I carry a gun. So you had no problems at Mount Vernon Junior High?"

"No. I didn't say that. On the final Thursday I stacked up all the homework and was looking around for a book I'd brought to read in the teachers' lunchroom. I couldn't find it, so I walked down the hall to the teacher's lounge and there it was on the table. But I forgot . . ."

"To *lock* the door." Baldy laughed. He was an affable man, in spite of the twists and turns his life had taken. Poor Dr. Mull. "So what happened?"

I told him when I got back the next day I pulled out the top drawer of my desk and it had been turned upside down. "All the stuff in the desk fell out. And there was the V.P. at the door. The kids all laughed, but the V.P. didn't think it was funny. 'I told you to lock the door of your room,' he said."

"So what happened with you and the V.P.?" he asked.

"They never invited me back as a sub," I said. "I got a real job. Full-time teacher."

"This is Longwood Avenue," Baldy pointed to a white stucco house with a carport and a large arched window. "This was Hank's house when I knew him as a kid." He stopped the car and shut off the engine.

"I don't drive by here much. Pretty boring place, right?"

I didn't want to insult him; Baldy lived in a house just like it only smaller.

He shook his head. "Still the same well-trimmed lawn. His father always made Hank cut the grass until it was perfect. The old man was a bastard. All Hank ever wanted to do was read books. His father would come along and nag him to get the trash out, or show him where the grass wasn't even. And Hank would say so the old man could hear, 'What a shame a man of letters has to demean himself cutting the grass.' We were in ninth grade then. The old man would get so mad . . ."

I asked if that was why Bukowski hated his father so much.

Bukowski's parents' house on Doreen Ave., in Temple City. Bukowski inherited the house and car in 1959.

Baldy told me it probably stemmed from little Henry's closeness to his mother.

"Hank felt sorry for her," he told me. "His father never went to church with her, so Henry had to go. She never really adjusted to life in America, and she was a pretty woman. She trusted Hank and she liked to talk to me. That made the old man jealous. She was really a bird in a gilded cage. A small gilded cage."

He said the old man was taller than Hank and really strong. "Hank used to shake when he saw his old man coming."

I asked Baldy if he could recall a particular incident, besides the ones Bukowski had already written about, that might shed some light on the father/son relationship. He thought for a moment, then started up the car. Neighbors were peeking out the window at us. Baldy felt uncomfortable. He suggested we drive over to Los Angeles High School.

"You know, Hank had a beautiful dog. They called it Igloo. It was a white husky. He really loved that dog and one day his father just got rid of him. Igloo. That was his name. He never told him why. He just did it. Hank always thought he did it just to hurt him. He was that kind of man. Hank never forgave him for getting rid of Igloo. No matter what his father wanted, Hank could never please him. Some fathers are like that. I remember his old man worked for The Golden State Milk Company. That was the name in those days. Later it changed to . . . I don't remember. Anyway, one day he got laid off. Hank was so ashamed. His father had lost his job. He was a failure."

Baldy drove north on Longwood Avenue to Olympic, then turned right. I was amazed at how close everything was in Henry Bukowski's young world. I asked if he could remember the names of any of Bukowski's teachers at Mount Vernon. "He hated all his teachers," he said.

"There was one, a Miss Duncan, she taught French and she really despised Hank. She had it in for him. He switched to Spanish. But Hank was a reader. He'd walk the streets all the time, headed for the public library on La Brea, and spend hours there. He read everything. Even medical books. In junior high I remember Hank was permanently consigned to the auto shop. Pop Elsworth was in charge. A fat Irishman."

Then Baldy drove me around Los Angeles High School. The 1971 earthquake had totaled the sixty-year-old building, and a new one had sprung up in its place. Baldy didn't like the architecture. "L.A. High, when we went there, looked like a high school. Now it looks like a prison."

He repeated what Bukowski had told me: "It was the best school in the city. The kids who lived north of Wilshire in Hancock Park used to drive over here to go to school. Some of them probably lied about their address so they could attend L.A. High. You know, you get an aunt to say you live with her. I guess they still do that with the best schools."

I told him they still did that. We didn't mention busing.

"Hank would always say 'environment shaped the guy,'" Baldy told me. "I don't know where he came up with this stuff. Maybe he was reading Darwin. He read everyone from Mencken to Dostoevsky to Schopenhauer. He liked the Germans and the Russians, but especially the Germans."

"What about this German thing?" I told him Bukowski described attending two Bund meetings when he and Baldy attended LACC. "He said you went with him."

Baldy told me that was completely untrue. "Hank mentioned it many years later," he said, "but I was already in the service when he went to those meetings."

As the afternoon buses started to line up, Baldy pulled his car around the corner.

"But why do you think Bukowski was drawn to the Nazis?" I asked.

"He didn't start that stuff till later. He loved the ROTC. He got me into it. When I get back I'll show you a picture of Hank in uniform. He was really into the military. Hank joined ROTC first. He was in Company A commanded by Harcourt Hervey Jr. Even in the ROTC, social strata determined who would be an officer or not."

As an LAPD car pulled up and shooed us out of the no parking zone, Baldy turned onto Edgewood Avenue and we looked out onto the athletic field. The squad car made another circle around the school and signaled us to move on.

"L.A. is all about automobiles," said Baldy. "Let's go back to the house. I've got something to show you. It's important if you really want to know who Hank was back then."

"So what was he like in ROTC?"

"He had to wear pajamas under his uniform because he had terrible skin, but I'll tell you a funny incident that happened back then, when we were both in the ROTC: I was in Company B, under the command of Captain John Nevins. Hank (he hated the name Henry because it was his father's name) had hall duty one day. That was a job for the ROTC. A lieutenant went by and Hank didn't salute. His name was McHargue. He humiliated Hank in front of the whole ROTC. He called him Henry Bukowski and made him apologize in front of the entire unit. Hank was always getting into little scrapes like that, but he liked ROTC."

Baldy parked his car in the driveway and returned his pistol to the closet.

Back on the sofa, he handed me his spring '38 Blue and White Annual. He showed me a picture of the three ROTC Companies.

"... he had dreams of joining the U.S. Navy."

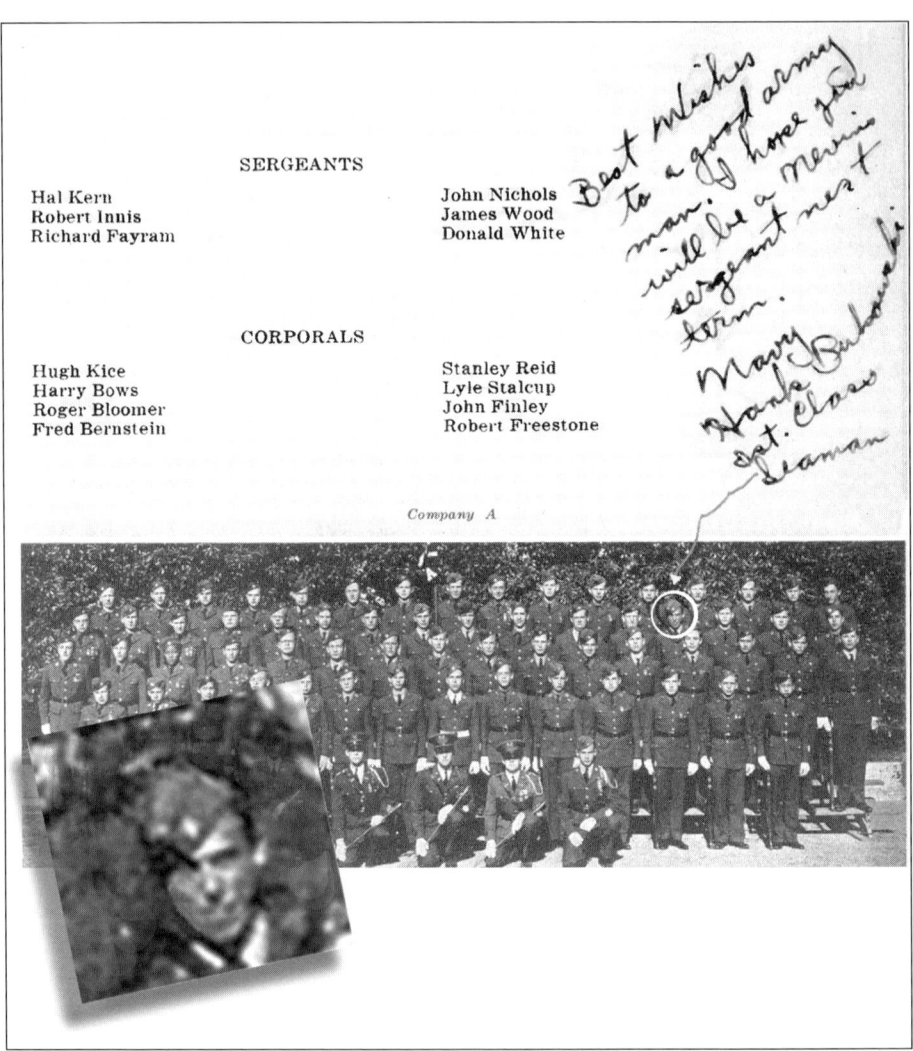

Company A
Charles Bukowski in uniform, under arrow,
L.A. High Yearbook, *1938.*

Henry Bukowski was in Company A, William Mullinax in Company B, and another friend, Jimmy Haddox, in Company C.

In the spring term of '39 Mullinax was a corporal and Haddox a sergeant. Bukowski was still a private. "But he had dreams of joining the U.S. Navy," Baldy said.

In the margin of the Company A photo Henry "Hank" Bukowski wrote:

"Best wishes to a good army man. I hope you will be a Nevins Sergeant next term. Navy. Hank Bukowski. 1st Class Seaman"

William "Baldy" Mullinax   Bob Stoner   Jimmy Haddox

L.A. High School Yearbook, *spring '38*.

"He wanted to go in the Navy then," Baldy told me. "He hoped he could sail away from his father and Los Angeles forever. But when the War came he changed. He took creative writing courses at LACC. Writing made him very strange."

I asked Baldy about friends killed in World War Two. He could remember two: Norman Weersing, killed at Pearl Harbor. "He graduated in 1936," he told me "and was a student at USC. And then there was Jimmy Haddox. That was really sad. Jimmy was the nicest kid I knew in school. He had a society mom who was always looking after him. She looked like the Mona Lisa. He was an only child. I don't know where he was killed."

Later, when I read through the yearbook, I found a chilling inscription written by Jimmy Haddox that read:

BILL:

You've been a swell friend and I truly hope that our friendship may continue infinitely—Good luck to you and may your medical profession become the outstanding success that I'm sure it will be. (Lay off the S.S. Arizona)

        Sincerely,

        Jim Haddox

  Next day I mentioned to Bukowski what Jim Haddox had written about the S.S. Arizona, sunk at Pearl Harbor on December 7, 1941— a day that changed Bukowski's life along with everyone else's.

"He wrote that in 1939?"

"1938." He just shook his head.

As Baldy poured me a glass of orange juice he began to talk about his years at LACC.

"They called it Los Angeles Community College then, not City College. That was where the kids went who couldn't afford to go to UCLA or USC. Hank graduated from L.A. High in the spring of '39 and started at LACC in the fall. I graduated a semester before and went to LACC in the winter term. I took pre-engineering; he became an *intellectual* and took creative writing courses. He was satiric and ironic about everything. He laughed at the Marxists who were everywhere and said, 'We're on their magic shit list.' I guess he said that because he was German. I took math and science, but by 1940 I was in the service. I guess he was starting to talk like a Nazi then, but I really don't remember it much. Except for gym we had completely different classes."

Baldy said the war changed him completely. "I came back a man while Bukowski was still a kid. When I left the service I went to USC and took mechanical engineering. After graduation, I worked for Northrop, RCA, and Fairchild. In the fifties my arthritis kicked up and I had a hip fusion. You can see what kind of job they did. I didn't see

Hank again until the late Forties. When he was living with Jane Cooney Baker."

I asked if he remembered her.

"Sure do," he said. "She made a play for all of Hank's friends, me included. I guess he told you. All they did was drink and fight. The first time I ever had a drink was with Hank. I was fifteen. It was New Years 1935. We drank half a pint of my father's whiskey. Hank could out drink any three men I know, but he couldn't out drink Jane. They were both alcoholics' alcoholics, in a class by themselves."

I asked if he could remember how Bukowski met Jane Cooney Baker.

"They met in a bar on Alvarado," he said. "Jane was something else. Once, in their place she kissed me and started taking off her clothes. She was heavyset and not well educated. That would be putting it mildly. She didn't work if she could help it. I was there alone with her and she stripped off her clothes and showed me her privates. I thought, 'This woman is crazy.' And then there was noise outside. Before I knew it a mob was milling around downstairs outside the apartment house. I looked out the window and they were pointing to the next window over. It was on the third or fourth storey. I looked over and there was Hank hanging out the window by his feet. He was gonna jump. He was so jealous over that crazy woman. Later he left her for a hunchback. Hank and Jane were together off and on from about 1948 to 1954. Then he dumped her for this rich woman from Texas. They never got along. Jane died around 1961, maybe early 1962. I think it was a perforated ulcer. Hank felt real guilty about dumping her, and he never forgave me for feeling her up. He always found the ugliest women."

I was about at the end of my interview. I could sense his punctilious wife on her way home from work soon, so I asked him the big question. Bukowski had told me once he and Baldy were in the same bed together after a long, drunken evening. Bukowski was having an erotic dream. Feeling a warm body next to him in the bed, Bukowski told me he stuck his erect penis into the nearest available orifice which happened to be Baldy's anus. I'd saved this question for last and I held my breath to see if Baldy would go for the gun.

Instead, he merely laughed. "You know, Hank writes this stuff when he's angry and drunk, late at night. It's his way of getting back at the world. I was never in bed with Hank. I guess he's still mad at me for feeling up Jane. It was no big deal, really. Everybody did it."

"But why do you think he'd write such things about you, his oldest friend?"

"He just uses the people he knows for his stories is my guess. Either that, or maybe he wanted to impress the queers."

I thanked Baldy for his help and I left before his wife got home. We never talked about his war years.

I wanted to arrange a meeting with Baldy and Bukowski, but when I told Bukowski what Baldy had said he turned cold. He said he'd forgotten the name of the dog, Igloo. That put a big smile on his face. "Baldy remembers what he wants to remember," he said.

I guess that was true with both of them.

A few years later, Bukowski told me William "Baldy" Mullinax was dumped by his wife and had moved into a trailer behind his daughter's home in San Diego. He said it with a touch of glee. William "Baldy" Mullinax died in the early eighties. He would appear in *Ham on Rye*, Bukowski's rites of passage novel, as Eli LaCrosse, but his nickname, used in the novel, was always Baldy. Bukowski knew he could get away with Baldy; that he and Black Sparrow and John Martin could not be sued for nicknames. Jim Haddox, killed in World War Two, the young man Baldy remembered with fondness, becomes Jimmy Hatcher. The portraits of each are stinging and cruel. Hatcher's mother is a sexy barmaid who satisfies Bukowski's sexual fantasies, and of Baldy he writes, "He was so pitiful I couldn't tell him to get lost."

When Baldy died, Bukowski said, "He did everything society tells you to do: he joined the service, went to college, got married, had a good job, and look where he ended up. He never got it right."

HAROLD MORTENSON: The Facts of Fiction

"Best of everything to a good baseball player and a swell student."

Henry Bukowski

L. A. High School Yearbook, *spring '38.*

I was on the phone from L.A. to Honolulu.

The first thing I noticed about Harold Mortenson was his passion for detail. At the age of 81 he could recall each member of his ROTC unit at UCLA, where they were stationed (U.S. Army: Tank Corps at Fort Hood, 104th Infantry at Fort Benning), those who survived and what they became; those who died in combat; where approximately, and when. In his mind's eye he could picture the faces of every officer in his L.A. High School senior class, especially one he had a crush on; hum the recessional to his high school graduation convocation from the winter term '39 (Mendelssohn's Recessional); knock off the lineup to the local triple A Pacific Coast League team, The L.A. Angels; sing the words to the 1937 hit "The Miller's Daughter, Marianne," and regale me with stories of the three winning seasons his L.A. High football team enjoyed, led by Al (Li'l Scooter) Cole.

From memory, he could circumambulate his high school campus, starting from the place he parked his bike and ending up anywhere I asked him.

"I was shy," he told me on the phone. "I was the youngest kid in my grade, but they elected me class treasurer. I had to collect the dues, so I got to know everybody."

I asked him my obvious question. "Did you know Charles Bukowski?"

"I knew a Hank Bukowski. In my last two years of high school."

So I had it. The guy in *Ham on Rye* Bukowski called that "idiot book reader." The same guy Bukowski slammed on tape and later in his novel. He was Abe Mortenson the Jewish whiz kid in *Ham on Rye*. Bukowski had hardly been kind to him.

I started slowly. I knew this was big. I held my breath.

"You knew a Hank Bukowski at L.A. High?"

"His real name was Henry Bukowski. His middle name was Charles, I think. I never heard him use it. I called him Hank. He was one of my closest friends along with Bill Mullinax. I hardly saw him in school. Hank was in the spring '39 graduating class, one semester behind me. He was quite a bit older. I hardly ever saw him in school. I mostly saw him after school when we went to his house. The place on Longwood."

"He's world famous," I said.

"Hank Bukowski is world famous? What at?"

"He was a writer. Died in 1994. Wrote more than fifty books, published in . . . many languages."

"Hank Bukowski? Amazing."

I was trying to be careful. I knew what Bukowski thought of friends: how disposable they became as they were whipped up into the batter of his "fiction." In chapter forty-five of *Ham on Rye*, Bukowski had described Mortenson as "a broom, a stiff, a wimp." I was on the phone to Honolulu after transcribing hours of tapes I'd done with Bukowski in the mid-seventies in the era of Cupcakes, the time between the two Lindas. Bukowski had rolled out his whole childhood seven years before *Ham on Rye* came out. There was quite a bit about Mortenson. He could not recall the first name.

There was a pause. Harold Mortenson broke the ice. "You knew Hank?"

"I knew him for more than twenty years and I also knew Baldy."

That got him. Baldy. Bill Mullinax with his retreating hairline. Baldy and Abe Mortenson and Jim Haddox. All savaged in *Ham on Rye*. What did the English philosopher John Locke say? "Bellum omnium contra omens." (War of all against All.) That was the world of Charles Bukowski.

I started slowly. There were delicate questions to ask.

"He mentioned you in one of his books. You were the straight A student," I said.

"You mean RH. Recommended for honors. We didn't have A's then. What was the book he mentioned me in?"

I knew from experience there was only one way to do this. Win or lose, I had to tell him the whole thing first. "He wrote some bad things about you, Harold."

"What?"

"He called you a fool and an idiot book reader. He said you had a saliva problem and he used your last name."

Mortenson was quiet. "How did you find me?" he asked.

"Through the UCLA Alumni Association. I read about your bequest. I'm a member."

His voice brightened. "So, what was my first name in the book?"

"Abe. He said you were Jewish."

Mortenson burst out laughing. "Really? He said I was Jewish? I'm Episcopal. Sang in the choir. What's the name of the book?"

"*Ham on Rye,*" I said. "I'll send it on to you if you want it. It might make you angry."

He laughed again. "Send it on. I'm a big boy."

First I sent him a book of poetry, *Mocking Bird Wish Me Luck*, and then I sent on the novel, with my telephone number and address.

There was silence for a week. I called him back. He told me he got the book. He found it funny.

"It opened up all my memory banks," he said "Like a flood."

For an hour we spoke together on the phone. I tried to get it all down:

The flood. Hank and Harold on their bikes rushing from L.A. High to Bukowski's house to war with their intelligence, brain against brain, in a complicated baseball game played on paper. Numbers, statistics. Bukowski mentioned it on the tapes I had done with him. "We had lineups. We had super sluggers." He considered Mortenson a worthy opponent. The guy on the other end of the line. There was more. Much more. Out it all came: classmates' teachers; baseball games played for real at Dorsey High till the sun went down; bike rides; touch football; flying airplanes with rubber band motors; Harold Mortenson's graduation ceremony where Bukowski said Harold gave Hank the finger; ("He wasn't even there"); and the grand prize: Mr. and Mrs. Bukowski at home.

In *Ham on Rye* it was all fire and rage, victims and tyrants, but Harold Mortenson spooled out the whole thing in cool, dispassionate tones.

He was the second character from *Ham on Rye* to emerge from the pages full of life. It was ironic. Bill "Baldy" Mullinax was the first. Bukowski had already told me much of those years on tape, but when I played it for "Baldy," he said it was false. He suggested I interview Bukowski and himself together. Bukowski demurred. When *Ham on Rye* came out, I saw how Bukowski crucified Mullinax as Eli LaCrosse, with the same nickname, "Baldy." Now here was Harold Mortenson, after the novel was published. The before and after. Both had been in the house on Longwood. Wasn't this something out of Heidegger? Being and Time?

Harold Mortenson continued speaking and I tried to get it down.

He recalled clearly Bukowski's house: the neatly cut lawn, Mrs. Bukowski preparing dinner.

"A few times when we were playing the Danny McFadden Game, I'd stay over," he said.

I asked about Bukowski's father, Henry Charles Bukowski Sr.

He said Hank and his father were much alike. "Rough cut. Gruff and gruffer." He recalled some of the repartee between father and son as Henry Senior came home from work.

"Competitive," said Harold.

I was struggling to get it all down: the one-car garage with the basketball hoop Henry Senior had put up for his son, the game the two friends played at Dorsey field called "Over the Line", flying windup engine model planes, songs they hummed together, the classical music playing on the Bukowski family radio.

I couldn't keep up. He could describe the bike ride from L.A. High to Bukowski's house block by block. In all the interviews I'd done over the years I always worked face to face with tapes. Kenneth Rexroth, Budd Schulberg, Ferlinghetti, Bukowski, Edward Dmytryk, James Laughlin, John Fante. Phones never worked for me. Phones I hated. Finally, I told him to stop.

"Where do you live in Hawaii, Harold?"

"Why? Do you think it worth your while to come out this far?"

"I owe my wife a vacation. A second honeymoon. I can't write it all down, Harold. I need to see you face to face."

"Well. OK. Come ahead. I'll tell you my side of it. You know the one thing he said that got me was what he wrote about my mother. That was cruel. I don't know why he would do that. We were very close friends. We spent lots of time together. We never even had an argument. Was he on drugs?"

"No," I said. "He was a lifelong drunk. A brilliant drunk. Maybe the greatest drunken writer who ever lived."

"Really?" He was impressed. "When do you want to come?"

"The last week in June."

He gave me his address. Not in the city. He said he'd been successful in life. Comfortable, but his wife Barbara had died a few years ago, and her death had left him bereft. "She was a smoker," he said. "I had it all planned out. She was provided for after my death, but she died first. Lung cancer. One terrible year. The whole nine yards. She was . . . my life."

That caught me. Bukowski would never have said something like that about anyone.

"In the book," I told Harold Mortenson, "he called you a one woman man."

"Well, that part he got right. I just lived an ordinary life and I did well. I had a passion for cost accounting." We both laughed.

The State of California was almost forty billion dollars in debt. "We could use some of that here right now," I said.

"Anything you want me to think about?"

"What about the broken arm?"

"That's a story. It was much worse than a broken arm. Actually Hank snapped the tendon and tore my triceps. It took me six months before I could drive a car. The way he wrote it was melodramatic. I mean . . . we were both in the outfield. I wasn't on second base. You can even look at the elbow."

Paula, my wife, booked passage the next day in Santa Monica. One of those package deals. We arrived in Honolulu on June 23, 2003 . . . The Sars epidemic was raging. Hotel rates were way down.

Harold Mortenson lives halfway up the Mauna Oahi Ridge in a retirement community with a full view of Maunalua Bay on the island of Oahu. Hawaii has been his home since 1977.

I met him in the well-appointed dining room while he was finishing his water. He rose to shake my hand: a precise man, white-haired, on the tall side, with piercing blue eyes, strong hands and a long Scandinavian face. He had on a red Hawaiian shirt that matched

Harold Mortenson, 2003.

his complexion. The dining room, almost empty, was surrounded by plants, flowers and a fountain of gurgling water.

"Ben? You're early," he says. "I thought you were coming at two."

"I hate to be late." He finished his coffee with a friend. I introduced my wife.

"Paula? Charmed."

He directed us to the elevator, walking with a cane.

"My knees are shot," he said.

His apartment, the largest one in the complex, has a panoramic view of the Pacific. It is on the second floor at the end of the hall.

"It's a little messy," said Harold, opening the front door. "Barbara . . . my wife . . . always kept our house just so. She made it a home."

Inside there was a kitchen, a long living room, two bathrooms, a bedroom and an office alcove. On his desk sat a brass plate that read HAROLD MORTENSON, VICE PRESIDENT, OPERATIONS & FINANCE.

Stacks of magazines and papers were arranged neatly on tables and on the floor. Harold offered us sodas from the fridge. Surveying his piled up material he said, "Most of this stuff is history and medical research. I have a hard time getting up, so I place them in strategic locations."

"Paula, my wife, is always moving my papers around till I can't find anything."

My wife said, "Paula's going down stairs to read her book." A good exit line.

I set up my machine, as Harold settles down into his sofa. "So you knew Bill Mullinax?" I ask.

"Bill introduced me to Hank. They'd known each other since junior high school."

Outside it's a perfect Hawaiian day, 87 degrees, the blue water clear and dazzling in its dual colored dance inside and outside the reef. I snap on the tape recorder.

"How specific do you want this?" Harold asks.

"As accurate as you can get it. Let's start with you. Your life before Bukowski."

"I was born at 10:05 p.m. on June 11, 1922 at California Lutheran Hospital on South Hope Street in Los Angeles. My father was Harold Mortenson, married to my mother Anna in 1918. Chicago. They were both from Chicago. My grandparents on my father's side were from Stockholm, Sweden. My father's mother was from Stavanger, Norway." He gives the Norwegian pronunciation.

"So you're half Norwegian and half Swedish?"

"Right."

"Not Jewish?"

"Hell no. I'm not Jewish. I don't know where the hell he got that from. Why would he make something like that up? I was baptized at St. John's Episcopal Church on West Adams Blvd. At Figueroa Street, across from the Automobile Club Southern California by the Reverend George Davidson. I sang in the choir in the fifth and sixth grades. My family went almost every Sunday." He points to a picture of his parents on the breakfront. Then another.

"That one's of my wife and my mother."

"Tell me about your parents. Bukowski said your mother made you study when you wanted to play baseball."

"My parents were wonderful," he says. "My father was a manufacturing optician. He made glasses. For a time he worked for Superior Optical Company. Then he had his own business for fifteen years. Sigmor Surgical Supply from stethoscopes to operating tables. It was located on West Ninth Street near Union Avenue, an outlet of A.S. Aloe Company, located on South Hill Street."

I persist. "Bukowski said your mother was a nag?" I read him the section in chapter 42 on pages 178 through 179 in *Ham on Rye*. Bukowski wanted Abe Mortenson to play baseball on a Sunday, but he was inside studying civics. According to Bukowski, his mother was forcing him to study.

He laughed. "Bullshit! My mother was a housewife. When I started school at Magnolia Grammar, she was the one who made sure I got there on time. She showed me how to organize my materials. Sometimes she helped me understand math. I did my homework because I wanted to. She never forced me. I was only at Magnolia for four and a half years. I skipped three semesters and graduated at ten.

Maybe that was a mistake. For the rest of my education I was the baby of my class. That penalized me right on through school because I was too young to compete in sports, but I made up for it with my ability to learn. My scholastic pursuits, which meant a lot to me."

For fun I asked if he could remember which semesters he skipped.

"B2, A4 and A5. The semesters were A and B. I graduated from Magnolia in January of 1933. By the time I got to Berendo Junior High School on Vermont, the kids in all my classes were two years older."

"You always went to Los Angeles schools?"

The tape was humming and I was enjoying the ride.

"Not always. My father was out of work for a year during the Depression in the early thirties. He had a job opportunity out East in Whittier, so I spent my junior high school years out there. John Muir Junior High School. It was a Quaker town. We came back from Whittier in January of 1935. High school in Whittier was grades nine to twelve, but in Los Angeles it was ten to twelve so I had to go back to junior high school. A year at Thomas Star King, from January 1935 to January 1936. When I started in at Los Angeles High School, my parents moved near the school. I began there in January of 1936 and graduated in January of 1939. It was the old L.A. High on Olympic and Rimpau. Before the earthquake. Right across Olympic was an L.A. Public Library branch. My house was west of there, between Rimpau and La Brea on Highland Avenue."

"And that's where you met Baldy, Eli LaCrosse of *Ham on Rye*?"

"Bill was in my class. His house was between Venice Boulevard and Washington Blvd. . . ." He closed his eyes for a better look. "Off of Overland Avenue. I remember riding my bike there. It was a modest house. We were all middle class then. I guess you could say that. Owned our own house."

"You and Bukowski and Mullinax?"

"Right. Each one of us was an only child. Another L.A. High friend of mine then was Robert Lopez. And Sid Noodleman."

"What was your course of study at L.A. High?"

"Math, accounting, commercial law and science. Science in its broad sense, biology and physiology specifically. Everything in math:

algebra, geometry, trig. I'm from a generation that still used a slide rule."

"Where did you first meet Bill Mullinax?"

"Bill was in my homeroom. Lucy Adams was our homeroom teacher. He was also in my physiology class. My lab partner. We dissected a frog together." He laughed. "I haven't thought about this for sixty-five years."

I asked about Mullinax and his family. Harold recalled "Baldy's" modest house. "I lived on Highland, a block and a half below Olympic. To get to Bill's house, I had to cross Venice, then Washington. Bill was near Washington and Hank was down the other side. Baldy lived between me and Hank. I remember Bill's father was a doctor, but I never met him. Baldy's mother I remember vaguely."

I read him the part in *Ham on Rye* where Bukowski described his high school as "a rich kid's school." Chapter 36, Page 154.

He laughed. "Not L.A. High. Beverly Hills, yes. Hollywood High, maybe; but L.A. High School was more like Fairfax or University or Hamilton. Middle class, not rich."

"He said the rich boys came from far away and drove cars."

"That's bunk. Some of 'em had cars. Not many. It was the Depression. I remember Pat Curry drove a 1934 Plymouth Roadster. There were more girl students who had cars than boys."

"Pat Curry?"

"I had a crush on her. She was Vice President of my senior B12 class. What Bukowski said was bunk. We all rode our bikes and parked them at the lock stand at the back of the campus. There was a driveway where they had athletic equipment. It was right near the football grandstand, by the cafeteria."

In his mind's eye, he could see it all.

"So it wasn't an elite school?"

He laughed. "The building was beautiful, but it was old even then. It had two beautiful towers. It was one of the GOOD schools with an excellent faculty. My grades there qualified me for UCLA. It wasn't a school for rich kids. One of our biggest rivals on the south side was Manual Arts. Jefferson was the Black school. There were few Blacks at L.A. High; we were mostly White, Hispanic, Japanese."

I asked again about Pat Curry. "I was a shy kid," said Harold, "but I got elected treasurer of my class. Pat Curry was elected vice president. The class treasurer carried on from one semester to another. B12 to A12. The other officers didn't. It was always that way with the treasurer. Continuity. Because of the financial records. I collected all the dues, so I got to meet everybody in the class. In 1938, when I met Hank, I was a B senior. He was still a junior, in the 11th grade. I was fifteen when I met him and he was almost eighteen. I don't know why he was behind."

I told him it was because of his acne. "He had to stay out a semester for treatment. It's in the book."

"I must have missed that part," said Harold. "I asked my father about his face and he told me he might have had smallpox. His face was really terrible. I never talked to him about it, but then he never mentioned my braces."

"How about with Baldy? Did you ever talk about Bukowski's skin?"

"Never. I saw Baldy mostly in school. We went to the football games together some times. I never missed a game. Hank I almost never saw in school. It was always at the house on Longwood or on the field where we played Over the Line at what is now part of Dorsey."

"Did you ever go to the movies together? You and Hank?"

"Maybe," said Harold. "I'll think about that later."

He was focused on L.A. High. I was thinking about the way Bukowski described the three of them in *Ham on Rye*: Abe Mortenson, Eli LaCrosse and Henry Chinaski.

"The three of you made a funny group," I said. "A bit odd."

"How do you mean?"

"Well, Hank was one of the oldest guys in the class and he had terrible skin; Baldy walked with a limp and was losing his hair; and you were the baby of the class and had braces."

Harold laughed. "When you put it that way, I guess you're right. Let's move on to Bukowski. That's what you came all this way for, right?"

"True and not true. The UCLA stuff interests me too."

"We'll save that for Thursday. What do you want to know about Hank Bukowski?"

"Everything."

"OK then. As I said, Baldy introduced me to Hank Bukowski in the spring of 1938. March. Hank and I became firm friends. We loved baseball. Baldy and I didn't have that much in common. Bill was always talking about the navy. Baldy."

I asked why Mullinax was always called Baldy.

"His hairline receded far back while he was a teenager. The front part of the top of his skull was just skin. Everyone called him Baldy. You know how kids are. Once they start in, they all pick up on the same thing. You said you met him."

"He was completely bald when I interviewed him and he walked with a bad limp. Baldy started Bukowski on liquor. That much they both agreed on. Did you ever see Baldy or Hank Bukowski drink?"

"Never. I never drank or smoked in my life. Healthy living."

"Maybe that's why you're still alive and they are both dead."

He pulled out his winter, '39 yearbook. "Bill and I graduated together. A semester before Hank. Here's what he wrote: 'Lots of luck to an old pal and a truly great guy. Bill Mullinax ("Baldy").' See. I don't think it bothered him at all being called Baldy."

"How well did you know Jim Haddox?"

"I don't remember him at all."

"He was a friend of Bill and Hank. They were in ROTC together."

Harold said he wasn't in ROTC in high school

"That came later, when I was at UCLA."

"Did you and Bukowski ever have a class together?"

"No. I don't think so. I hardly ever saw Hank in school, it was always at his house or on the playing field."

"And you remember the house on Longwood?"

He had a clear memory of it room by room. "The house was white. It had a one-car garage. Hank had a basketball hoop over the door. His mother was an attractive woman. At age fifteen I wasn't much interested in women's figures, but I remember she was a very sweet woman. She had a slight accent and she was into dieting somewhat. Proper foods, I mean. I remember the carrot juice. She used a press to get out the juices. I'd never seen anyone squeeze carrots before. The kitchen was a comfortable room. You looked out the window onto the backyard and you could see the garage. They had a back lawn between the garage and the hedges next door. It was a nice, well-kept lawn."

"Which Bukowski complained about cutting. He said his father was very tough on him. Did you ever see Hank cut the grass?"

"No, but I met his father several times. His father was Billy Goat Gruff. Hank was a chip off the old block. Gruff and gruffer. The best way to express the relationship of father to son was they were both rough cut off the same bolt of cloth. They spoke gruffly. His father, Henry Senior, was about six foot. He was burly. I think he was around forty years old. I'd go over there during the week. My family always had something doing on the weekend. His mother was more genteel than his father. She liked to cook. Back in those days they were mothers. They did what mothers do. Today, they're career women."

I asked him to compare Mullinax with Bukowski: "Hank was roughhewn compared to Bill Mullinax. Bill was a sweet, soft-spoken guy. He didn't get his feathers ruffled very easily. Hank did. He was excitable. He was self-conscious about his face. We never discussed it, but he played with it a lot. He'd put his fingers on his cheeks, feeling the pockmarks. I felt sorry for him, having smooth skin."

"Did your parents meet Hank? Did you have him over to your house?"

"Never. That stuff in the book about my studying in my room on a Sunday is all made up. The closest he ever came to my house was the field where we played baseball, about a block away."

"But you went to his house."

"Many times. We'd ride our bikes over there after school."

"Did you ever go with Bukowski to the football games?"

"Bill and I sat together at the football games sometimes. Maybe Hank came with me once or twice, but I can't remember him at any football game. Always at the house or playing baseball or touch football or basketball outside."

"What about the movies nearby? Can you remember the movie theatres in your neighborhood?"

"Clear as a bell. There were three of them. On Pico there was the Victoria and the Empire. The Boulevard was on Washington, one block west of Vermont. And there was the Rialto on Sunset. That was farther away. I went there only when I was enrolled in junior high school."

"You never went with Bukowski to the movies?"

"I don't think so. I usually went with my father on a Saturday afternoon."

Harold spread out a stack of yearbooks. He told me he'd looked for Bukowski's signature in all of them, but couldn't find it.

"So, sport is what drew you together?"

"Baseball. First it was the Danny McFadden Baseball Game. The game was played on paper. There were two books. Pamphlets, really. Each page had a different set of plays following specific numbers on special red and green dice. The red and green dice were numbered one through six. For how many bases and so on. The white ivory die had black letters on it. N, H, B, and S. H was a hit. S was strike and B was for ball. If it was a hit, you would throw the colored die to see if it was a single or a home run or whatever. We would play it on the dining room table at Hank's house. We'd trade players from the lineups. I gave him Wayne Adrahall, a pitcher, and he gave me Mel Sherwood from left field. We had complete lineups. Pitching staffs. The whole works. McFadden was a Boston Braves right hand pitcher. From the 1930s. It was a complicated game."

"So you played it on paper?"

"Yes. It was mostly numbers. Hank was good at it and so was I. We'd play it for hours until dinner was ready. His mother would ask me to stay. His father would come home for dinner. I had dinner there a few times. We were right in the middle of the Danny McFadden game. His mother would let me eat there. Everything was perfectly normal. Teenaged boys and their parents. His parents were cordial to me. They made me feel comfortable in their house. Once Bill Mullinax was there. The three of us. My father made sure I had a light on my bike. Sometimes it was dark when I rode home."

I asked if he could remember what was said at the table.

"Nothing memorable. Probably we just talked like kids."

"Did you ever help Bukowski with his homework?"

"Maybe once or twice. I might have showed him how to study. I can't remember any details."

I asked if Bukowski told his parents Harold Mortenson was an honors student.

Harold laughed. "I never talked about that with them. I was a shy kid."

"So you played baseball on paper with Bukowski?"

"We played outside too. In the field. Football, basketball and baseball, and Over The Line."

I asked him to describe the game.

"It was played with a baseball-sized softball. Hank and I played it together at Dorsey play field. It was a two man game. You had to hit the ball over a line between second and third base and not have it caught by the defender. The defender stood on the other side of the line between second and third. If he caught you, you were out. If it went past him, you got different points. Once in a while I could whack it over his head. Hank didn't run fast. We were about on a par with each other. We had such fun playing that game. We'd be out there till it got dark, till you could hardly see the ball. Sometimes, in the winter, we'd play touch football in the street in front of his house with kids from his block."

I asked if he ever talked about girls with Bukowski.

"I was into sports. When I was 15, I was very shy. Girls would frighten me to death. In my own class, Don Brubaker, the class president, would push girls on me. They'd come over and touch me and smile sweetly. Seventeen and eighteen year olds. I couldn't run away fast enough. I was terrified. A girl touching me? I felt like shrinking into the floorboards."

"Except for Patricia Ann Curry."

"She was class vice president. We worked in the same office on class matters at L.A. High. And yes, I had a crush on her."

"Did Bukowski ever talk about girls?" I asked.

"He was more frightened of them than I was. Because of his face. Bill may have had a girl friend. I think he went to dances. I never went to dances. My dad even sent me to a dance studio to learn the latest steps, but at the age of 15–16, I was petrified when a girl touched me."

I took a break as Harold continued looking through his yearbooks. I was ready for the head-to-head stuff. The real Harold Mortenson and the fictional Abe Mortenson of *Ham on Rye*.

"Next."

"Let's turn to the novel. *Ham on Rye*." We both had our copies.

"How about chronology? What happened first, the baseball accident where Bukowski broke your arm, or your graduation?"

"I graduated in January of 1939. The accident was in May of 1939. Hank was still in school."

"Do you remember breaking your arm?"

"You bet. It was my left arm. We were both going after the same fly ball in the outfield. Our arms were outstretched. Hank and I collided. It wasn't a regular bone break. You see this knob on my elbow, to which the tendons are attached. They snapped. It hurt like hell. The way he hit me, my arm was overextended. The muscle and the tendon snapped off along with the knob of the bone. My dad took me to an orthopedic surgeon, who put it in a cast. It was a lot more serious than a bone break. It was a year before I could use my arm again."

Harold held out his left arm and showed me his elbow.

I thumbed through *Ham on Rye*. "Did your mother call Mrs. Bukowski and threaten to sue?" I read him the part about the Jewish lawyer. Page 184. "He said he did it on purpose."

"Of course not. It was an accident."

"Page 185. Your mother and Mrs. Bukowski on the phone. The Jewish lawyer."

"We didn't even know a Jewish lawyer."

I read him the section where they smacked together in the field. Bukowski wrote the ball popped out of Mortenson's mitt and Bukowski caught it

Harold laughed. "It was a fly ball. Neither of us caught it. We were both down on the ground. He said he visited my apartment when I was studying so we could play baseball. I had graduated in January. Why would I study civics? I always lived in a house. Not an apartment. He never met my mother. He was never in my house."

"Well, he said you were Abe Mortenson and you were Jewish."

"Maybe he was jealous of me. I don't know! I never knew anyone named Abe at that time. I'm Harold Richard Mortenson."

"Maybe because you were the class treasurer, he thought you were Jewish . . ."

"God. I never thought that way. I didn't care what people were. We were all just Americans."

"Well, he did spell your last name right, anyway."

"That's true. He got the son right. Son is Swedish and sen is either Norwegian or Danish."

I asked if he wanted to stop.

"Certainly not," he said. "This is getting to be fun."

"Bukowski spoke about you for about ten minutes on the tape I did with him. He couldn't remember your first name, but he did describe in great detail the Danny McFadden Game. And the accident. In the book he said his father would be proud of him for breaking your arm."

"Oh, bunk. That wasn't the Hank I knew! It was an accident and he was sorry. He helped me up. Hank sometimes used vulgar language, but we had fun together. I had a problem with my teeth: braces; so maybe he was right about the saliva. We both liked to read. We both liked to sing. To me what he wrote about is amusing. My arm was banged up so badly I couldn't use it for almost a year. My parents moved to Sherman Oaks and with my arm so bad, I put off college for a year. I couldn't drive over the hill to UCLA."

I wondered one more time why Bukowski would write with such anger about a friend who'd been one of his closest companions, who'd been invited over to meet his parents and even stayed for dinner.

Harold smiled and shook his head. "To me it's amusing. My life was full of scholastic priorities. The comments he made about me . . . I don't know if it was frustration or if he wanted to be a scholar too. Do you have any idea?"

I did. Bukowski once discussed the director Taylor Hackford with me and he held two things against him: one that he was good looking and had perfect teeth, and two he'd been the president of the student body at USC. "At least that's what Bukowski told me," I said. "He always talked about the standard American type. I don't think you were it."

He laughed. "What's next?"

"His chapter on graduation. Chapter 45 of *Ham on Rye*. Bukowski's farewell to high school."

Harold had not read that section. I read the whole thing aloud as the tape rolled on. It was mostly dialogue. Bukowski was seated next to Jimmy Hatcher (Jim Haddox) as the names of the graduates were read by the boy's vice principal. I didn't know his real name.

"His name was Ralph C. Noble," said Harold. "He was a disciplinarian. I always walked quietly by his door."

"According to Bukowski, the music at his graduation was Wagner."

"When I graduated, it was Mendelssohn." He hummed it. "Go on."

"Bukowski describes the honors students seated separately."

"Bullshit," said Harold. He was starting to get angry.

As Noble rattled off the names, Hatcher mocked each future graduate. One would be a dogcatcher, another a madhouse attendant, and Abe Mortenson a cost accountant in an auto parts plant in Gardena.

Harold smiled at that. "I do love cost accounting," he said. "But not in Gardena." He'd worked for top corporations like Federated Department Stores in New York, Cincinnati, Albuquerque, and Tucson.

I continued reading: Abe Mortenson would have a lifetime job.

"Not true."

"A lifetime wife."

"The only woman I ever loved. He got that right."

"As they left, Abe gave him the finger."

Harold smiled. "All made up. A complete lie. I graduated six months before Hank did. He did not attend my graduation and I was not at his. After I graduated, I never went back to L.A. High."

"Never?"

"Not once."

"Did you see Hank after that? I mean after the accident? After he graduated?"

"Yes. Once. At the Owl Drugstore and soda fountain at the northwest corner of La Brea and Wilshire. I was there to get my braces off. My orthodontist's office was upstairs. It must have been . . . 1941. I think he told me about LACC and it was then I must have mentioned cost accounting at UCLA. Math again. I never saw him after that. Everything changed after Pearl Harbor."

There was one more missing piece. First I asked about politics. Harold remembered listening to FDR's Fireside Chats, but he never talked politics with Hank Bukowski. They never spoke about the Nazis or world affairs.

"Anything else on Bukowski?"

L.A. High School, spring '38

Al Cole — Small but speedy. Al was a dangerous competitor in all low hurdle events. He also ran in the relay.

"The halfback on the L.A. High football team. Bukowski wrote about him too."

"Al Cole. We called him 'Li'l Scooter.' He enlisted in the Army Air Corps. He was killed in a training accident south of San Francisco Bay early in the war."

In *Ham on Rye* Al Cole is Jimmy Newall. Standard American type. I read what Bukowski wrote: "He had been the halfback on our football team, undefeated for three years. His hair was a beautiful yellow, the sun always seemed to be highlighting parts of it, the sun or the lights of the schoolroom. He had a thick, powerful neck and above it sat the face of the perfect boy sculpted by some master sculptor."

In the book, Al Cole goes after the lowly Chinaski and mocks him as he works in his smock at Sears. According to Bukowski, Newall and his friends are all headed for Stanford or USC, where standard American types go to school.

"So many of the things Bukowski wrote were twisted and warped," said Harold. "They were fantasized, cruel, half true or outright lies. Mullinax was a wonderful friend to Bukowski. Maybe it was the pockmarks on his face that made him so bitter, or the fact that he was older. I can't be offended by something that wasn't true. I only feel sorry for the writer. We had fun together. Do you know why he wrote those things?"

"Maybe. Bukowski liked to have it both ways," I said, pointing out a line in chapter 52 where Chinaski said "I avoided any reference to Jews and Blacks, who had never caused me any trouble. All my troubles had come from white gentiles."

Then I read him the part where Chinaski's mother is hugging Mrs. Mortenson: "My mother went over and threw her arms around Mrs. Mortenson. It was Mrs. Mortenson who decided not to sue after many, many hours of conversation."

"You were Abe Mortenson, Jewish whiz kid. Then you gave him the finger!"

Harold laughed. "Never happened. I graduated the semester before he did. I wasn't even there and our parents *never* met. Hank had a vivid imagination."

We were done with Bukowski. I saved the UCLA stuff for the next day. Harold graduated summa cum laude in October, 1944, after military service. He served at Fort Benning, Georgia, with his ROTC class at the end of his junior year in June of 1943.

Calling me back a month later Harold Mortenson discovered what Bukowski had written in his yearbook in January of 1939.

"Best of everything to a good baseball player and a swell student. Henry Bukowski."

It was right above Sid Noodleman's "Lots of luck to a fellow office holder and a swell basketball player."

Harold asked me if Bukowski had any kids. "One," I said. "Very bright. Her name is Marina. Good in math. Except for his wife Linda Beighle, I think she was the only person in life he really, truly loved."

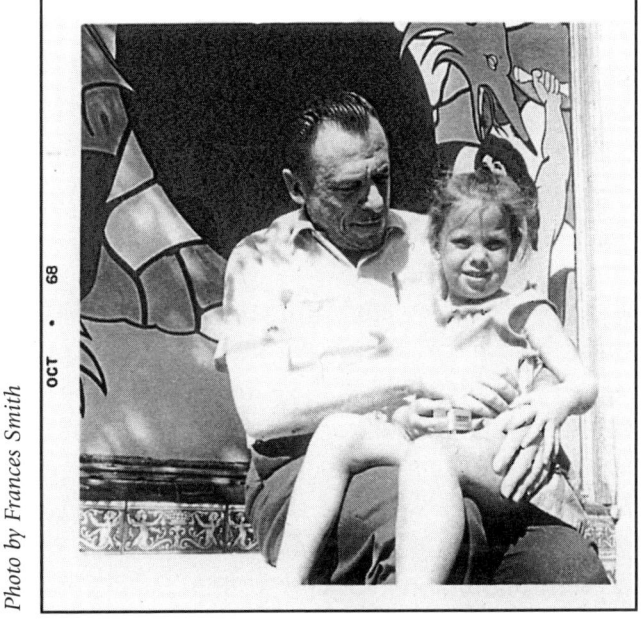

Hank and Marina.
(courtesy of Charles Bukowski)

When Bukowski was a Nazi

> "As school became boring and drab for him, Bukowski was drawn more and more to the 'Nazi trip.'"

I

The subject of Nazism came up first at Canter's, a famous Jewish restaurant on Fairfax. Bukowski and I were both working at the *L.A. Free Press* in Hollywood, and we were preparing a symposium on L.A. Poets including Gerald Locklin, Steve Richmond, Ron Koertge, and Bukowski, all *Wormwood* poets. I was to conduct the interview.

"Symposium means with drinks," Bukowski barked at the editor, Penny Grenoble. "Beer in bottles. Pabst Blue Ribbon."

Penny, who had graduated with a PhD. from RPI, agreed. "We'll have lots of beer in bottles, I promise. And don't worry about your column. You'll get your regular pay. The Symposium will fill the space of 'Notes of a Dirty Old Man' next week. You'll get paid and you won't have to write a thing. Okay, Mr. Bukowski?"

They had a playful relationship, the slender and beautiful editor dressed in high fashion and still in her twenties, and the fiftyish satyr in down-at-the-heel shoes and khaki pants.

Bukowski gave her a mock grimace: "You're not trying to edge me out now, are you?"

The editor of the *Free Press* laughed. "You're the mainstay of our adult pages. How could I do that? And we'll require the usual Bukowski drawings."

We agreed to conduct the interview on tape. Bukowski suggested the two of us meet a few days before to go over the ground rules. At that time he was living on Carlton Way in East Hollywood and I was in Beverly Hills on South Doheny Drive. When he suggested Canter's, somewhere in the middle, I told him I didn't much like Jewish food. He said he found the place entertaining, especially the hefty waitresses in gravy-stained uniforms marching around with huge trays of roast beef and whipped potatoes.

"They have good pastrami," he said. "And besides, they have a bakery."

He knew I had a weakness for pastry.

We showed up at noon a few days later, both ordering pastrami on rye with whipped potatoes and beer. One of the hefty waitresses took our order. It was a hot L.A. day and she was sweating in the heat.

While we were waiting for our food to arrive, Bukowski gawked at the predominantly Jewish diners and, swigging down a brew, yelled loud enough so all could hear: "TURN ON THE GAS."

No one looked up. I shook my head and refused to laugh.

On heavy drinking nights at his place in Hollywood, he had often howled at the Hollywood Jews and how they had ruined one writer after another, from Fante to Saroyan to William Faulkner. I agreed with him, it was not a nice business.

The sandwiches on the menus were all named after Hollywood Jews: moguls, directors, actors, and comedians. One was the Buck Benny. That was a hot dog, the cheapest meal. I tried to change the subject by mentioning the time I saw Jack Benny on Spaulding Drive floating along with that delightful walk he had.

"Never mind," said Bukowski, dismissing the subject. He didn't want to talk about Jack Benny. "If those guys [Hollywood Moguls] did a film about the garment industry, the bad guys would be Eskimos."

That did make me laugh and spit up my beer. I didn't disagree, but pointed out that Jack Warner and Louis B. Mayer didn't justify Hitler.

"What do you have against Hitler?" he asked. "Ever read him?"

I told him no, then confessed a little secret: "I'm a quarter Jewish on my father's side. My grandmother's family came from a little town east of Frankfurt on the Main River."

Bukowski laughed. "Being a quarter Jewish is like being a quarter crazy; it only matters if you take it seriously. My parents were both German Catholics and I could give a flying fuck about what they believed. It means nothing. The important thing is who you are. The Beverly Hills Anarchist."

He always called me that, even after I'd moved from Beverly Hills. We ate our pastrami on rye, drank our beer and went on planning The Symposium.

The Symposium came off as planned on October 14, 1975, with bottled beer spiced with great humor and vulgarity, decorated with Bukowski's delightful illustrations and a few amusing photographs.

A few weeks later I suggested to Bukowski that I might want to write his biography. That was probably the biggest mistake I ever made in my life: getting the facts from a writer of fiction is about as easy as curing herpes, but as time went by, Henry Charles Bukowski Jr. began to open up the Pandora's box of his life, Nazis and all.

This is what he told me.

From the time he was a small boy, Bukowski was super-conscious of being German. He was an only child whose parents spoke German late into the night as he slept in his room next door. At the dinner table, when they didn't want him to know what they were saying, his parents would "turn on the Deutsch." It was all around him. His grandfather, Leonard Bukowski, and his grandmother Emile (they were divorced and lived separately), both spoke German when they came to the house for Christmas.

Leonard, who was from Prussia and had fought in the Franco-Prussian War, was also a heavy drinker. "When he got drunk," his grandson recalled, "he would sing old German war songs and put on his war medals."

Then there was Bukowski's mother. He described her as "the prettiest girl in Andernach." When she received letters from her parents and brother back home, she would read them over and over, missing her family. This would occasionally annoy her husband, who would shout at his wife: "You think you're so great because your brother is the Burgermeister of Andernach." (That proved false, as Heinrich Fett told me himself when I met him in 1977.)

When he was little, Charles Bukowski was a momma's boy, coddled by his mother; what irked him most was the intimate conversations his parents had late at night in a language he could not understand. Henry Sr. was fluent in German while Henry Jr. could not speak a word of it.

Sometimes, when Katharina was especially lonely and craved German company, Henry Sr. would take her to the local German meeting place, the Deutsche Haus, located at 634 15th Street, close to their home. Here, when he had a little money, he would treat his wife to a meal, buy her a German magazine, listen to a German band, or watch a travelogue on what was going on in Berlin. If they came for lunch on a Sunday after church, Henry was dragged along, but the long hours of watching people speaking a language he did not understand, bored him.

Bukowski was always very touchy when people asked him why he had not learned German. He said his parents discouraged it; they wanted him to speak perfect English.

He said that after World War One, German was not taught in most public schools; but both L.A. High School and Los Angeles Community College offered German.

Bukowski always resented the fact that his father could read and write German. When I asked if that's why they kept his father on in Coblenz after the war, he got angry and said, "No. He was only a typist, not a translator."

Whatever attitude his parents had toward their son learning German, they did expose him to the Deutsche Haus, a little island of German culture in a sea of American white bread. There Bukowski discovered German music, German films, German food, and German books and magazines, some written in English. It was there he first observed the German-American Bund in full uniform. His parents even took him on an outing to Hindenburg Park in La Crescenta where he celebrated Hitler's birthday with a torchlight parade. It was the year of the 1936 Olympics.

At his most forgiving, he would say of his parents, "Living in that house I never learned German except for the songs."

What brought Bukowski around to the Nazi viewpoint is hard to say. It began in the depth of his solipsism, at the time of puberty when his skin erupted and in the eyes of many he became deformed. Though he says over and over that he was some kind of leader among the friends he had, in fact, he was an outcast and a loner. In *Ham on Rye*, he refers to an essay he writes about the value of no friends at all.

This taught him the lesson of the gifted misanthrope: writing can be the avenging sword. All the bitterness that welled up in him as he broke out in boils and huge, exploding pimples, became the fuel that drove his writing. He looked for writers with similar views and found Celine, Ezra Pound, Jeffers, Hamsun, and Adolph Hitler.

Bukowski told me he had a gym teacher named Wagner who had it in for him:

> My friend Mullinax and I were always in trouble over little things. We were put on the garbage can crew. I forget where we were carrying them. I guess where they got loaded. There was a place where the trucks would pick them up. We had to go around carrying these garbage cans to the loading area. And pick up little pieces of paper with a sharp stick. It was small things, but we were always on the outs.
>
> Especially with this guy Wagner, the gym guy. He was always on us and we would have to stay after school. We did nothing, really. We were just outcasts. We felt it. We didn't have it; they landed on us. I remember one time I had to stay after school and rake out the sawdust pit. You get stuff that's fallen in. I made all kinds of money. I got dimes and nickels. The money looked good. It always did. I remember that was interesting getting all that free money from raking up the sawdust pit.
>
> Then, on Graduation Day, I was standing on line with my friend Baldy and this guy Arnold Woodchurch and his buddy, who had the longest cock in school. I forget his name. He was always in trouble because the girls were after him. Anyway, Wagner came up to us in the graduation line and he walked over to me and said: 'Listen, you guys are graduating. You think you can get away from me, but I'm gonna get you! You can't get away from me.' This guy was crazy.

When I played back the tape for William "Baldy" Mullinax, he replied: "One or two times it happened. That's what he remembers from Mount Vernon?" Mullinax recalled the first dance he ever attended, his first girlfriend, his growing interest in science, while Henry Charles Bukowski Jr. could only recall his humiliations, his battles against authority, his struggle.

Bukowski's one triumph of childhood, according to him, was his essay on President Hoover at the L.A. Olympics, though Bukowski had to admit to his teacher, it was a fiction; he hadn't attended the event.

School for Bukowski was always torture. Later, speaking of poetry, he told me his one great mission was to "get the bullshit out of it; the stuff about learning." To Bukowski teaching was a dishonest profession and those who were scholars were phonies!

Life on the page was about three things: the battle for position, money, and sex. Out there in the arena of life those were the three things that mattered.

When I came back with Baldy's objections, Bukowski got angry and curt and commanding: "Go find Arnold Woodchurch," he said. "Woodchurch was laying all the girls. He was doing a lot of fucking and the guy with the big cock was doing a lot of fucking. I wasn't and Baldy wasn't. Baldy's pathetic."

Much of Bukowski's high school career in his words and others have been carefully altered to conceal his humiliations, failures, and loneliness. The myth that his father forced him to attend Los Angeles High School is just that: a myth. Bukowski lived walking distance from campus and was assigned to L.A. High along with his companions, Jim Haddox, Bob Stoner, Ray Shuwarge, Bill Cobun, Hal Ortner, and Bill Mullinax.

On paper Bukowski was a bright student. He tested well, especially in language and mathematics, and his father had high hopes that his son would find his way in the one of the professions. Henry Sr. felt his son's abilities lay in technology, science, and engineering. He thought that if he applied himself and kept up with his homework, Henry Jr. might make it into a good college and become the "success" he was not.

But his son had other ideas.

"My course," Bukowski told me, "was mixed up. My father wanted me to be an engineer. I was taking drafting and Spanish and all. I ended up in a vocational program because I couldn't pass Spanish and I didn't like drafting. My father just gave up and said, 'Okay, give it up.' So I took whatever was easiest. My mother just went along."

Oddly, when I read Hitler's *Mein Kampf* upon Bukowski's request, I came to the following passage:

> My father forbade me to entertain any hope of ever becoming a painter. I went one step farther by declaring that under those circumstances I no longer wished to study. Naturally, as the result of such declarations, I got the worst of it and now the old man relentlessly began to enforce his authority. I remained silent and turned my threats into action. I was certain that, as soon as my father saw my lack of progress in school, he would let me seek the happiness of which I was dreaming. I do not know if this reasoning was sound. One thing was certain: my apparent failure in school. I learned what I liked, but above all I learned what in my opinion might be necessary to me in my future career as a painter. In this connection, I sabotaged all that which seemed unimportant or that which no longer attracted me.

[p.14 of the 1940 Reynal & Hitchcock edition]

I pointed the passage out to Bukowski. "Yeah, I know," he said.

With little homework and no interest in team sports, no job, no clubs, few friends, and only his chores—which included taking out the garbage, going to the store, and mowing the lawn once a week—Bukowski had his afternoons free. These he spent alone at the library at La Brea and Adams, or as a hanger-on with Baldy, Ray Shuwarge, and Jim Haddox.

Bill Mullinax, who he describes as pathetic in his poems, stories and in *Ham on Rye*, his childhood novel, was really the popular one. Both Mullinax and Haddox were in the ROTC Officer's Club by their junior year. Mullinax had various girlfriends including Marla Morton, who wrote him: "To more and better astounding stories." Lonetha Davidis congratulated him on his skills in chemistry. Hal Ortner called him his "bosom pal," while Bob Stoner congratulated him on his success in ROTC and Elaine Lettice consoled him as a "fellow-sufferer in Geometry." A girl named Betty wrote: "To a boy who tried to change me and did." She left her telephone number. Ray Shuwarge wrote: "Be sure and don't join the navy as you have a good future in the medical field, and I wouldn't like to see our trio (Lobdell, Ray, Bill) broken up."

> "Bill" be sure & don't join the navy (Mary) as you have a good future in the medical field, and I wouldn't like to see our trio (Lobdell, Ray, Bill) broken up. Lots of luck. Ray Shuwarge

Ray Shuwarge does not mention Henry Bukowski, who did not take chemistry or geometry, did not join Buildings and Grounds along with Mullinax, Haddox, and Shuwarge, and ran away from girls. Mullinax said:

> Bukowski did nose around the newspaper, *The Blue and White Daily*, but disliked the editors: Matthew Rapf, editor; Morton Cahn, managing editor; sports editor Melvin Durslag; and news editor Robert Weil.

Bukowski told me he had read the *Examiner* at the time because William Randolph Hearst published Hitler and Mussolini, though he fired Hitler because he missed his deadlines!

In *Ham on Rye*, he taunts his friend Jim Haddox, who is Jim Hatcher. Haddox lived at 1782 W. 22nd Street with his mother, Nina Ruth Haddox, who Bukowski described as "café society." She becomes the grotesque sex object in chapter 38, Claire, the barmaid, whose husband had committed suicide. The real story, the one Bukowski held back, is far more interesting, more tragic and ironic.

When Bukowski reached his eighteenth birthday on August 16, 1938, he was heading into his senior year with serious problems. Publicly he showed interest in military service. Privately, as Germany gobbled up the Sudetenland and moved into Austria, Henry Jr. cheered Germany on to war in Europe.

All this came to a head in the summer of 1938, when he had to prove his citizenship. Was he German or American? On August 1,

1938, he wrote to the U.S. State Department requesting a record of his birth in Andernach through the offices of the U.S. military. On August 9, the division chief of the Foreign Service Administration wrote back:

My Dear Mr. Bukowski:

In accordance with the request contained in your letter of August 1, 1938, I am pleased to enclose a certified copy of the Report of Birth of Henry Charles Bukowski, who was born August 16, 1920, at Andernach, Germany.

His final year in school was not memorable to him, though he did give me some insights into his mindset in June of 1939.

L.A. High School was a rich man's school at the time. They all had sports cars. We walked or rode bicycles. They came from huge distances just to attend this special school. The women wouldn't pay any attention to you. The other guys got the girls. We were the outcasts. I didn't allow myself to like girls. The report cards were very important to my parents. They were always disappointed. It was not so bad. I had mostly C's and a couple D's.

But in typical Bukowski fashion, he did recall one bit of zaniness:

This one time there was a teacher in high school. I was making good grades and I was passing her tests. It was the next to the last day before report cards.
She said, 'Henry, I'm going to flunk you.'
I said, 'Why?'
'I'm going to, that's all.'
Strange, I thought. She must be in love with me. She wanted me to stay in high school. See me another term. She was an old thing. That was my only thought. I felt the hate, like she didn't want me to go, but I also felt the love. That was the first time I felt somebody really cared about me.

I looked for that wrinkled smile of his when he was being ironic, but I could see he was dead serious. I asked for the teacher's name. He couldn't recall it. It all seemed so pathetic: MACHO BUKOWSKI, the Hemingway warrior, and here he was telling me this old lady was the first person who ever loved him.

I asked if she carried out her threat and flunked him.

"No," he said. "My mother found out. She went over there and cried and cried for hours. So she gave in. It was so strange. I was getting passing grades and she wanted me to stay."

I had to laugh. "So you were saved by your mother!"

He nodded. "It wasn't the last time, either," he said.

Though he remembered in detail this crazy, deranged event, he could hardly recall his graduation from high school. "They played Wagner," he said. "I went up and got my diploma. This gets sadder and sadder. I'm about to weep. I should have been traveling with Stravinsky's grandson and going to operas."

In *Ham on Rye*, Bukowski mourns the state of his lonely life as he watches through the windows as the senior class enjoy their prom. He neglects to mention that Jim Haddox, Bob Stoner, and most of the friends he knew in ROTC were all at the dance, and that all of them would be in the military before Pearl Harbor.

After describing Jimmy Hatcher (Jim Haddox) as "soft and standard" in *Ham on Rye* (p. 160), and telling him to his face "I don't like anything about you," he lines up the rest of his acquaintances for fictional assassination as they dance at the prom:

"I hated them. I hated their beauty and their uncontrolled youth . . ."

While Jim Haddox went directly into the Army Air Corps, Bill Mullinax was preparing himself for a career in engineering at LACC. Meanwhile Henry Charles Bukowski Jr. remained in the same bedroom he'd been in since childhood, drinking, nursing his anger, without a job, afraid to be seen with women, waiting for that blinding light that would propel him forward into greatness.

His epiphany came on September 1, 1939, as the armies of Adolph Hitler marched into Poland, dividing it up with their new partners in crime, the USSR.

II

When he enrolled at Los Angeles City College, located on Vermont Boulevard in Hollywood, Bukowski said, "It was like I never left high school. I just went from one place to another. I was supposed to be taking a journalism program, but I just took the courses I wanted to take. It was basic journalism. I'd open the book, but I wouldn't follow it."

His parents gave him a typewriter and their blessing. They just wanted their son to get a job and survive. Bukowski never blamed LACC on his father; he had others to blame: the nonpublished professors who held good writers back.

The first issue of the school paper, *The Collegian*, on September 18, 1939, gives us a taste of what Bukowski experienced. First there was the Howdy Hop, a dance Mullinax attended and Bukowski did not. Then there was the note from the Journalism Club from president Irwin Simon: "Our purpose is to better acquaint new journalism students." And then there was the German Club, Deutscher Verrien, headed by Lillian Morrill, "a girl for Christ's sake."

Again, I asked Bukowski about his interest in the school newspaper, *The Collegian*, a tri-weekly. After all, he was a journalism student. Did he try out? He said no. "I walked in and looked around. There were these guys with little paper hats on. Tremendous egos. I couldn't stand it. So I walked right out. I never did get into it. Never liked the look of the place. I got into the Nazi trip instead."

I tried to follow the logic of that: Nazism instead of journalism.

I asked what he meant by the Nazi trip. He said he'd been thinking about Hitler's Germany ever since the 1936 Berlin Olympics. He looked me straight in the eyes and asked: "Tell me who won them?"

"The 1936 Olympics?" All I could remember was the Hitler slight of Jesse Owens. "I guess the U.S. did. Right?"

He laughed. "Hollywood propaganda. The Germans won by a mile. The U.S. wasn't even close. Look it up."

I did. He was right. The Germans had an overall medal count of 89, while U.S. had 56.

It all fit. His anger at women, his hatred of the standard American go-getter type with straight teeth, like Jim Haddox and his father. He felt the Germans had been slighted by the U.S. newspapers, except for *The Examiner*, the one Hitler wrote for. I tried to understand. He was sensitive about his German birth, he said. In 1936 it wasn't very important, but when the peacetime draft bill was passed, in September of 1940, he started to worry. His worst fear was to be drafted into the army and sent to Germany to fight against his own people. That was the way he put it.

I reminded him that in 1940 the U.S. was neutral.

"They were and they weren't," he said.

He learned to be careful about expressing his feeling on the war. In his political science and history classes he said most students favored the British and the French over the Germans. As he read *The Examiner* and delighted in the German victories in Poland and France, he discovered an odd fact: Most of his teachers were against the U.S. getting into a war.

"I think they were Marxists," he said. The Moscow line was all about peace. They'd signed a treaty with the USSR. A Non-aggression Pact. "As for myself, I have the feeling that any creative person is a rebel. Whichever way his country goes . . . everyone is saying this one thing . . . believing this one thing. There's a tendency to believe the opposite. What the hell are the masses? They read the papers and are easily fooled!"

Bukowski even recalled a peace demonstration on campus where Dalton Trumbo, the famous Hollywood screenwriter, attacked the U.S. government for being too friendly to Britain and France.

As school became boring and drab for him, Bukowski was drawn more and more to the "Nazi trip."

The only place he could express himself comfortably about his admiration of Hitler and his growing distaste for the U.S. was at the Deutsches Haus, which was just a walk from his home. Now it was no longer a boring place. The D.H., as it was called, had become a front for Hitler. Here he could find books, magazines, and pamphlets in German and English praising Nazism. They were available cheap at the Aryan Bookstore, which was located on the first floor of the D.H.

It was at the D.H. that Bukowski viewed the German war film, *Blitzkrieg in the West*, a Nazi propaganda feature that depicted the crushing defeat of Holland, France, Belgium and Denmark before the advancing German army. It played to packed houses of enthusiastic German sympathizers who roared with delight at the triumph of the Fatherland, Bukowski among them.

His parents by that time were not enthusiastic and did not attend. His father openly opposed Hitler and when Bukowski defended him his father would say, "Why don't you find a job? You live in this house and do nothing but read." It was a sore point.

The D.H. gave Bukowski his introduction to the German-American Bund, Hitler's front organization for American youth over eighteen years of age. While fellow students at LACC tried to forget the war, drowning their fears in the swing music of the era, petting in the parking lot, or dancing at the Howdy Hop, Henry Bukowski showed up with pamphlets from the Aryan Bookstore and defended the Nazis in class. It made him feel unique!

Meanwhile, the same old problems with teachers occurred. In an English class with a Professor Richardson, who "played Gilbert and Sullivan and was big on enunciation," Bukowski brought up the usual complaints:

> The class started at 7:00 a.m. I never showed up till 7:30 'cause I was drinking, even though I was living at home. The first piece of writing I turned in, Richardson said, 'This is great writing, Bukowski, but women aren't that bad.' But then the grades dropped down. Finally, three-quarters of the way through the class he said, 'Well, Bukowski, you're showing up at 7:30 again. I'm gonna give you a "D" whether you show up or not.' So I stopped showing up. It was a strange class.

It was standard American fare. It bored him. On the other hand, the Nazis offered him excitement. Whenever he spoke of them, his eyes brightened:

> At LACC, Veloff and I got into the Nazi trip. We were drinking hot buttered rum and Veloff had an actual gun. He wanted it to be a Luger because that was a German gun, but it was a revolver. He used to play Russian roulette with it. He wanted me to play but I refused. Together we attended a Bund meeting in Glendale. Of course it was Glendale. We went down into a cellar. They had this great big American flag there. They had all these chairs. It was an upper middle class house. Very large. The speaker (Hermann Max Schwinn, Los Angeles Bund leader) had his desk onstage. We all stood up to pledge allegiance to the flag, which I didn't like to do. Then he started talking about the Communist menace. How we had to fight force with force. These guys were ready.

When he stood up and shouted for the Nazis he got noticed. He was outrageous, he was frightening, and he was funny.

Henry Bukowski dropped out of LACC in the fall semester of 1940. He was drinking a great deal. By that time his father had had enough. With no job and LACC an incomplete, he told his son to get a job, go into the service, or pay rent while living at home.

Henry Jr. moved downtown and took handouts from his mother. He spent all his time reading in the library and walking through Pershing Square at night where he hoped he would find John Fante. By early 1941 he was on the Nazi track and the stories he wrote reflected that point of view. None survive! When he was hungry he would sometimes sneak back home for food when his father was at work.

That summer, the summer of 1941, Bukowski's mother came through for him again. He was twenty-one and he had never worked. As he tells it:

> My first job was with the Union Pacific Railroad. My mother got it for me through a friend of hers. He took me down to the railroad tracks in his car. I was supposed to work in the roundhouse, which had a little sense of dignity, but I ended up scrubbing the sides of trains. Boxcars and all that. I had to go to work on the bus. I didn't much care for it. I turned out to be the clown; one of those guys who was always fucking up.

He laughed. I asked him how old he was.

"I was pretty fucking old. I was twenty-one."

"And your mother got you the job?"

"Yeah." He laughed but looked ashamed.

Along with *Mein Kampf*, he was reading Knut Hamsun's *Hunger*, just the right fix on work and starvation. He also read John Fante's *Ask the Dust*, the book that changed his life, and Hemingway's *Men Without Women*, a little Nietzsche, some Schopenhauer, D.H. Lawrence, and a hell of a lot of Robinson Jeffers, especially the long poems.

On June 18, 1941, Germany attacked the USSR and the fragile peace between the world's two most powerful dictatorships collapsed. Overnight, Marxists like Dalton Trumbo went from peace doves to war hawks, and Henry Charles Bukowski Jr. found a new hero in Charles Lindbergh and his America First Committee.

Lindbergh complained that American Jews, especially in Hollywood, were egging America into a war with Germany. When Lindbergh, the famous aviator, came to Los Angeles and spoke to an overflowing crowd at the Hollywood Bowl, Bukowski and some of his Bund companions led a torchlight parade up into the Hollywood Hills, where they could watch their new hero from the heights as he moved the enormous crowd to their feet over and over again. That was a memory he could recall vividly, from beginning to end.

The crowd was estimated at 20,000 plus and the FBI were on hand to keep tabs on the audience. In his speech that night Lindbergh made three points and Bukowski agreed with them all:

> (1) We are still unprepared for war, and it would take us years to prepare adequately for the type of war we now consider entering. It would mean turning this country into a military nation that exceeds Germany in regimentation.
>
> (2) Even if we were fully prepared at this time, we would face the superhuman task of crossing an ocean and forcing a landing on a fortified continent against armies stronger than our own.
>
> (3) We in America have the best defensive position in the world. No foreign power can invade us today.

Bukowski was thrilled. With Fante the humanist in one hand and Hitler the monster in the other (both published by the same publisher) he was writing up a storm, and without his mother's help he switched to a more civilized job as a stock boy at Sears Roebuck in Hollywood; his boss liked him so much he gave him a reference when he left.

The pay was poor, but he wanted a job that demanded no security clearance. "In 1941, before the war," he said, "jobs were hard to get unless you went to work in a shipyard. I could never do that. Those guys with lunch pails and tin hats and badges making the big money. I couldn't bear to do that 'cause that was again being part of the flow."

I knew exactly what he meant.

In October of 1941, the California State Assembly opened an investigation into Un-American Activities; the German-American Bund was first on the list. Next came The America First Committee.

Bukowski nervously read the newspaper as Hermann Max Schwinn and Hans Diebel were dragged before the committee and required to testify. They were both born in Germany but unlike Bukowski, Schwinn and Diebel were not American citizens. Still, Bukowski was a German-American, born in Andernach to a German mother who still had family in the old country, some of whom were now serving the military of Adolph Hitler. At the end of the hearing charges were filed and papers were confiscated.

On December 7, 1941, a Sunday, Bukowski was sitting downtown reading a book. He heard the news of Pearl Harbor with alarm. The whole city of Los Angeles was on alert. Two days later Schwinn and Diebel and a number of other German and Japanese sympathizers were arrested. His hero, Charles Lindbergh, with help from friends, later wormed his way into being a pilot and was a hero no more to Charles Bukowski.

As the draft went into high gear, Bukowski grabbed up all his Bund materials, his copy of *Mein Kampf*, and his grandfather's medals and threw them down the sewer. Tossing his writings into a bag, he climbed on a bus headed for New Orleans. Much of his travels can be found in *Factotum*; much cannot.

His major fear was the FBI. A few months after he left he returned to Los Angeles to see if the Feds were looking for him; to his relief they had bigger fish to catch. His second fear was his draft board. He told me he had a high number and it had not come up, but he wasn't waiting around until it did. For almost two years he played cat and mouse with his draft board.

"I kept going back and forth," he said. "From the East Coast to the West. I hit New Orleans three times. New York once. I was in Philly two or three times. San Francisco twice. There was St. Louis twice and a little stop in East Kansas City. Then Charlotte, North Carolina, Atlanta, where I nearly froze to death. In Houston I stayed quite a while."

In each city he would use his reference from Sears to get a new job. Since most of the young men were in the military, jobs were not hard to find. "I'd stay a few months in each place," he said, "dragging my typer along with me."

He worked as a stock clerk, a sorter in a dog biscuit factory, a packer in an auto parts store. Again, no security checks. Those types of jobs were going begging as half the men in America were in the service and the other half were working in defense plants; women too! Lugging his typewriter from city to city, still hating the government and hoping the Nazis would win the war, Bukowski had found a crack in the universe where he could crawl in safely and write.

He said of his short stories during that time: "They were full of complaints. I wanted too much too fast, and I was weeping in the wind. The unrecognized artist shit. THE WORLD SHOULD KNOW THAT I HAVE THIS GIFT! I wrote a lot of that out of me then."

He returned to Los Angeles in early 1942 to pick up his mail, check on his friends, and see if the FBI had been looking for him. To his delight they were not. His friends were all in the service. Jim Haddox was training as a pilot; Baldy Mullinax was in the Navy along with Eugene Fife who was a naval officer. Harold Mortenson, who Bukowski had no interest in finding, was at UCLA getting all "A's."

So back and forth across the country Henry Charles Bukowski went.

"When I was absolutely broke," he said, "I'd come home. My parents would put me up. I still had my bedroom. They'd bill me for food and lodgings, which I had to pay when I got a job."

Henry Bukowski Sr. became more and more impatient with his son. What was wrong with Henry, he wondered? Why did he not enlist in the service? Was he sick or unbalanced or simply a coward?

Only his mother had some sympathy for him with her family on the other side of the world and her former country at war. Her brother, Heinrich Fett, would later be appointed head of the Volkssturm for the Third Reich in Andernach, their local commander, but that was toward the end of the war when Germany would welcome the Americans (they hoped). They needed a man who knew them and could speak English . . .

With no letters from the FBI, Bukowski had no intention of enlisting; his loyalties were elsewhere. In 1942 he read D.H. Lawrence's short story, "The Prussian Officer," and that helped him write. He had found his subject: "Ultimate human cruelty. It could have been anybody," he told me. "It happened to be the Prussian officer. The way he did it was sooo very good. There's a tightness of line there."

Bukowski loved the story and he loved what it said: human beings are vicious animals. He went looking for his own Prussian officer and found it in his namesake, Henry Charles Bukowski Sr.

In later years, Bukowski would blame his father for everything that went wrong in his early life: he was a brute, a philanderer, a child beater, a cheat and a liar; he could not hold a job. He sent his son to a school where rich boys teased him; he took poor care of his mother when she was ill and did not appreciate his son's great gifts: "My father was standard American type. Dull, holding a job, showing up to work on time."

For the purpose of his fiction, and as a vengeance upon him for eternity, Bukowski turned his father into the Prussian officer. His Uncle Heinrich Fett had very warm things to say about Henry Charles Bukowski Sr. when I met him in 1977, things Bukowski did not want to hear.

Bukowski told me on tape he only got to write what he really felt after his father died. "When I could get out all the poison." Much of Bukowski's poems, stories, and novels are all about getting out the poison. "It saved me from madness," he said. It also saved him from World War Two!

When Bukowski was arrested by the FBI seems to be a problem. In his biography, Howard Sounes says he was arrested on a July evening in 1944.

Sounes got the month right but not the year. On July 7, 1942 the FBI and the Justice Department launched an all-out push on members of the German-American Bund, including Hermann Schwinn. Bukowski was caught in that net and taken to federal prison.

Here is what he told me about his adventures in Moyamensing Federal prison in Philadelphia. Verbatim.

> Pleasants: You had one big-time stay in jail when you were a draft dodger.
>
> Bukowski: Oh, Moyamensing. Yeah, seventeen days.
>
> P: That was when?

B: Hell, I don't know. It must have been . . .

P: 1944?

B: Uh-uh. Much earlier. 1942.

P: I'll have to research that.

B: Moyamensing. You think they'll still have the records? Henry Charles Bukowski Jr.

P: You'll be in there. They'll have your photo and everything.

B: It was quite nice after a while. You've read it. I won all the money with the craps. Food. After lights out. Better food than I ever ate on the outside. It's real ancient. When they take you in it's like a castle. These great big gates. They must be sixty feet high. They open just for you as you go inside. I made more money in there than I ever made on the outside. I almost hated to leave when they let me go.

P: You were in there on draft evasion. Right?

B: I guess that's what they called it.

P: Did you go to court?

B: No.

P: Did you have a lawyer?

B: No.

P: You just went in there?

B: They figured I was nuts. What they did . . . they made me go to the draft induction center. They said, if you make the draft, if they draft you, okay, you're in. If they don't draft you, we'll let you go. I said okay I'll go along with that. But I couldn't get past the psychiatrist's three questions.

P: What were the three questions?

B: To begin with, they raided my room after I was gone. They found all these writings. These mad, garbled writings. So eventually, the psychiatrist had read these ahead of time.

P: Your short stories.

B: Yeah (laughs). My short stories. Jesus. So I sat down and he said, "Do you believe in the war?" I said, "No." "Are you willing to go to the war?" I said, "Yes." "By the way, we're having a party next Wednesday at my place. Artists, writers, intellectuals, doctors. All kinds of interesting people. I know you're an intelligent man and I'd like you to come to my party. Will you come to my party?" I said, "No." "All right, you can go." I looked at him. He said, "You don't have to go to the war. You didn't think we'd understand, did you?" I said, "No." That was all. Pass on through. That was after jail, except I had to wait for a ride back to jail to be signed out. There were a whole bunch of us sitting there. Hours went by. I just got up and I walked out of the doorway. I just walked out into the daylight."

The fact that Bukowski remembers specifically it was NOT 1944, but much earlier, he says 1942, is important. It means from that time on he could travel where he wanted with an UNFIT FOR SERVICE

draft rating and not worry about the FBI any more. The writings they took from him they kept; they were his Nazi ravings coming off his reading of *Mein Kampf*, his experiences in the German-American Bund, his participation in the America First Movement and his hatred of Hollywood. All three, much to my amazement, would appear in his work later in life.

On December 11, 1943 his friend Jim Haddox was shot down over Emden, Germany. He and all of his crew but one perished. He had made pilot and was a First Lieutenant of the 100th Bomber Group, 351st squadron, training in Thorpe Abbots, East Anglia. He left only his mother, Nina Ruth Haddox, who Bukowski described as a barmaid and an oversexed temptress.

Baldy later said of Haddox, "He was a real war hero. A damned decent guy." Peggy Harford, who worked with me on the drama desk at the *L.A. Times* and graduated with Ray Bradbury from LAHS a year before Bukowski, said she could not remember Bukowski at all, but she did recall Jim Haddox as "gracious and brave."

Bukowski never mentioned Haddox's war record. To him, Haddox was the standard American, a hanger-on who followed the great writer around because "I always draw the weak instead of the strong." He hated Haddox because he worked hard and was liked by the girls.

In 1943, with the draft board off his back, Bukowski sat at his typer and the stories rolled out week after week. "I just pushed them along, four or five a week," he told me. "And I didn't keep carbons."

Still roaming from city to city, he sent on his manuscripts to *Harpers, The Atlantic* and *Story*. Every short story he ever sent to *Harpers* and *The Atlantic* came back with the usual form rejection, but *Story* was different. *Story* had published John Fante and Hemingway and William Saroyan. *Story* showed interest in his work.

For the first time in his life Bukowski was thrilled about writing:

> Whit Burnett (the editor) always sent me a hand-written note. They were fairly short. He'd say, 'Send more.' He kept saying it. He'd say, 'Hell, this one is very, very close.' I think he meant it. There was an awful lot of competition at that time. He was the only one who cared!

After Bukowski hocked his typewriter and hand-printed his fiction, Whit Burnett continued to read him and write back. "*Story* was the only one who responded," Bukowski said in animated tones. "The others, *Atlantic* and *Harpers*, must have thought, 'Here's that nut again who prints his own stuff.'"

Finally, in their March/April 1944 issue, *Story* published "Aftermath Of A Lengthy Rejection Slip" in the end papers of the magazine. Bukowski was disappointed. The piece shows wit and brilliance, and he was approached by an agent who wanted to represent him; but there is something else all his biographers have left out: the bio Bukowski wrote himself in *Story* magazine:

> CHARLES BUKOWSKI was born in Andernach, Germany in 1920. His father was California born, of POLISH parentage, and served

in the American Army of Occupation in the Rhineland where he met his mother. He was brought to America at the age of two. He attended LACC for a couple of years and in the two and one-half years since has been a clerk in the post office, a stockroom boy for Sears Roebuck, a truck-loader nights at a bakery. He is now working as a package wrapper and box filler in the cellar of a ladies sportswear shop.

Three things jump out at the reader: the fact that he mentions his German birth, the lie about his father's POLISH parentage, and the change of name.

If Sounes is correct with his dates, the story that Bukowski changed his name in 1944 from Henry to Charles because he hated his father is as much incorrect as the comment about his father's Polish parentage. He changed it because he knew the war was still on and he was worried that his draft board had ruled him emotionally unfit to serve. There was always a fear during WWII that his draft evasion status would hurt his career as a writer.

If Bukowski's dates are correct, it's more than likely he did it to protect his father's job.

Whichever way it went, he published no more work during World War II under any name.

When I asked him where he was when World War II was over, he said, "I can't remember. Really. It didn't mean anything to me. It wasn't important."

I told him even I remembered the end of World War II, VJ Day. My parents set off Roman candles. I was five. He just laughed uncomfortably. When I showed him the bio lines in *Story* about his father being Polish, he looked back sheepishly and said, "You got me."

My view about Bukowski's fascination with Nazism at the time was simply one of youthful rebellion; his desire to shock. That's what I believed at the time. That's what I wanted to believe.

Sometime after The Symposium, when we were returning from Santa Anita in his little blue Volkswagen, I began to have different thoughts. Bukowski liked to drive, but he had the habit of avoiding the freeways when he could. "Too many DUIs," he told me.

On our way back, he took a little detour to Hollywood proper and stopped the car. There were two teenagers in uniforms, one male and one female, blonde and attractive, looking almost like Brownies until I saw the armband. It was a swastika. They were Nazis.

Jeannie Cordova, a reporter for the *FREEP*, had been doing articles for weeks on all the organizations that were beyond the limits of good taste in politics, but protected by the First Amendment: The KKK, Jewish Defense League, Black Panthers, and the American Nazi Party.

There they were in all their glory. Nazis collecting for their party. I turned to Bukowski laughing. What a joke, but he had tears in his eyes. I shook my head in disbelief. "See those two? That could have been me," he said. Then he started up the car and drove off.

I was beginning to wonder if writing his bio was the right thing for me. I'd recently bought him a hard to find Celine novel: *Nord*. He loved Celine. *Nord* was about Celine's flight from France after the Nazi defeat.

"Maybe YOU should write a novel about it," I said.

"About what?"

"Being a Nazi."

"You write it," he said. "But make it funnier."

For years and years I thought about doing it, and then I did.

In Andernach, in 1977, when I met his Uncle Heinrich Fett, I found the name *Israel* in the family plot. I asked Bukowski if he was part Jewish, and he said no.

Many years later a member of the Fett family confirmed that Bukowski's grandmother was named Nannette Israel. Andernach is on the French border and has many French-speaking people, so that would explain the Nannette. "The Nazis investigated and found nothing," said Heinrich Fett's nephew. "But who knows?"

In the eighties, when Bukowski and I attended a reading given by Lawrence Ferlinghetti at Occidental College, a fan rushed up to Bukowski and said, "All that suffering. So much pain in your work. You must be Jewish."

"Not a drop," said Bukowski. "Not a drop."

By Jewish law, if Bukowski's grandmother was Jewish, his mother was Jewish and so was he.

On the first page of his novel *Hollywood*, Bukowski gets back at all those old movies he hated and all the old Jews who produced them:

> There we were down at the harbor, driving past the boats. Most of them were sailboats and people were fiddling about on deck. They were dressed in their special sailing clothes: caps, dark shades. Somehow, most of them had apparently escaped the daily grind of living. Such were the rewards of the Chosen in the land of the free. After a fashion, those people looked silly to me. And, of course, I was not even in their thoughts."

The Chosen, Jews in America, MOST OF THEM, did not work. That's what Bukowski thought. They got money through deals and false promises and schemes. That's what the whole book is about. It's right out of *Mein Kampf*.

The last time I saw Bukowski was at the track at Hollywood Park. I took a girlfriend, and introduced her to Bukowski. I wanted to tell him she had met John Fante, was also a diabetic and John had been fond of her; but before I could open my mouth Bukowski drew me aside and said, "Get rid of that one. Too Jewish!"

My four great heroes through history have been Spinoza, a lapsed Jew who preached reason and was ex-communicated by the Jews of Amsterdam; Edmund Husserl, a Jew who converted to Lutheranism in order to invent Phenomenology and was kept from the university library by the man he mentored, Martin Heidegger; Hannah Arendt, author of *Eichmann in Jerusalem: A Report on the Banality of Evil*, Heidegger's lover, and a philosopher of great merit in her own right, loathed by many Jews; and Mary McCarthy, Arendt's best friend, the great novelist and critic who hid the fact she was one-quarter Jewish until half her lovers were Jews.

An understanding of Bukowski's Nazi loyalties is key to everything he ever wrote.

Maybe he was right when he said, "Being a quarter Jewish is like being a quarter crazy. It only matters if you take it seriously."

I doubt he ever did.

LACC

"Come on, Ben. You want to see something?"

In early October 1975, Charles Bukowski was a columnist for the *L.A. Free Press* and I was the Special Arts editor in charge of drumming up new readers, those who looked beyond the sex ads. I had a salary as a teacher, but Bukowski was struggling to make it as a writer. We met for late lunch on a regular basis at The Sizzler on Hollywood Boulevard, where Bukowski would devour green steaks or chops or something called Malibu Chicken. We were both drinking quite a bit and neither of us was trying to lose weight. Bukowski was up to 215 pounds and I was about 195.

Penny Grenoble, editor of the breakthrough alternative newspaper in Los Angeles and a practicing feminist, was looking for alternatives to the alternatives, especially when it came to the selling and exploitation of the female body. Bukowski didn't know how to read her. "She put my column in the adult part of the newspaper," he complained.

"That's the part that most people keep. The rest they throw out."

He was telling me about Robinson Jeffers, the only poet beside himself he liked to talk about. The subject was sex and men and women. That's what Jeffers wrote about. That's what Bukowski wrote about. He had a friend named Sheri Martinelli who lived up north in Pacifica, near Carmel and Jeffers' home. One day, he told me, Sheri showed up at Jeffers' door. She was a looker, he said, and she wanted a chance to bang the master up in that great tower room where he wrote. When he opened the door, she introduced herself, showing off her body in the sunlight. She thought Jeffers might like that. Instead, standing in the doorway of Tor House, that marvelous pile of rocks that he built with his own hands, Jeffers said, "I built my house; you go build yours." Then he closed the door.

Devouring an overcooked pork chop, Bukowski told me it sounded almost Biblical, so grand and final. He told me he loved writers who looked at their fame and laughed at it. Jeffers must have known that the fame of a poet is fleeting at least (my words, not his) and ridiculous at most. I told him Euripides, the most prolific of Greek tragedians, was torn apart by dogs.

We talked about Jeffers' *The Roan Stallion*, where the woman named California makes it with a horse. We both had too much beer, and even in that part of Hollywood a conversation about a woman having sex with a stallion was a little much. But not for Bukowski. When people shhhhhed him he got louder.

I asked him what he thought of the coast around Carmel and Monterey, where Jeffers lived. He told me he'd been up there for a reading, or somewhere nearby, but scenery was just scenery to him. What he needed as a writer were human collisions.

Then he told me about Jeffers' problems after World War Two. He said there was one book that got him into trouble with his publisher, Random House. He wasn't sure if it was *The Double Ax* or *Be Angry at the Sun*. Random House attached a warning to the reader, explaining that they didn't agree with Jeffers' poetry, complaining that Jeffers was calling for human annihilation.

Bukowski wanted to show me the warning. He didn't have the book, but suggested a quick drive down Sunset to Vermont, then over to LACC. I'd never been to LACC with him before, although I'd taken a few of my older students there to inquire about enrollment.

As usual, he drove. His little blue VW with the Iron Cross on the front mirror. He parked in the handicapped section. "They never check," he said. We headed for the library, turning left at the administration building. I asked him where the newspaper office was. He pointed. "*The Collegian* it was called when I went here."

We were up the steps in a few jumps. He found the book; it was *The Double Ax*. He opened it up to the preface page and there it was. He read it aloud. "Random House feels compelled to go on record with its disagreement over some of the political views expressed by the poet in this volume."

"Because he was against the wrong war," said Bukowski. "Like me." I told him I thought Jeffers' poems concluded the world would be better off without humans. Bukowski agreed. He said so many times.

While he was wrestling with Jeffers' *Double Ax*, something about *The Collegian* clicked in his head and he started to laugh. He put the book back on the shelf and went over to talk with the reference librarian. He wanted to know where he could find back issues of *The Collegian*. Way back. Back to 1940.

"That would be in serials," she said. "Upstairs and around the back."

"Come on, Ben. You want to see something?"

We found the serials desk on the second floor. Bukowski asked the clerk if she knew where we could find old issues of *The Collegian*.

"How old?"

"1940."

"They come in giant folio volumes. Do you know which term?"

He thought for a moment. "Spring term."

"Month?"

"April or May."

She came back with a library cart filled with giant dusty volumes. "I can't lift them," she said. Bukowski pulled out three volumes and spread them out on a large table. It was about five in the afternoon and the place was empty. He blew off a coat of dust and began to work his way through the crinkled yellow pages. Big chunks of faded newsprint fell out onto the table, but Bukowski kept searching.

"What the hell are you looking for?" I asked.

"'Cubby Hole.'"

"What?"

"'Cubby Hole.' It was like letters to the editor. You had to pay five fucking dollars for the snots to publish your letter, and it had to be typed and . . ."

"There." I pointed. "'Cubby Hole.'" He laughed that Bukowski laugh. A HA HA HA HA HA. The clerk looked up.

He read one but it wasn't the right one. "And?"

"It had to be approved by an editor." His hands were now smeared with newsprint.

"There was a guy out here at about that time. A famous writer. It sounded like Dumbo. They had this big peace rally and . . ."

"You paid five dollars to get published in 1940?"

"Shut up. See. Trumbo." He pointed to a headline:

DALTON TRUMBO, JUDGE DAWSON ADVISES STUDENTS 'KEEP OUT OF WAR' AS 1,100 ATTEND ANNUAL PEACE RALLY

I read aloud the following from the front page: "Trumbo told the students, 'We should be neutral in thought as well as action. How can American people really believe in U.S. neutrality when our president publicly condemns Germany and privately praises England and France? We are operating under a neutrality bill that is skillfully designed to deprive one belligerent from our supplies, while supplying the others . . .'"

Bukowski laughed again. He read the date. April 5, 1940. "That was the year the Nazis and Commies were on the same side. Jeffers must have been right."

He finished off April, checking every page just in case, then moved quickly through May. He was stirring up enough dust to make the serial clerk, if that's what she was, withdraw to her office.

Almost to the end of the volume, on May 24, 1940, Bukowski found it. He pointed to the column: "Cubby Hole." I read the headlines of three letters: "Romeo Answers." Nope, that was signed Juliet. "Just One Dance." Hardly. Signed Disillusioned. The last one was his: "Why Crab?" Here's what he wrote:

ROMEO'S ANSWER:

Dear Cubby Hole: G.B. of Wednesday's paper certainly does need help. "Hi Babe" is no way to get acquainted with girls except streetwalkers, and City College girls aren't streetwalkers.

I haven't heard of many fellows crabbing about being snubbed by our girls. About the only cure for him is a good black eye; but even then some of them never learn.

Juliet; L.H.

JUST ONE DANCE

Dear Cubby Hole: What happened to the dances which were to be held in the Student Union during Men's Week? According the Collegian, they were to be daily events. Being students interested in the social life of this institution, we as others, anxiously looked forward to such events.

One dance alone would have added greatly to the spirit and success of Men's Week but to everyone's disappointments none were held.

Disillusioned J.E.S.; M.A.L.

WHY CRAB?

Dear Cubby Hole: In answer to R.D complaints about our street car service. would like to step forth as a valiant defender of that vehicle.

I find that the violent rocking not only awakens me for class but also allows me to kick heck out of the guy next to me, if I don't like his looks. I never have to give my seat to a lady—I never get one; I have developed a marvelous muscular coordination by the continued process of holding a strap with one hand, my books with another, while treading heavily (and of course accidently) upon some person's feet in an effort to blitzkrieg my way to a seat.

All this for 7 cents! Why crab?

Henry Bukowski,

from The Collegian, *May 24, 1940.*

I told him the letter was really a short story. A Bukowski short story. He checked to see that I'd written it all down. "Get the date," he said. I carefully copied the letter and the date into my notebook.

144

"I wrote another one," he said. "At the end of the semester. It wasn't as good."

He looked for a few minutes, covered with dust, but he couldn't find it. He said it felt funny to see his real name in print: Henry Bukowski. But what he loved most, after all those years, was to see the word "blitzkrieg."

I told him Jeffers would have approved. He thought not. He thought Jeffers was anti-war all the way. Reading Jeffers in later years I agreed.

Wormwood

Americans in Exile, Salt Spring Island, Canada, 1976.
Wayne DeVane (L, friend, son of FBI man), Ben Pleasants (C), Charles Tidler (R)
Buk called Tidler the "greatest poet in Canada."

Bukowski liked to talk about women and I liked to talk about writers. In fact, Bukowski liked writers to talk about their women, and then he would talk about writers. I knew the risks. The more you told him, the more it would end up in his poems and stories; but I reached the point in my life where I thought Bukowski might do a better job of writing about the women I'd known than I could; I was writing about death at the time—suicide. He'd passed that years ago.

In the sixties the women I knew were mostly well within the range of what Bukowski would call nonstarters; with romantic attachments right out of *The Great Gatsby*; I knew Bukowski hated Fitzgerald. But in the seventies, as my marriage came to an end, I began to experience types Bukowski liked; he wanted me to talk about them. "Turn off the tape if you have to, but tell me."

So I told him about a woman he could relate to. I'd met her while working for a magazine specializing in literature.

"Already boring," he said.

"Turn on the tape," he said. It was my tape, not his. I told him I'd turn it on when he talked about Malone. First he showed me his steel file cabinet and pulled out three drawers, each with several feet of manuscripts. "All poems" he said. "Malone read them all. The ones in here are the ones he didn't want." He showed me several and told me Black Sparrow would publish them all; Martin wanted every scrap. He'd be picking them up soon and Black Sparrow would be publishing Bukowski books until the year 2020. And there'd be more; every night he was writing more.

Bukowski told me he sent stuff to *Wormwood* in the early sixties, piles of them; and Malone read them all, kept the ones he liked and sent back the rest. He told me he usually got it right, and the poems and stories Malone didn't take for *Wormwood* he'd send on to other magazines; but he knew Malone had gotten the best ones. Then he told me to turn off the tape. He wanted to know more about the female. Something different.

"She was into it." I told how I ripped off her panties and she came just like that. In spasms. And then she wanted me to bite her nipples; she sat in the chair in the living room and told me to hit her on the tits with a wooden spoon. She really wanted me to smack her. Finally, I did and she started spurting a piss-smelling liquid right up into my face.

Bukowski didn't believe me. I told him I didn't believe it either, but it happened. I was on her all night and half the next day. I could hardly walk.

Bukowski liked that. It embarrassed me to talk about it; but I knew it was what he wanted to hear, and I told him there was more, lots more, but I turned on the tape and asked him to talk about Malone. He said he was looking for an early issue of *Wormwood*, the one where Malone wrote the first Bukowski bibliography, or maybe it was the second. I told him I had it; it was the second one Malone had published me in: number 24 with the Bukowski drawing of the three sailors and the woman with the bobbing tits. I told him I'd look for it. I asked if we could get the Malone down on tape now that my own little adventures had stirred his imagination. I told him he was making me work too hard, but he wanted to know more about my female friend. "There must be more." I told him there was a lot more. That made him happy and he finally began to open up about Marvin Malone.

He said most editors were idiots; they published names, not poems. They looked for the names before they read the poems. He told me the two editors who did not fit into that mold were Jon Webb and Marvin Malone. He said if I wanted to know what he thought about Jon Webb I should look up the *Wormwood* Malone did in tribute. Bukowski couldn't remember the number, but I later found it: number 45 titled *Jon Could See True*. He compared Webb to Mencken and Whit Burnett, pretty good company. But the one who mattered most to Charles Bukowski, he said, was Marvin Malone.

"He said he was looking for an early issue of Wormwood, the one where Malone wrote the first Bukowski bibliography, or maybe it was the second. I told him I had it; it was the second one Malone had published me in: number 24 with the Bukowski drawing of the three sailors and the woman with the bobbing tits."

He referred me to a *Wormwood* chapbook titled "Night's Work, Including Buffalo Bill." He said it had one of his best poems in it; the one about the Watts Riots. He told me I was in the same issue. "That Chinese stuff you stole from Pound." He said he wrote a poem called "finish" about the stupidity of violence of the Watts Riots. He needed a copy for a future book of poems. He was concerned that poems in book form would not be exactly what he'd written.

I told him I'd check and find the poem. I remembered it. I told him when I'd read it I thought he was a Communist. He told me he wished he was; that if he were a Communist he could call out all his comrades and catch the guys who were stealing copies of his *Wormwood Reviews*. He mentioned a few suspects.

Checking at home in my pile of *Wormwoods*, I found the poem in number 20. I read it over several times and found it spellbinding. I gave him one of the two copies Malone had sent me. Bukowski was right; it had one of my Chinese poems.

In my journal on that date I wrote the following:

> Had a long night with Buk. Drinking warm beer—he was not in good form—complained about money (for good reason), talked about a publisher (who was holding back royalties), talked a lot about ending up on Skid Row downtown. Told Richmond he was writing garbage.
>
> Listened to a long, boring tape—Buk laughing all the time—of some character from Texas talking tough. Buk's novel still sitting with publisher.
>
> Gets the only satisfaction from his little girl, plus his poems which are going well now. Check *Wormwood* #20 for Buk poem on Watts Riots.

He wanted to know more about the female. I told him to finish up Malone first; my batteries were low. He said that Malone was an old-fashioned editor like Whit Burnett, who read every manuscript and answered every letter. He told me Malone might be publishing *Wormwood* in a run of six hundred to a thousand copies, but writers he dealt with couldn't have been treated better if they'd been dealing with H.L. Mencken. Bukowski thought Mencken was America's greatest editor. I told him my grandfather had worked with Mencken at the *Baltimore Sun*.

Bukowski nodded. He said that a real editor had staying power; his magazines lasted like *The American Mercury*.

That proved accurate for Marvin Malone. Little mags came and went, but the *Wormwood Review* survived for thirty years, putting out more than one hundred and twenty-five issues.

In 1974, when he was revising *Factotum*, Bukowski added this:

"I don't send him as much stuff as I used to. I used to send Malone everything that I wrote. He would take it from there. What he sent back I'd send somewhere else. When the *New York Quarterly* showed up," he said, "I got sucked in on that. Now they're not coming out and they have tons of my crap."

But through the years, Bukowski went back to the *Wormwood Review* again and again. There would be quarrels with his editor at Black Sparrow over *Wormwood* chapbooks. Martin wanted all things Bukowski. When Linda King smashed his Underwood typewriter on the sidewalk outside his place on Carlton Way, two kids tried to put it in their wagon and haul it away. Bukowski stopped them . . . He told them no. "That goes to John Martin," he said. I carried it in for him and put it down.

Here was Marvin Malone busting his ass publishing real poets, nonacademics with no money, and Martin was complaining because Malone might make a little money from Bukowski's chapbook! It bothered him. Martin's proprietary nature.

Then he told me a story about his paintings.

"I paint when I'm too drunk to write," he said. "I throw them away. I give them away. I really don't have the drive to paint. It's a good thing to do when you're drunk. You can't write when you're drunk. Not when you're real drunk. You can paint when you're real drunk. If I have paints around I'll use them. If somebody said you could never paint again, I wouldn't drop a tear. It's not a drive."

He told me a few years back John Martin had arranged for an exhibition of Bukowski's paintings with an eastern bookstore. "In New York City. It's quite famous." He couldn't remember the name, but it was perhaps the Gotham Book Mart. He said they were going to do a show. "Martin gave me a bunch of paints and papers. So I started painting. Martin came over and looked at 'em. He took a few." Bukowski laughed. "Martin didn't say anything. These are good or okay, or I failed. I got drunk one night and kept looking at 'em and I said, 'I don't like these. They're too bright.' So I turned on the hot water in the bathtub and threw all the paintings in there. Then I took them out and I liked them less. I tried to save some by painting over them; finally, I just threw them out in the garbage can. Martin phoned about two or three days later. He says, 'How you doing with those paintings?' I said, 'I got a sad story for you.' He said, 'What is it?' Well, I threw them all in a bathtub full of hot water.' He said, 'What?' I said, 'I didn't like 'em. I threw them in the garbage can.' He says, 'Do you realize what you've done? You've thrown away at least two or three thousand dollars.' I said, 'Come on.' He said, 'I'm serious. Have they collected the garbage yet? Are they still in the can?' I said, 'The garbage man came two days ago.' And that's the story of my painting career. Your turn."

So I told him the rest about the female: How she made it with her ex-husband's two cousins with a crying baby down the hall; how one was in one room and the other was in another, but they finally got together. How she'd go out with a guy who owned a limo company and they'd make it in a drive-in movie with the windows so steamed up that no one could see them in the back seat. And how the limo driver used to call in the middle of the night when I was on her and interrupt her on purpose to make her more hot; and how the guy in the limo gave us both the clap. And there was more, much more, and it was even worse, but I didn't tell him about it. I told him I was trying to love her but it was hard.

He said I was being stupid, acting like Fitzgerald. He quoted the title of his best book of poems: *Love Is A Dog From Hell*. Then he finished up on Malone. He said a good editor was more important than a good woman; that longevity was the thing; that Malone's *Wormwood* was his kind of little mag, free and open to new ideas. It had writers he liked: Steve Richmond, William Wantling, Gerald Locklin, Diane Wakoski, and Doug Blazek. He said one of the best of his works in *Wormwood* was "Grip The Walls," a detachable booklet published in an edition of six hundred copies included in *Wormwood 16* (1964).

I asked what he liked about Malone the best.

"He doesn't take himself too seriously," he told me. A few weeks later I showed him the poem "finish." I asked him about not using caps. He said everybody was under the influence of E.E. Cummings. e.e. cummings. He said it was just a fad that would pass. He read the line aloud: "the worst men have the best jobs / the best men have the

Covers from Marvin Malone's The Wormwood Review, *volumes #16 (bottom), #45 (center), and #20 (top).*

worst jobs or are / unemployed or locked in / madhouses." Then he said: "Sometimes Martin will change a word. The color of a car he'll change from blue to green and I'll just change it back."

He said he remembered writing that poem because the stores were out of food, and he was sweating in the terrible heat of late August L.A., watching as the National Guard patrolled the streets. I pointed out the lines "we have done this to ourselves, we / deserve this." He went and referred back to the title and then to Jeffers. Because Jeffers thought we were finished as a species; but for the poet Charles Bukowski "finish" referred to the bestial state humans had sunk to. "Sure, you can be a Beverly Hills anarchist," he said, "but the riots never got to Beverly Hills." He told me he was very low when he wrote that poem; he was broke and sick and still working at the post office, but even then it had its good side—the Watts Riots shortened the amount of mail he had to sort.

And then he talked about his latest girl; how she stole money from his wallet and wanted him to buy her food and clothes and lipstick. It was before I met Cupcakes, but it might have been her. I never asked him if she wanted him to bite her nipples or beat him with a wooden spoon. He told me once how Jane Cooney Baker had beaten him with a cold cream jar until he was covered in blood; but the beatings he gave women, I thought, were for his pleasure, not theirs.

A Day at the Races

Charles Bukowski goes to the races because he no longer has a nine-to-five job. He writes at night and gets up late in the morning, usually at eleven-thirty or twelve o'clock: the ride to the track on a warm day stimulates his sense of daily purpose. To Bukowski that turnstile at Hollywood Park is like a time clock.

When he first showed me the way around the racing world in 1975, he was driving a beat-up Volkswagen with an iron cross ceremoniously hanging from his front mirror. He lived in a two-room apartment in the worst section of Hollywood and grumbled about a ten-dollar-a-month rent increase.

> "When I first began to frequent the track he gave me a few rules: Don't take a book with you. Don't talk about literature. Watch out for prostitutes. Never bet on the Daily Double. Don't take a woman."

We would sit in the grandstands, far away from the finish line where the crowd was thinned out and there was space to do serious work. After purchasing a program, a *Pasadena Star-News* for doping out the consensus, and a copy of the *Daily Racing Form*, Buk would begin his compilations, computations, and calculations, circling horses with a black pen, numbering the consensus, and adding the odds as they flicked on the tote board. I rarely spoke to him during that half hour, concentrating instead on all the long shots that never came in.

Things have changed a bit for Bukowski now: He no longer drives a Volkswagen or lives in Hollywood or sits in the grandstands. Now his new BMW is parked in valet parking. He sits in the clubhouse and makes larger bets, but he is still intense and the inner man is very much the same as he was in 1975. He no longer, however, runs with the hunted.

When I first began to frequent the track he gave me a few rules: Don't take a book with you. Don't talk about literature. Watch out for prostitutes. Never bet on the Daily Double. Don't take a woman. Somehow along the way I've managed to break every rule except for the one about prostitutes.

When he sits down in his seat before the first post, Bukowski begins by checking the consensus "because I want to know where the dumb money is going." Usually he has studied the horses the night before in the newspaper. He never gives tips. "If you win with a horse I give you, you'll think I can do it every time, and if you lose I'll get the rap." From my own experience, I'd call that sage advice.

Bukowski doesn't write poetry at the track, but he does write poems and stories about his experiences there. He doesn't much care for racing types. "You'll see the worst kind of people out there," he says. "I'm there, aren't I?"

At bottom, Charles Bukowski believes a racing fan can be a winner, but he has to be plenty smart. "A guy who wins at the track can do anything," he says. "You have to know everything to be on top of this game."

"Bet to win" is Bukowski's motto, but he does it his own way. In the last season at Hollywood Park he had twenty dollars on the second consensus favorite. I had five on a six-to-one shot. When the thirty-to-one long shot came in on a short field I tore up my ticket, but Bukowski pulled out a two-dollar bet on the long shot and said quietly, "I had it as an insurance." When he wins he wins quietly. His biggest day was about five hundred dollars, but you wouldn't know it

155

by the expression on his face. "Amateurs yell about winning," he says. "They'll lose it all on the next two races betting baseball combinations. When a veteran player wins a big exacta, he'll come back the next morning and cash when there's no one around. It's pretty dumb to stand at the window in a crowded space and put nine one hundred dollar bills in your pocket, right?"

"Right."

I've asked Bukowski why he doesn't write a novel about the races. It seems a natural for him, but he shrugs the idea off, saying "It would be too boring. Someone loses the rent money and goes home and strangles his mother."

In the summer Buk looks forward to the Del Mar season. It is his vacation in the sun. The ride on the train to Del Mar and the ocean breezes give him a small degree of pleasure. "I take Linda (Beighle) along on that run. It's one of the few times I break my rule about women."

Another informal rule: Charles Bukowski, who has been dragged out of bars on his hands and knees and personally awakened by police on city sidewalks in the early morning, never drinks at the track. He will take two or three cups of coffee with cream and eat a salad, but no beer, no wine, no whiskey. He smokes little Indian cigarettes that look like pieces of rolled up brown paper bags, but disapproves of drinking at the track. "You get out there in the sun with a beer or two in your belly and you just make the whole thing harder for yourself. I drink when I write because it makes the words flow. Out at the track I just need to concentrate."

Technically Bukowski doesn't bet on the jockeys and he doesn't bet the horses. His system has to do with the smart money. "I lost $10,000 learning how to bet," he says. He likes to bet late on most races. Three minutes before the flag you'll see him in the clubhouse watching the inside tote. "That's when the smart money goes in," he says. "They go to the ten-dollar window." (The new system at Hollywood Park has thrown that off somewhat, though there is still a fifty-dollar window for the high rollers.) "I want to know what the numbers are, down to the last minute."

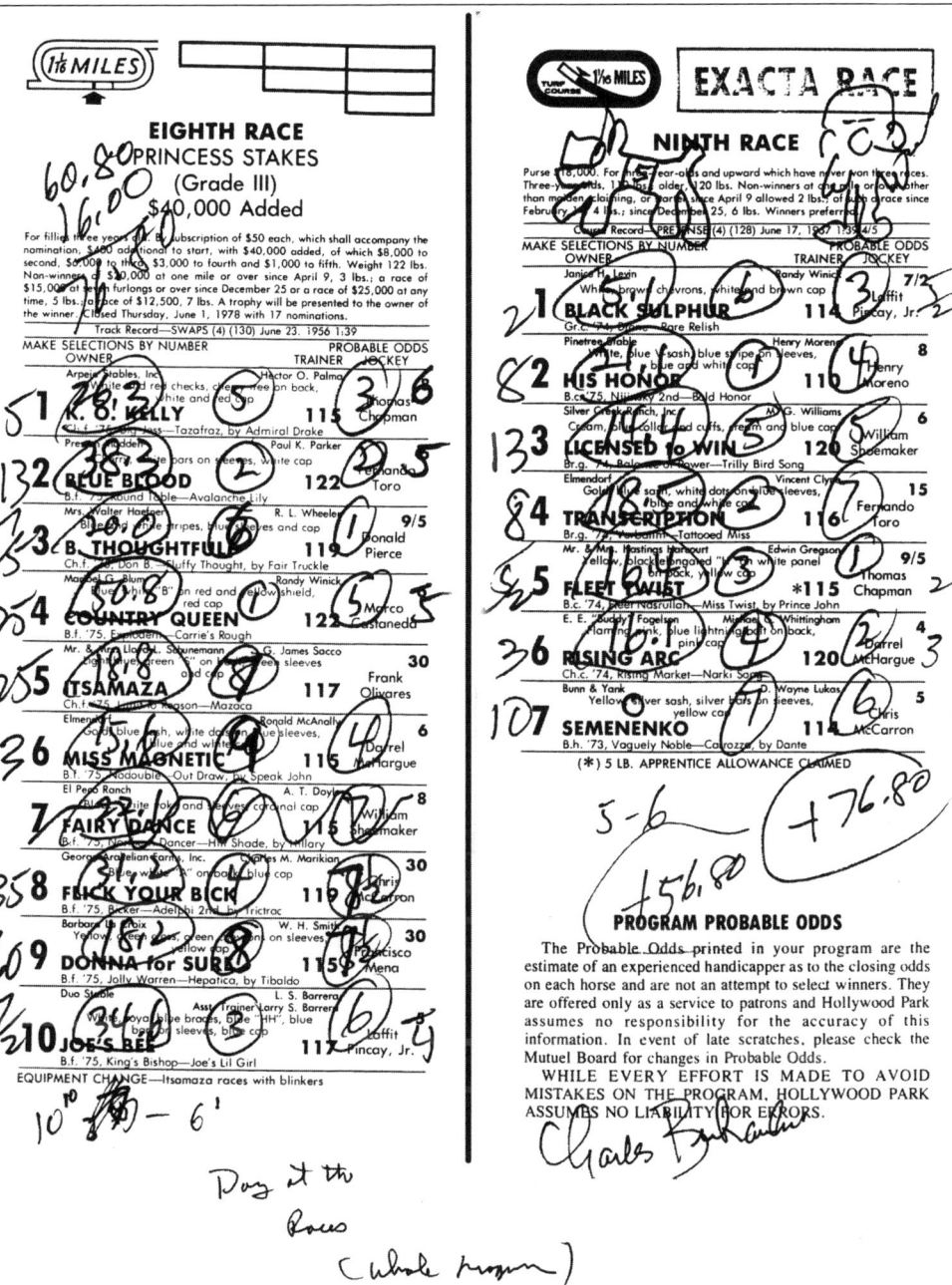

Just before the race goes off, his mind is going like mad. His mouth is set and his eyes never leave the numbers. He doesn't speak at all. He is busy figuring amounts. On some races he will bet three horses and he wants to know if a five-dollar bet on a four-to-one horse will cover a twenty-five dollar bet on the second favorite if he should fail. In the last minute he might tag five dollars on a medium long shot. On some races he will have one horse and bet it down solid, always to win. He likes the quinella and frequently wins the exacta, but he never wheels a horse (bet every horse as second against the one he thinks will come in first).

"It's all agreed," he says. "Look at the faces of the losers and look at the faces of the winners. The losers are saying 'I knew I should have bet the six horse. Why did I bet the eight?' And the winners are saying 'I had that six all along. That was a sure bet.' But there's no sure bet. You can have a two-to-five favorite that's won ten straight races and the horse can stumble or the jockey can fall off on his ass."

The worst day I ever had at the track was when Bukowski broke one of his own rules and brought his Texas girl friend along. She talked the whole day.

"What do you think of Pincay today?" she asked.

"The jockeys don't mean that much," Buk answered.

"But he's won two straight." Buk went back to his form.

"How about that horse? Look how big he is."

"His times are terrible." He handed her the racing form. She didn't look at it.

"How about the horse with no tail?" Bukowski strained his eyes looking for the horse with no tail. "Steve Richmond would bet that horse," she said. Bukowski laughed. Then he went back to his figures.

She began again. "The guy in front of me in line said the nine horse is the one. He bet two hundred on him to place."

"Why to place?"

"I guess he thought he was the one to place."

Sure enough the horse without a tail won and the nine horse placed and Pincay had four winners. Buk and I both went home losers and she was seventy-five dollars ahead.

"You see, Pleasants," said Bukowski, climbing into his blue Volkswagen, "that's why I told you never to take a woman to the track." The lady from Texas smiled.

The next time I went out to Hollywood Park Bukowski wasn't there. I decided to break another rule. I brought a book to read. *Don Quixote*. I hadn't realized Cervantes had written a Quixote II and I enjoyed especially the chapter on "How Don Quixote Resolved to Turn Shepherd and Lead a Rustic Life." I cashed more tickets than I tore up that day and I selected horses only on the basis of those that had the most r's in their names. I even had a beer, but I didn't talk about literature. That's one rule even I'm not stupid enough to break.

1926, Bukowski on Tommy. (courtesy of Heinrich Fett)

William Wantling and the Meat School of Poetry

> "Bukowski liked Wantling because he was 'a non-literary type.' He was the loser's loser. . . . He drank too."

If Charles Bukowski was President of The Meat School of Poetry, then William Wantling was his Vice President. For years they had known each other through Doug Blazek's magazine *Ole* and they were much alike. Neither could hold a job; both had trouble keeping their women. If Bukowski was the alcoholic's alcoholic, the drunk all drunks looked up to, then Wantling was the substance abuser's abuser. Both had been arrested and reveled in it. Wantling's rarest book, *Heroin Haikus*, salutes the life of the jailed addict.

Though they corresponded since the early sixties, they only met once. That was in 1974 when Wantling was teaching at the University of Illinois in Urbana. His health was poor, his career was in decline, but he'd written a roman á clef titled *Young and Tender* in 1969, published by Bee Books, about a character who was obviously Charles Bukowski. Bukowski never mentioned the book, but he was always on the lookout for writer's wars.

In 1976, Bukowski took me downtown for a tour of his youthful haunts. First we stopped at the L.A. Public Library to visit the fiction room, where he first read John Fante's *Ask the Dust*. It was filled with drunks and street people reading the newspaper. "Same as ever," he said. Not one Fante book could be found on the shelves.

Then we walked along the heights of what was once Bunker Hill, and he pointed down to a cement stairway near what had been Angel's Flight, a one-minute train ride from the top of Bunker Hill to the central city below. Arturo Bandini, Fante's protagonist brought the place to life for Bukowski. He told me it was the first time he knew he didn't have to go to Paris to write a novel. "Fante did it right here in Los Angeles."

As we walked down the hill toward the Grand Central Market, I asked if he knew another writer who'd taken his surroundings and made them come alive like Fante did. He said Wantling. William Wantling. We grabbed a beer at the standup bar in the Grand Central Market, and Bukowski told me what he knew about Wantling; how they'd corresponded for many years and only met once.

He said he got to know Wantling from the little magazines, especially *Wormwood* and *Ole,* which, he said, everyone mispronounced. Blazek told him *Ole* rhymed with soul, but everyone called it Olé. I asked if he'd ever discussed the Penguin Poets Series, since Wantling was in *Penguin Poets 12* and Bukowski followed in *13.*

He told me the subject never came up; that Wantling hated discussing poets and books and poetry more than Bukowski did.

"No. It didn't go that way." When Bukowski got a reading gig at the University of Illinois in Urbana, where Wantling was teaching. Wantling found out he was coming. He called Bukowski to ask if he'd like to stay with him and Bukowski agreed.

The President of the Meat School of Poetry and the Vice President would have a little time together under one roof to talk about what they wrote about: whores, cops, addicts, busted marriages, jail, lost jobs, and dying.

When they met at the airport Bukowski thought they both were in a race for the graveyard. From the very beginning, Bukowski told me, arrangements were awkward. Wantling was recently separated from his wife and living in a one-room dump on skid row. There was only one bed. Wantling told him, "You can either stay with my wife or stay with me." Perfect. Just what Bukowski needed: a drunk, an addict, and a pissed-off wife in the middle.

Bukowski suggested they all stay at the house. "I don't want your wife," he told Wantling.

Together for the first time, they drank all night. Wantling was on speed and codeine, Bukowski said, and when they woke up Wantling was really sick. Bukowski was pretty sick, too, but Wantling's wife, Ruth, was perky and awake and went off to teach a class somewhere.

Bukowski said he was feeling really hung over. He was telling me this on a sunny day downtown after three glasses of beer, and he was laughing at the memory of himself and Wantling standing in the kitchen in their shorts.

"Wantling suggested we eat something," he said. "He made soft-boiled eggs. A few minutes after we'd eaten, Wantling was out in the back yard throwing up the soft-boiled eggs."

I asked if he'd been disappointed coming upon Wantling in such a state.

"The letters were good," said Bukowski. "When he'd get high he'd go off into this heady philosophic jargon. He'd try to explain things, but he'd get way lost. It sounded all right, but he didn't quite know what he was getting at."

"We all do that," I told him. Bukowski laughed. "As a writer," he said, "he was best when he wrote about dope. Even though his lines were hard and good, I told him you always manage to throw in one old-fashioned poetic line as if you're ashamed of what you said. And he'd do it almost every time; usually the last line. He'd write all this stuff:

'Peggy took the ladle and it crashed between the commode and the toilet paper rack. Florence called and asked if she could have a hit.' Better than this, you know. And then the last line he'd say something like 'The roses of jeopardy always astonish us.' He'd try to clean it up. There was a subconscious fear of saying it straight on through."

"The toughness collapsed and he became Wordsworth."

"Something like that." Bukowski recalled Wantling saying they would both live to the year 2000.

"And a month later he was dead," he said.

Bukowski liked Wantling because he was "a non-literary type." He was the loser's loser. The Meat School of Poetry was filled to the brim with nonstarters. Wantling had a part-time teacher's gig. According to Bukowski, he lasted about six weeks. He'd fallen off his bicycle. He was on pills: speed mostly. And codeine. He drank too.

We were walking up Bunker Hill. Bukowski pointed to the place where Arturo Bandini had crawled out the window of his rooming house. At that time I had not read John Fante and had no idea who Arturo Bandini was.

"Wantling was okay," said Bukowski, "but I'm the one who will make it to the year 2000."

Friends

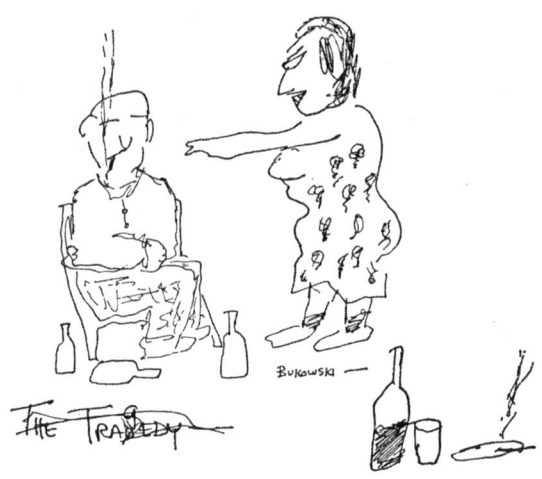

"Now that I'm nuts, everybody wants me," Bukowski told me. "Except women."

It was wintertime and the cutout cardboard snowmen with their crooked beards and paste stained boots were up in the windows of the court apartments that surrounded Bukowski's little studio. A Bukowski Christmas! Beer and tinsel. There was a card from Larry Flynt and you could find his signature by pulling out the vulva of the blonde model with her tongue sticking out.

He was between Linda's. Linda King was gone and Linda Beighle had not yet arrived.

He was still on Carlton Way, but the money was piling up. Most of it came from Germany, he said. A number of women got through his door that year, but no one stayed.

I had two tickets to the fights at the Olympic Auditorium, a freebee from the sports editor at the *L.A. Times*. When I got there, two women were fighting over Bukowski.

"So, OK kid, friends are more important tonight than getting fucked."

"You sure you wanta go?" I told him I could find someone else to take to the fights, but by then the two women had stormed out, taking the liquor, the cigarettes and the money on the table.

"They'd probably just give me blue balls anyway," Buk said.

Things were starting to work for Bukowski. He told me he had more than a hundred grand in the bank and his books were really selling in Europe. "And *Hustler's* paying me two grand a story."

Every month he had offers of readings, some with advances stuffed in the envelope. Now he needed a house and a woman to run it for him. Not Cupcakes or Georgia. Someone with smarts who could cook and fuck and get the grass cut. We climbed into his little blue Volks and headed downtown for the fights. Buk took surface streets. He hated the freeway. Too many cops. Too many DUIs. He had a place he always parked under a freeway ramp on Olive, around the corner from the Olympic Auditorium.

"How they hangin'?" he asked.

I told him I was heading for a divorce.

"Got your steel?" As we climbed out of the car, I showed him my knife. "Ever tell you about my divorce? From Barbara? I'll call her up some time and you can talk to her. You're my Boswell. OK?"

"OK."

It was one of those downtown Red nights. Indian Red Lopez or Little Red Chavez or Irish Red Fong. I forget which one. A Red was the main event and he did have red hair. Really, really red hair. We had good *L.A. Times* seats, almost ringside and I bought us two shots of whiskey. We both liked guys who paid their own way. Maybe we talked about Willy Pepp before the prelims or maybe it was Carmen Basillio. It was one of those fighters with a hundred scars on his face. Their names always came up if we got there for the PRE lims—"the pathetics" Buk called them. "The losers like us! HA HA HA." The young and inexperienced fighters or the old and finished. "I love to watch failures," Bukowski laughed. "Reminds me of myself."

"Not anymore. Not with a hundred thousand in the bank."

"OK, well let's not mention it here. We might not be among friends."

Halfway through the fights, before the main event, we ran into a poet Bukowski had tangled with somewhere before. Paul Vangelisti. He was taping the fights for a radio program. "That fuck owes me money," Bukowski yelled. Right into the tape recorder. Right into Vangelisti's face. Vangelisti got up to shake Bukowski's hand and Buk went purple. "You owe me three hundred bucks, you prick."

Van got red in the face.

"For the anthology, remember?" said Bukowski.

"No. I don't owe you . . ." Vangelisti replied.

"Buk, three hundred bucks. You got . . . how much in the bank?" I asked.

He pushed Vangelisti back down into his seat and headed to the mens' room to take a piss. "I just wanted to scare him. HE IS MY ENEMY. And you're my friend. My Boswell. Bought you a shot." He handed me a whiskey. We drank several more and washed them down with beer.

Little Red or Indian Red or Irish Red lost that night and his blood was all over the ring. It got on Bukowski's shirt and in my hair and the women at ringside were scooping it up in their hands. Rubbing it on their tits. For good luck, as if it were the blood of Jesus or something.

On our way back home we got out our steel and looked for the car. It was still there. We were both wobbling drunk. Bukowski got in and started it up. Three blocks later a cop started following us. "Oh shit. I forgot my license."

"Just keep the yellow line on the left. Drive slow."

We both held our breath and Bukowski babied it. After half a mile the cop peeled off in search of another drunk. In Hollywood we stopped in at an all night liquor store and bought some beer. I paid. I bought a box of cheap cigars too and some peanuts. We drank until four in the morning and then Bukowski picked up the phone and dialed. Before he could answer he handed me the receiver. "Yes?" It was a woman's voice. "My wife," Bukowski whispered.

"Hello."

"You know, it's six in the morning. Who's this?"

"My name is Ben. I'm here with your ex-husband. Charles Bukowski."

There was dead silence. "I'm his biographer."

"Oh." Another pause. "I don't want to have anything to do with him. Put him on."

They spoke for a minute or less and then Bukowski hung up. "I guess your job as a Boswell is gonna be tough."

"How about tonight if I just be a friend? No wives. No family."

He laughed. "Family. My parents had to die before I could really write!"

"Where is it six o'clock?"

"Tyler, Texas."

"She sounded really pissed."

"She was . . . She was never a friend. Wives become relatives. And friends don't last either. Not forever."

He looked at me seriously. "Know what I mean?"

"Tell me."

He took a pull on his beer. It was almost dawn. "I say that human relationships do not work between a man and a woman, a man and a man, a woman and a woman, a man and a dog, a pig and a dog. I say any human relationship at its given best, I'll give it six years. How long we been friends, Ben?"

"God, ten years."

"Two and a half is average. When you get up to six, look out. I've known a great many who've been friends for six years and they don't make the seventh."

Sam the Whorehouse Man. (courtesy of Charles Bukowski)

"I guess we don't take each other very seriously then."

"Maybe. Still, you'll know. But you pay your own way. I like guys who pay their own way."

When I left, Sam the Whorehouse Man was just coming home.

"Rough night?"

"Rough Night."

A month later Linda Beighle showed up. I met her the morning after they'd spent their first night together.

167

I could see he was sizing her up for his hausfrau. She was blonde and good looking. She could cook and keep the house clean. She could even help him with real estate.

A few months later Bukowski moved out of Hollywood and bought a house in San Pedro. He took Linda with him. "As a what?" I asked.

"Don't ask," he said. "Anyway, remember you're four years past the limit."

"OK," I said.

"OK, then Ben. OK."

(Photo by Ben Pleasants)

(Printing by Charles Bukowski)

Andernach: 1977

Hello Ben--

o.k., have a good France. things here are about the same--that is, I'm always on the edge of something: insanity, defeat, discovery, death, boredome, fear, so forth. you know that deck of cards. in fact, I'm low down right now, so this is short. to awk. your letter and to hope you a ####happy France. jesus christ, the dogs bark knives.

Letter to Pleasants, 1977, on the advent of Ben's trip to France and then on to Germany to meet Bukowski's German relatives.

In the spring of 1977 I went on sabbatical leave from my teaching assignment at Shriners Hospital in Los Angeles. My wife and I were married in name only; a radical newspaper I'd helped found, the *Los Angeles Vanguard*, had closed due to the lack of advertising revenue; the local branch of the IWW I belonged to as an anarchist was splintering into three factions; and I was stuck in dead-end relationships with women who ranged from Radical Feminists to members of the Revolutionary Communist Party. It was time for a change.

I decided to take six months off and live in France. I chose Paris, where I had interests, and Grenoble, where I had friends. Everyone agreed it would be a good move for someone who had just given a poetry reading at a local college where every poem was about suicide.

"Have a good France," Bukowski told me. "And if you get a chance, look up my Uncle Heinrich Fett in Andernach. He's probably in the graveyard." Then he handed me copies of several letters his uncle had written him in English. "I don't know how he got hold of me. We started writing back and forth. He found out I had a daughter. At Christmas he'd send me these wonderful German presents. They were well made, things you can't buy in America. Wooden toys. He'd send a big box. There was candy in there. It was really well done. His letters were very warm, but kind of corny. 'I hope your little girl is all right and I hope you're happy.' Stuff like that. He seemed like a very old man to me. Then I sent him a copy of *Notes of a Dirty Old Man* in German. That was the last time I heard from him. He died or he hates my guts. He's probably in the graveyard at Andernach. Anyway, if you have time . . ."

I told him I'd make time.

In March of 1977, after a torrid affair in Grenoble with a beautiful French woman named Annie, I finally set out for Andernach. Europe had worked its magic on me and I was happy, maybe even in love. The weather in Germany is usually cold and wet in early spring. I had on a heavy plaid coat and I'd done a little homework on the town. I located a book called *My Rhineland Journal*, written by Henry Allen, that described the town of Andernach under the American occupation after World War One, when Bukowski's father was there. "Returning to Andernach," he wrote, "I inspected and reviewed a battalion there which was not particularly well set up, nor did it pass by in review with sufficient snap; in fact, neither officer nor men were as smart as they should be for one of the regular divisions kept over there."

I showed the book to Bukowski when I got back and we both had a good laugh. He had told me earlier how his father and mother met. The older Henry was guarding a bridge which Katharina Fett was trying to cross. He gave her some trouble. Henry Senior spoke German. She told him her family had no food. So Katharina Fett invited Henry Bukowski Senior home to dinner provided he bring the food. That was the story Bukowski told me. As I found out later, it was all wrong.

On March 23, 1977 I left Paris for Andernach, Bukowski's birthplace. In a letter to my wife, I told my daughter Alexandra "Just now I'm sitting in the Gare de l'Est waiting for a train to Germany, where I'm going to take photos of Bukowski's birthplace." I'd asked my wife three times for Bukowski's address. I'd lost it. I had a bad cold. The weather was raw and I hated the poorly heated waiting rooms in Paris train stations. I was low on money, but my wife sent me $80 in American Express checks and a note from my daughter which I'd picked up at American Express. They had a rule: they'd hold your mail for you if you had $20 in travelers' checks. I had the minimum. I put the hundred into francs. While I was waiting in the cold, I wrote my wife a card: "Arrived in Paris today. Received your letter with Sandi's note and the $80. Glad to get all three." That was it. There was nothing left of our marriage. Only my daughter and the money taken from my sabbatical check.

The journey by train from Paris along the Rhine was somewhat difficult. On the French side of the border the trip was restful. I read Whitman. I was traveling light. Most of my luggage was back in Grenoble; the rest was checked in a locker at Gare de l'Est. I carried only a small bag with a notebook, a change of underwear, a camera and a letter of introduction from Bukowski to his Uncle Heinrich, just in case he was alive. I wasn't planning to spend the night there. German trains are not French trains. German trains run on time. The passenger has ONE MINUTE to get off the train with luggage in hand. No one told me that at the Gare d'Est. That's the disadvantage of having a Eurail Pass. You just hop on the train and go. No questions asked.

Andernach is a tiny town on the Rhine between Bonn and Cologne. From the moment I sat down on the German train things changed. My seat was not reserved. I needed a reserve seat, the conductor informed me in German. He spoke little English. Price: four marks. I had only French money. My German, which was worse than my French, consisted of a few words I'd picked up from American war movies: Achtung, swinehundt, sig heil and yah vol. None of these helped me much. I could also throw in schnell, mach schnell and

Deuchland, Deuchland uber alles. That didn't help either. The conductor explained to me in German I had one minute to make my connection to the local train to Andernach.

I missed the connection and found myself in the station at Cologne. There I found a ticket agent who spoke English and had read Bukowski. He knew he was born in Andernach. I showed him the letter Bukowski had written out in his own hand. The agent touched it as though it was something from the hands of Jesus, then he punched out an itinerary and put me on the right train, the train to Andernach.

This time the ride along the Rhine was pleasant. There was a light rain. But the boats on the river and the old castles on the hillsides made me feel better. I arrived just about lunchtime. The town itself was impressive. In a cold light rain I clambered off the train and made my way up the ramp from the Rhine to a dark walled fortress where both French and German were spoken. I looked around for anyone who might speak English. "Do you know Charles Bukowski?" I asked. This was the town of his birth. Out of the rain popped a young man named Rolf Degan. "I know Bukowski," he said in English. "He was born here in Andernach."

I'd found my man. Rolf was tall, with dark hair and bright eyes. He was barely out of high school. He had a few friends with him. Some spoke English. I told them my name. I said I'd been sent by Bukowski to look up his uncle, Heinrich Fett. One of Rolf's friends, a Turkish German named Arif, had heard the name before. I said I needed to change francs into marks. They took me to a local bank where the teller spoke German and French. She knew the name Fett. They still lived in Andernach, she thought.

Rolf and his friends were now jumping up and down telling people I was sent to Andernach by Bukowski. We sat down at a café and ordered some beer.

"Tell me again, why are you here?"

"Bukowski sent me." There was a crowd by now. The beer was excellent.

"You know Bukowski? Really?"

"He sent me here to find his Uncle Heinrich. Heinrich Fett."

I showed them the letter Bukowski had written to his uncle. They stared at it reverently. I said the last time Bukowski had heard from his uncle was in 1970. That his uncle was old and might be in the cemetery. I asked if they knew where the cemetery was. They told me that was easy. I finished my beer and tried to pay for it, but the waiter refused my money. He'd read Bukowski's *Post Office*.

Then Rolf and Arif and their friends took me to the cemetery. It was close by. One of the girls asked "When is Bukowski coming to Andernach?"

I told them I didn't know. "When they pay him," I said.

They wanted to know who *they* was. I told them the *they* were his German publishers.

They wanted to know if Bukowski was poor. I told them he was doing better. They asked if Bukowski had been back to Germany as an adult. I told them no. They wanted to know what he did during World War II. I told them that was a long story. They asked if I was his biographer. I said I was trying to be. I asked if they knew of a hotel I could stay in Andernach. They told me they'd find me a place to sleep. They asked if there was anything Bukowski needed from the town. I told them I'd get back to them on that.

We walked around the town until we found the cemetery. Rolf pointed out the Fett family. There they were. He mentioned a famous Russian writer whose name was Fett. We looked at the stones. They were dark and solid and well carved. Uncle Heinrich wasn't there. I did locate a "somebody Israel," and almost asked the obvious question, but I held my tongue. I looked at Arif, who was an auslander, a Turkish German, but I thought twice about asking if Bukowski had Jewish blood.

Then we went back to the town and drank more beer. Dark beer. They asked if Bukowski drank German beer. I told them Bukowski drank any beer you put in front of him, but he hated beer in cans, and German beer, real German beer, was expensive in the U.S.

"So," said Rolf Degan, "let us find Uncle Heinrich." We took a walk down to the town hall and Rolf made inquiries. "He's still alive," he told me. "Very old. They say he goes to a certain café every day for a glass of white wine. Let us see if we can find him." By now there were just three of us. Arif, Rolf and me.

We entered a dimly lit room in an old hotel. Rolf asked the barmaid if she knew a Heinrich Fett. She pointed to a well-dressed man in a suit and tie sipping a Gerwurtztraminer. Rolf and Arif introduced themselves. As they said the name Bukowski, they pointed back at me. The old man smiled. In English, he asked me my name and told me to sit down. "You have a pleasant name," he said. "So, you are Henry's friend. We once wrote letters. Is he well?"

"He's very well," I told him. "He asked me to look you up."

"Look me up?" He had trouble with the concept.

"Find you." I gave him the letter Bukowski had written. He read it and shook his head. At this point Arif left. He had an appointment.

When Heinrich finished his wine, he invited Rolf and myself back to his home for a chat. My hair was wild and my coat had remnants of the forests of Grenoble on it, where I had lain among the leaves with my lovely friend Annie. Heinrich was polite and introduced me to his female companion Louisa. He told me she was not his wife. Heinrich asked me if I were a writer too. I told him I wrote about writers.

We talked first of Andernach. Uncle Heinrich told me it was a sleepy town located strategically on a major river and the residents watched conquerors come and go, keeping their distance.

I asked him if it were true that his father had been the Burgermeister of Andernach. Both Heinrich and Louisa laughed. No, he said, his father had not been the Burgermeister of Andernach. He mentioned another Heinrich Fett, his namesake and grandfather. "He went to America in 1889 and landed in Hoboken. You know the place? New Jersey."

I told him I was born in the next town up the Hudson, Weehauken.

"Oh." He was surprised. America seemed so big. "His children stayed here in Andernach," he said. "Two sons and a daughter. The oldest was my father, Wilhelm." He told me his father played a gypsy violin, often on the streets. And he was a chronic drunkard. "Sometimes he drank so much, he would fall asleep in the middle of a melody and the violin would fall from his hands. I was the oldest son. Wilhelm, the next son, was killed in the Battle of the Marne in 1918. Katharina Fett was born on May 4, 1899." He described their childhood in the small family house in Andernach. He said the family had always been poor, living a hand-to-mouth existence for generations. "We attended the Roman Catholic Church in Andernach," he said. He gave the German and tried to translate it into English. Rolf did it for him. "Our Lady of the Heavenly Flyers is what it means in English," Rolf said. "Sounds funny, no?"

I wrote down the name in my note pad and laughed. It did sound funny. I started to make a joke about the word Luftwaffe, but bit my tongue. Instead, I asked him about his sister, Katharina. He sighed. He said his sister was a dreamer, a little shy and very pretty as a girl.

Then I told him what Bukowski had said about his parents' first meeting. She had given Bukowski's father trouble on the bridge he was guarding and she had invited the American soldier home. Uncle Heinrich remembered it differently. He said his future brother-in-law met his sister at a YMCA victory dance in the spring of 1919.

"She was still a school girl. It was a dance the U.S. Army gave for the defeated. Us. The young Henry took to her immediately. They courted for only a short time," he said, "walking along the Rhine hand in hand, picnicking on the nearby hillside and talking about their future together."

I asked Uncle Heinrich if he was in the war, World War One. He said he was stationed in Berlin, where he greased planes for the Luftwaffe until the war was over. He returned to Andernach in 1919. He said that his sister was always fond of him. They were close and she introduced him to Henry Bukowski immediately. He recalled a trip the three of them took to Coblenz in 1920. "We attended a fair. We were both very young." He was best man at their wedding. He neglected to mention Katharina was five months pregnant on her wedding day. Uncle Heinrich recalled that Henry was born in August of 1920. Then he showed me a letter Bukowski had written on January, 1966 requesting the exact hour of his birth. Bukowski explained that a friend was casting a horoscope for him and needed the exact time. He began his life as Henry Bukowski Junior," said Heinrich. "He was a very lively little fellow. Always running around.

175

They called him Sonny Boy." He said that in German and Rolf translated it into English.

"Is that so in English? Sonny Boy?"

I told him I had a cousin who was stuck with the name into his sixties. It was easier than calling him Junior. I said at present Sonny Boy would not suit Henry Bukowski Jr. He's changed his name several times. First it was Henry, then Hank, then Charles. I said that Bukowski hated his father.

Uncle Heinrich reached up into a bookcase and pulled down a book in German with Bukowski's picture on the cover. Bukowski had had it sent by his publisher. He said it was vulgar, not to his taste. He told me he stopped writing his nephew after he read the book. The drunkenness reminded him of his father and the violin that slipped from his hand when he was drunk. There was an awkward pause. I looked at Rolf. I said that Bukowski thought his father was ruthless and cruel. He would beat his son if he failed to cut the lawn properly.

Uncle Heinrich shook his head. He said he liked his brother-in-law. "He got me my first job with the YMCA. As a chauffeur. It lasted from 1920-1923. Then I went to sea. The English I got from working with the YMCA helped me much. The Americans were good to me."

He recalled the last Americans departed in 1923. He felt sad "when they packed their bags and left Germany." He told me Henry Bukowski was employed as a civilian for the U.S. Army until the spring of 1923. "He was in the R.R. & C. Service at Coblenz." He told me what that stood for, but I didn't write it down. "Yes," he said, "Henry and Katharina left in the spring of 1923. Henry wanted to see Europe and England before he returned home, but the army wanted him back in the U.S."

He showed me a sheaf of letters his sister had written him in the Twenties all in German. And he pulled out a postcard of the boat they sailed on, The Millard Fillmore. He said it was little more than a troop ship. Rolf translated the brief inscription. Katharina wrote to her mother consoling her and asking that she not make it hard on herself. She would be well provided for. In Germany, the days of wild inflation had come and Uncle Heinrich told me he went to sea to escape the madness of it. "I never saw them again," he said. "Not my sister or my brother-in-law or my nephew." I told him I thought he'd see his nephew before too long. "He's famous," Rolf told him. "Bukowski is known all over the world!"

They fed me a few cookies and offered me coffee. Uncle Heinrich checked to see if the address was right. I gave them the one in San Pedro my wife had included in her letter. Then Uncle Heinrich wrote out his telephone number and address. As he walked me to the door he said "Please say hello to Henry and his wife and Marina." I said I would. Bukowski would have to explain all that.

That night Rolf and Arif and their friends entertained me at the local youth hostel. We talked about everything. Nazis and Hitler and World War Two. Israel and Henry Ford and Stalin and what Germany was reading that year. They asked me about Bix Beiderbecke and Bob Dylan and Jim Morrison. Arif told me what it was like to be a Turk in Germany. Rolf asked if he should get Bukowski's birth certificate and send it on. He said he would read all the letters Uncle Heinrich had showed us and translate them into English. With his permission. I gave him Bukowski's address and phone number. I told him to call. Bukowski would love it.

Rolf did everything he said he would. When I returned home in May, after a poetry reading at Shakespeare and Company in Paris and a trip back to Grenoble to see my friends, there was a large envelope from Andernach filled with photos, the photocopied letters Bukowski had sent to his uncle, English translations of Katharina's letters to her brother, a letter from Bukowski's father to Uncle Heinrich, and a copy of Bukowski's birth certificate. To my surprise, the date was a few days off. Bukowski told me it must be a clerical error. His mother knew what day he was born!

All through the rest of 1977, the year before Bukowski returned to Germany, Rolf Degan continued to flood me with information. He wrote me on May 13, 1977 that Germany was experiencing a Bukowski boom. He asked Uncle Heinrich to photocopy more family photos and letters, but Heinrich finally drew the line between what he considered of value to the world and what he felt was personal. I wrote Rolf back to say that Heinrich had been wonderful. That Bukowski had spoken with him several times on the phone. Rolf said

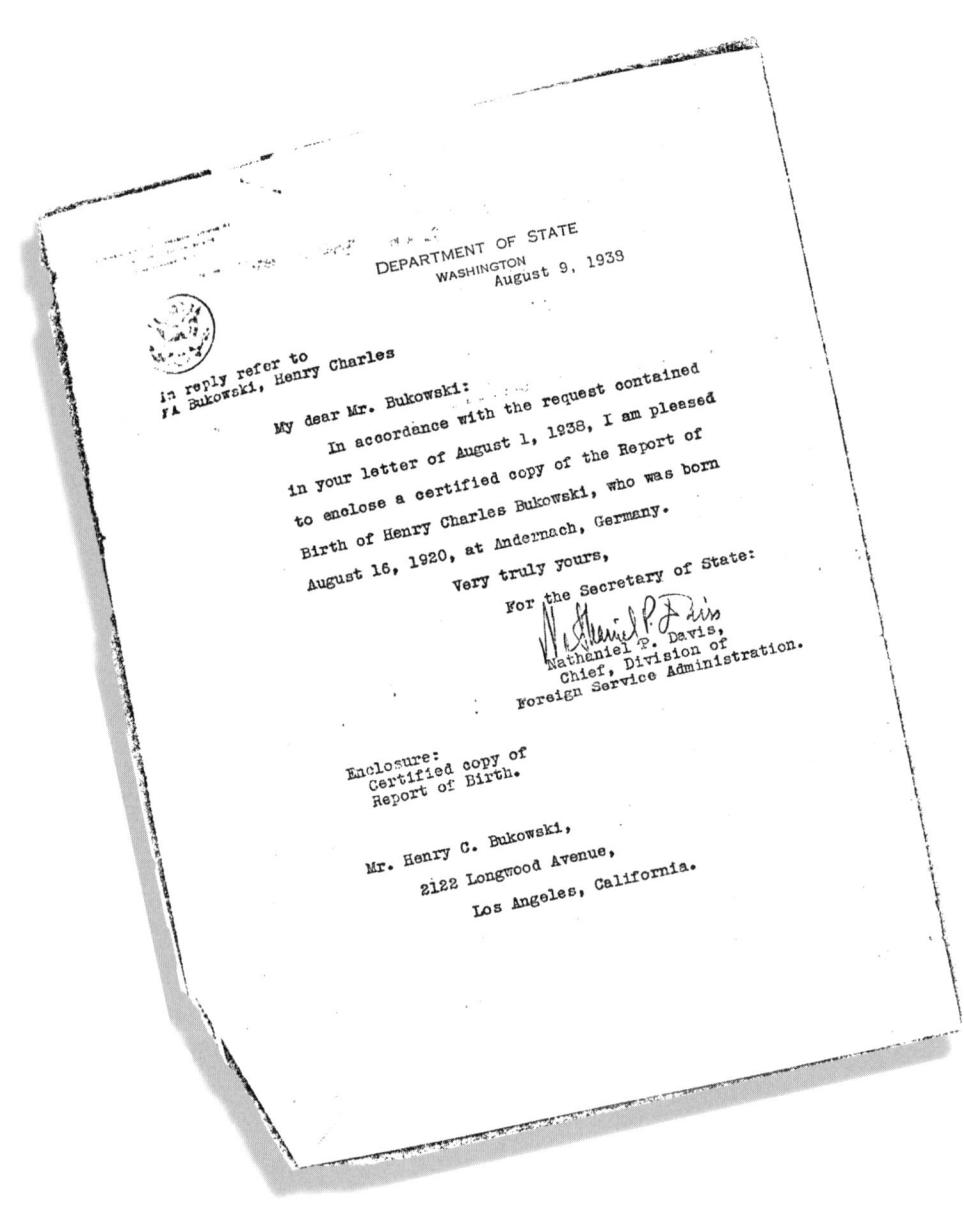

Report of birth of Henry Charles Bukowski.

he was making a super eight movie so Bukowski would know what Andernach was like. He filmed the house his family had lived in and said it was up for sale. Meanwhile Bukowski sent copies of *Post Office* and *The Fuck Machine* to his uncle in German. Rolf said Uncle Heinrich was not impressed. "This is for boys in their puberty," he told Rolf. Heinrich liked Thomas Mann's *The Magic Mountain*. Did I know the book? I told him I didn't.

A few years later when I read it, it changed the whole way I looked at the world, not just my view of literature. I asked Rolf if he wanted a little money for all the work he'd done. He said not to send him money. If I could find him a book, that would be enough. He wanted *The Effects of Mass Communications on Political Behavior* by Sidney Kraus and Dennis Davis. I ordered the book and sent if off. In the note he sent back thanking me for the book, Rolf wrote "Uncle Henry has seen a photo of Bukowski and his girlfriend in a magazine. I've got the feeling that in some way he now feels ashamed to have a nephew like this." It was the picture of Bukowski and Georgia where she looked like a streetwalker and Bukowski looked like a drunk.

I never showed the note to Bukowski, but I told him, as he readied himself for a trip to Germany in 1978, that Rolf had spent his own money to obtain all the letters and photographs, that he paid the costs for Bukowski's birth certificate and he was making a little film about Andernach in super eight. I suggested he should spend some time with Rolf when he got to Andernach. It was the least he could do.

I should have held my breath. When Bukowski got to Andernach he pushed past Rolf, barely acknowledging him, finding another local to drink beer with.

Rolf Degan was a new German; he disliked violence and saw in Bukowski a writer who was pushing back the frontiers of sexual honesty with powerful prose, but he missed the dark side. Bukowski told me once he was buying a piece of jewelry that had belonged to Eva Braun. For Linda. He bragged about singing "Deutchland, Deutchland Uber Alles" in a German tavern even after he was told it was forbidden. Uncle Heinrich was from the old Germany, the one that predated Hitler, the Germany of Thomas Mann, of elegant subtleties and subplots. Not *The Fuck Machine*. The letters Rolf Degan translated and sent on, disturbed the myths Bukowski had written about his parents. Henry Senior wrote Heinrich of his deep love for Katharina. How he was there all through his wife's hospitalization and was deeply moved by her suffering and pain. The letters proved Bukowski's parents loved each other and felt concern for their son, mixed with a sense of humor.

The seven letters written between 1965 And 1970 show Bukowski's duplicity when it comes to his family:

In the first letter to his uncle in 1965, Bukowski tells him he has a wife, Frances, and a daughter Marina, who was thirteen months old. He says he is a writer who publishes poetry in magazines, but makes little money from his writing. He explains that a German publisher (Verlag) wrote him a few years back with a plan to publish his work, but he never wrote them back. He gives his uncle the name of the publisher and the address in Germany. He speaks glowingly of his little girl. He describes her as a beauty and adds "I am not so beautiful myself." Mixing up his Uncle Wilhelm with Heinrich, he writes "Somehow—in my mind—I had always thought of you as being killed in a bombing raid." He tells Heinrich he did not go to the war. He does not say why, but bringing his uncle up-to-date on the death of his parents, he states "The loss of my father was hardly great. We did not get along, but I did have a good and innocent mother." Bukowski is putting out feelers, looking for his uncle's reactions. Since Heinrich liked Henry Bukowski Senior, who got him his first job at the YMCA, he does not pursue the point. Instead, he sticks to the wife (they weren't married) and the little girl.

In Bukowski's second letter dated December 20, 1965, he complains about overtime at the post office with no days off. The Christmas rush. He says he is suffering from dizzy spells and weakness. Then he mentions a poem of his that has appeared in a German magazine, *Vagabond*, and again gives the address. He wishes his uncle a good Christmas and "peace on earth forever." He explains he does not know German and would therefore be unable to read a letter from Heinrich's nephew, unless it was written in English. He mentions his daughter; there is no mention of his "wife."

In that third letter, dated January 28, 1966, Bukowski thanks his uncle for a box of candies and cookies sent to Marina from Andernach. He speaks of his current book, but explains he will not send it on "due to the content." He feels the reticence on the part of his uncle to get too close:

"There is little we can say to each other for we do not know each other very well. But it has been a very strange and wonderful thing—hearing from you after all these years." Bukowski seems to be waiting for his uncle to open up.

In the fourth letter, dated November 21, 1966, Bukowski returns to his theme. He describes his mother's slow death from cancer and his father's quick and easy death from a heart attack. He complains about his job again and tells his uncle he often misses work. He doesn't mention his drinking, but again lets out with the hearts and flowers. "My wife and little girl are very healthy. And that's something. We do not have very much money but we do not need very much money. We do not need the cars and trinkets and TV sets and things most people desire. We have each other. I hope to get my daughter, Marina, a tricycle for Christmas. I think I will be able to."

This is all very melodramatic. "Queen For a Day." As a result, Uncle Heinrich sends money in his next letter, but Bukowski tells him it was stolen from the envelope. The letter is undated. He goes on with his charade about wedded bliss: "Yes, my little girl is healthy, very and happy too. We give her much attention because seeing her happy makes us happy. She is really joyful, cheerful and makes us laugh and wonder and she teaches us things." Then Bukowski throws in a line about the Vietnam War. "I guess you've seen quite a few wars. They don't solve anything." Another opening. What did you do in the war, Uncle Heinrich?

On June 7, 1968, after a two-year break, Bukowski scrawls a printed note: He apologizes for not answering his uncle's letters. He speaks warmly of his daughter, who is now three years old. "We love each other very much and it is a wonderful feeling." He mentions the Robert Kennedy assassination at the Ambassador Hotel in Los Angeles and closes with: "This land is torn apart. Be glad that you are not here."

The last letter Heinrich received from his nephew before May 1977 was written on May 10, 1970. Bukowski tells of his recent success in the German book business. He gives him the name and address of his translator, Carl Weissner, and suggests he write for a copy of his new book, *Erections*. He says he has quit his job at the post office. He is now a writer. He speaks of his father as "cruel and blustery, yet a coward for it all." He describes his mother as "confused." Again he describes her death: "She died of cancer. A terrible and slow death. He died quickly, without pain. What does it mean?" Heinrich did not write back. Bukowski wondered why. He thought Heinrich had died, but there was another reason. After all, what was Bukowski asking his Uncle? Tell me the old man was a prick, so I can slam him in print, so I can turn him into D.H. Lawrence's "Prussian Officer." The Bukowski's were Prussian, Bukowski told me over and over. That's how they got the *ski* on the end of their name!

There's another side to all this, Henry Bukowski Senior's side. On December 31, 1956 Bukowski's father wrote a long letter to his brother-in-law in German. Enclosed was the announcement of his wife's death:

> BUKOWSKI—Mrs. Katharina of 9025 Guess St. Rosemead, passed away December 23, 1956. A native of Germany, she has been a resident of Rosemead 3 years. She is survived by her husband Henry C Bukowski, her son Henry C. Bukowski Jr. of Los Angeles, a brother Heinrich Fett and sister Mrs. Miller both of Germany. Funeral arrangements by Turner & Stevens Co.

In his book *Ham on Rye* Bukowski portrays his father as an unfeeling swine who runs around with other women, can't hold a job and is brutal to his son. Contrast that to the letter Bukowski's father writes to his brother-in-law Heinrich:

He gives the details of the cancer that destroyed his wife. He says that the problem began in her ovaries and spread to her bladder. He describes the two surgical procedures she received in August and September. "It was very, very hard for me, as we have been married for thirty-six years." He then mentions radiation and Katharina's final decline. He tells Heinrich the surgeries and hospital stays cost $5000. He had to borrow the money from his sister and brother-in-law in

Monday, december 31st
My dear brother-in-law Henry

Translation

Now I have to write a very sad letter. I kept it back so long, as I didn't want to spoil your holidays. Only now, one week later your dear sister and my ever loving wife isn't here any longer. [the death announcement] She died sunday, 23rd. It was very, very hard for me, as we were married now for 36 years. We had bought a new home in Temple City, as I wanted to work for only one more year. Then we wanted to live together our last days gladly. But God had it another way.

The costs were about 4-5000 dollars. But that means nothing if a life is at stake. I don't know what to do. It's very sad for me. I don't know Marie's address and beg you to tell it to me. In these ensuing days, I'll write you more of our whole life, and then you'll have a complete picture [he never wrote, R.D.]
I hope, you can understand everything
  greetings to all
    your brother in law
      Henry

Translation of letter from Henry Sr. to Heinrich Fett on the death of his wife, Katharina Bukowski.

Palm Springs. When a heavy bleeding sent her back into the hospital at the end of November (1956), the doctors told him she had no chance of survival."

Bukowski gave me another version. He said that he spoke with his mother in the hospital when she knew she was dying and she confessed to him "your father was not a good man." Katharina died on December 23, 1956. The mass was held in the Catholic Church in Temple City on December 27, at 9:00 a.m. Bukowski Senior mentions the burial at Mountain View Cemetery in Pasadena at 10:30 a.m. "I don't know what to do." He writes Heinrich, "It's very sad for me."

And then there's the other side to all this: Katharina herself.

Rolf Degan was allowed to copy and translate only two of Katharina's letters to Heinrich. There may have been others. Both letters are strange, yet humorous.

The first was written on February 27, 1956. Katharina joyfully tells her brother she is not Hilda Zeigler. She had evidently been told that her real father was a Mr. Zeigler, not Wilhelm Fett. After receiving documents from Germany she declares "It has all been cleared up. I am not Hilda Zeigler. It was an old gossip who whispered this. My papers are all right now. I was born on May 12, 1895 in Weibenthurm, Rhineland, Germany. That makes my papers all right." She tells her brother she is nursing herself back to health after a troublesome midlife. She begs him to come visit them. This was the year of her death. Did she have a premonition? "Airplane is faster," she says with a sense of urgency.

The second letter is dated March 19, 1956. Katharina mentions mental illness and an expensive operation on her leg. She also mentions her son: "Our son Henry is living with his wife (Barbara Frye or Jane?) in Los Angeles. They have no children. We let him think for himself. It always costs us money when we try to think for him."

She is proud of their new house in Temple City where there is a large garden for her husband to work. She mentions her sister-in-law, Eleanor Hofstetter, who lived in Palm Springs with her husband. "It takes us two hours to drive in our car," she said. Then there is the other Bukowski, the writer's namesake who lived in Indiana, Charles Bukowski. "Henry's brother and his wife have come to visit us several

Death certificate of Katharina Bukowski, Bukowski's mother (upper).
Death certificate of Henry Bukowski Sr., Bukowski's father (lower).

times. Indianapolis is a university town like Bonn in Germany. We plan to travel there this summer."

All this fails to jibe with the descriptions of Bukowski's parents and their marriage in *Ham on Rye*. Henry Senior is close to his sister and brother. They see the Bukowskis regularly. They have a new house with a garden and they seem to be ready for retirement. There are suggestions of darkness here, Katharina's possible menopausal problems, but the sadness of Henry Senior over Katharina's illness and death and the happiness Katharina expresses over relatives, a new house, vacation trips and Henry Senior in the garden, are not what the writer Charles Bukowski gives us in the description of his parents in *Ham on Rye* or in the stories and poems he wrote about them.

Nights at the Post Office

"He told me the rhythm of the work, the cruelty, the constant badgering from his supervisors and co-workers, white and black, kept him from sleeping, kept his mind awake half the night until it filled up the blank pages he fed into his Underwood."

Charles Bukowski's first novel, *Post Office*, isn't really a novel at all; it's a long complaint about working eleven years in a job that drove him crazy. In early 1970, on a warm afternoon with the windows open, Buk popped open two beers, showed me the novel in manuscript, and asked me to read it right there in his apartment.

At that stage it was about one hundred and twenty typed pages. I sat there on his broken couch and slowly worked my way through the novel as Bukowski banged out a few letters on his Underwood.

When I finished reading, I waited a while before I spoke. I felt there was something missing. After draining another beer, probably Pabst Blue Ribbon in a bottle, Bukowski asked me what I thought of the book.

I told him it wasn't really a novel; that it lacked the usual Bukowski humor, sarcasm, and feeling; that the hard profane line that made his work unique was missing. I thought *Post Office* might be a hit with postal employees, but it would never make him a famous novelist.

He agreed. For some time he'd been complaining that John Martin was refusing to feature his salty prose in Black Sparrow. He'd had to go to Essex House, a porno publisher, to get *Dirty Old Man* published. He told me Martin didn't like his newspaper stories, the ones published by *Open City*. To Martin they were too smutty. Black Sparrow, after all, had respectable poets; serious poets like Clayton Eshleman and Carol Berge and Robert Kelly: intellectuals. *Post Office*, he told me, had to be clean, free of the macho prose Bukowski spilled freely into stories like "Six Inches" or "The Fuck Machine."

He confessed it wasn't full-strength Bukowski.

I asked him if the novel was the whole story. He told me, "No." It was only part of the story. The rest he held back. Yes, there was the battle with his supervisor, whose name was Johnson "His first name evades me." There was something else there, something nasty. Something he wouldn't tell me.

We kept on drinking and he thanked me for the reviews of his prose and poetry I'd written in the *L.A. Times*: *Dirty Old Man* in the Essex House edition, before City Lights got it; *The Days Run Away Like Wild Horses Over the Hills* published by Black Sparrow in 1969; and *Penguin Modern Poets 13*, which included Bukowski, Harold Norse, and Philip Lamantia. Nineteen-seventy was pretty early in the game for the big newspapers to be taking on Bukowski. I got kicked around quite a bit by what Bukowski called the "lit/crit shitters" for reviewing his books. The Marxists hated him, the feminists hated him, and so did the academics. But I was learning to take my shots and not complain.

Under the headline "Three Volumes of Poetry from the Pen of Charles Bukowski," I wrote the following:

> For ten years Charles Bukowski has been hiding out in the back alleys of this American avant-garde, king of the mimeo presses, a squatter on the poetic badlands of Los Angeles racetracks and the bars of Alvarado. Ten years of sorting mail at the L.A. Terminal Annex, a surrealist postman in suicide pajamas, while Jean-Paul Sartre and Jean Genet have called him the best poet writing in America; while Henry Miller has praised him to the skies; while every important young poet in the English-speaking world has been hanging around in outlaw bookstores like Earth or Either/Or, searching for limited editions of Bukowski's works from presses like *Open Skull* or *Hearse Chapbooks*.

Bukowski was pleased. First he wrote me a note to thank me for the review. He told me life was tough, but he was still learning how to lay down the line and every bit helped. Then he called and told me he was surprised the *L.A. Times* would publish a review about his work, especially the prose. I told him I had a good friend who ran the Book Review named Digby Diehl, a pal of mine from my old UCLA *Daily Bruin* days. Bukowski called me a few more times. He spoke about his current women friends. Bukowski loved to talk about women. He said he wanted to see me. To talk about *things*. About women and literary enemies and exploding grenades. And about the post office—the real post office—the one that wasn't in the novel.

He told me to bring my tape recorder. And some whiskey.

I'd tried that twice before, getting it down on tape, but things always lapsed into drunken madness, and once he put my tape recorder in the oven. It melted.

This time he told me he was serious. He said he liked my line "a postman in suicide pajamas."

I brought over a bottle of Haig & Haig in the pinch bottle.

We drank a few shots and then he started in again about the review. He was especially happy about the Sartre and Genet lines. He laughed. "They never read my work," he told me. "Genet was in something Black Sun Press published and I was in there, too." It was called: *Portfolio III* published by Caresse Crosby. He described it as a large folder with single sheets on fancy paper by famous European writers and artists.

He'd told me the story before: how his father took the page with the name they shared on it, Henry Bukowski, and claimed he wrote it himself, getting a job advance at the L.A. County Art Museum, where he worked. He told me his father could have the story, "20 Tanks from Kasseldown," and hoped it would never be republished.

"And from that point on," he said, "he was Charles Bukowski. No more Henry."

But the thing about Genet and Sartre reading his work made him laugh that mischievous laugh of his. "AHHH HA HA HA HA HA." If there's one thing Bukowski liked it was mischief, and the thought that the *Los Angeles Times* had reported to its million-plus readers that Sartre and Genet were reading Bukowski made him deliriously happy; it made him choke up his scotch.

I asked him where the whole thing started. Was it Caresse Crosby?

"No," he said. "I just made it up. I think the Webbs said it first in one of their blurbs for *It Catches My Heart in Its Hands*, and now it's in print for a million readers to see. And you wrote it. AHHHH HA HA HA HA."

He liked that. That made me part of his little joke.

Then he asked me to turn my machine on. When I showed him it was running he "turned on." He energized. We both drank our Haig & Haig.

I had to admit I felt a little uneasy passing on misinformation to the readers of the *Los Angeles Times*, but he laughed and said, "The *Los Angeles Times* misinforms people every day." It was smack in the middle of the Vietnam War so I had to agree.

He tasted the scotch and made a joke about the word "neat." He was trying to stick with beer, but that evening we'd drink the scotch. Neat.

"Let me get you a clean glass," he said, in a room full of his dirty underwear, filthy plates, and muddy socks. The glass was almost clean and with screams coming from the alley outside—they're on the tape—we started in.

After adjusting the volume on my machine and testing it twice, Bukowski began talking about the post office, the downtown Terminal Annex, the real story.

"The real story isn't pretty," he said. "It's just real."

He asked if I had any questions.

I told him I remembered an object he once kept above his desk. It was a mail-sorting box with apples, his kid's toys, and letters and drawings and poems. I was curious about the carry-over from his Terminal Annex days. Why did he keep it? Did he bring it home to remind himself of the eleven hours of torture he experienced every night at the post office?

First, he said, it was part of his job. He told me the sorting box was where he used to practice his scheme for the post office.

"At home?" I asked.

"On my time off." But after he quit his job, he said, it became the halfway mark of something he couldn't decide to keep or throw away.

He said it was almost a wastebasket, and psychologically it was necessary at that time. It was for things he was keeping on hold. It had a special meaning: Because he'd switched jobs from mail sorter to full-time writer, it gave him a focus. It reminded him of where he'd been and where he was going.

He asked if I'd ever picked up something and wanted to throw it in the trash. "You don't quite want to, but you finally do anyhow? Well, something about that move hurts a little bit." The mail sorter, he said, was symbolic of order: a job, a salary, a place to go every day, something safe he no longer had. And then there was just the usefulness of it.

We finished our next glass of scotch and sat back down on the broken couch.

"Okay," said Bukowski, "now let me tell you about the Post Office."

"Terminal Anus?"

"Terminal Anus. The real story."

He talked for quite a while, and I listened while the tape recorder turned. He told me the problems he had at the post office, the ones he never wrote about, were mostly racial.

"The guys at the top were white," he said, "and the guys at the bottom were black. I was the white guy at the bottom." I laughed at that, but Bukowski wasn't laughing. He was serious. It still stung him.

"In order to survive I became the building clown. Mostly, I was jousting with the blacks. There was a lot of racism going on." He pronounced it raysh ism. He said that on bad days, when the supervisors swung their whips, Bukowski was Whitey to the blacks he worked with; on better days he was Brother Hank.

"We'd go back and forth like that," he told me. His voice got tougher.

"Nights and nights and nights of it. That took up most of my eleven years. That black/white jousting. I'd come through the back way and punch in. You'd put your coat away in a tray and 'BROTHER HANK! BROTHER HANK!' I caused a stir." The muscles in his face grew hard remembering it.

191

"It got funny and it got vicious. We went around and around and around. I more than held my own." He then retold the story about the time he asked for a truce. It's in the book.

"I said, 'Look, I wanna say something to everybody. This job is hard enough the way it is. The supervisor is rough on us. Let's treat each other like human beings. Why always this cynicism, these cutting remarks? Let us get along.'

"Then some guy said, 'Hank, you've got the worst mouth of any man in the Annex.' I sat down, turned around and started sticking mail." That was perfect Bukowski. The clear and funny line he could reel off aloud or on paper. I'd heard it before, but I laughed at the irony. He had that in spades. And he could also jive. One thing eleven years working at Terminal Annex with mostly blacks taught him was how to jive. He said it often came in handy at poetry readings.

"When I'm jousting with the audience, this background of lashing back and forth has come in handy; it's toughened me to this type of situation. I'm ready for the viciousness," he said. "It was damned good training." I told him it could be the same with teaching; he understood.

And that wasn't all he got out of the post office, I told him. There was something else: the actual lingo he heard all night long, the tough verbal warfare raging just below the surface of physical contact. That, I suggested, was the kind of tension that ran through all his work: the hard talk, the battles of little people. It seeped into the way he talked, the way he held himself, the way he thought.

Bukowski questioned that. He wanted examples.

"You say, 'Hey, baby,' without thinking," I told him. "You talk jive and write jive: black lingo, the language of Coltrane and Charlie Parker, of street-smart hustlers and hard-time cons. You even walk jive."

He liked that. He considered what I said. He lit up a cigarette and smoked it halfway down. He scratched his face. "Okay," he said finally, "being at the bottom can be a good thing."

He asked me how far I wanted to go into that. Being at the bottom. I told him as far as he liked.

He said, in *Post Office*, he describes the working conditions in comic terms, but to me he confided the truth as he saw it: the intense cruelty of working "another man's game," the constant battle for money and survival, "dogs in the dust fighting for scraps of meat."

In my opinion, those were the plot lines of all Bukowski's poems and stories. That's what his father had taught him with his razor strap, the taunts of bullies and bad teachers, the tough jobs where he was always the factotum, always at the bottom. And then there were the women he knew who laughed at his ugliness, at his worn out clothes, his bad teeth and yellow eyes and awkwardness.

He agreed with Jeffers and Celine and Hamsun that human beings were thoughtless, greedy, miserable, selfish creatures. I quoted a Jeffers' stanza that caught Bukowski's feelings perfectly when he wrote:

> Men suffer want and become
> Curiously ignoble; as prosperity
> Made them curiously vile.

Jeffers had got it right for Bukowski: the guys at the bottom were good because they fought back, and the guys at the top were rotten because they didn't care. Jeffers was one of the few poets Bukowski could always talk about. Jeffers was writing about humans in the Twentieth Century demolishing the earth; he thought humans had deteriorated in the Twentieth Century. Bukowski was less generous than Jeffers; he told me humans as a species weren't much. They'd always been cruel and selfish and worst of all were the literary types.

For some reason he didn't include me. What he liked about me, he said, was first the fact that I worked all my life at little jobs; at a tying machine at *Country Life Press* in my last year of college, at a box factory when my wife got pregnant, and finally as a teacher of handicapped children at Shriners Hospital and Children's Hospital. When I told him I worked with students with brain tumors who did their work every day without whining or crying, and I'd been doing that for almost twenty years, he was moved. He said it made him sick when he heard writers crying aloud or on paper about their sorry state, their struggles with the universe, their nonrecognition. Then he reeled off a long list of suffering poets we both knew who never worked and never would.

"How can they write about life if they've never lived it?" he asked.

I simply nodded my head.

He told me poets run on ego and viciousness, and what he hated most about them was their absolute lack of a sense of humor.

Gerald Locklin and Ron Koertge, he said, were the exceptions. They were funny.

"But working at the post office made me ready for the viciousness; it was damned good training at the Terminal Annex," he said.

I asked him for more details, for what he'd left out of his novel.

"You want the long version or the short version?"

"As much as you can stand."

He drew up close to the tape machine and laid down his drink.

I asked him what it was like when he began as a mail sorter.

"Okay. This is the way it went: They'd first put you in a certain group called the city mail. They'd keep moving you around all over the building. They had different types of mail. You had to learn these schemes. Sorting schemes. The zone numbers. You'd pick up a piece of mail without a zone number, and you had to know just where it goes. You had to study this shit on your own time. That's what killed you. It took hours and hours of your own time. You're working eleven hours. I asked the supervisor one time, 'Well, look, you work eleven hours and you still have to learn the scheme. When do you sleep? When do you eat? When do you take your laundry out?' He said, 'Man, if you want your job, you just figure it out.'"

I asked about unions. Bukowski laughed. He told me they were paper locals. "You just find your own way," he said. To pass the exams the post office ordered for schemes in sorting mail, Bukowski told me, "I used sex as my key. Like this guy lived on a certain street; he lived with three women and he dealt with them every night. His name was Smith and he went from sixty-four to ninety-four. I learned the whole thing through sex. And I got a letter from the Postmaster one time, telling me I got 100 percent. He was congratulating me for getting 100 percent on my scheme. He never knew how I did it. It was all sex. It was just a nightly grind that beat the shit out of me."

He asked me what my toughest job was. I told him they weren't very tough. My last year in college I worked for *Country Life Press* in Hempstead at a tying machine from six to midnight without a break. I stood at a tying machine and bound up junk mail all night. He wanted to know the details.

"It was an easy job," I said. "I'd just take the bundles of junk mail and tie them by zone number and throw them into a mail bag. I was at the end of a long conveyor belt. It was an easy job. The girls liked me. They'd come by and rub their tits against me to see if they could get me excited." That made Bukowski laugh.

"I was twenty and I was just married, in my last semester at Hofstra, and the women there thought I was hot. They didn't know Hofstra from Harvard. I stood there and read Ezra Pound all night. His *Cantos* and *The Confucian Odes*. All that Chinese stuff. The women thought I was crazy, but I tied up all those bundles every night at the end of the conveyor belt, reading Ezra Pound. It was a really easy job."

"Not like the post office," Bukowski said. "If they caught you reading on the job they'd give you a warning. If you did it a second time the supervisor would call you in. If you did it again they'd put you on suspension. I needed the money so I never read on the job. And the women there never rubbed their tits against me. I'm glad they didn't."

He asked me how long I lasted on the tying machine. I told him seven months. "The girls gave me a party when I left." I asked how long he worked at the post office.

"Eleven years," he said, "working the night shift and trying to find a few hours a day to write."

He told me the rhythm of the work, the cruelty, the constant badgering from his supervisors and co-workers, white and black, kept him from sleeping, kept his mind awake half the night until it filled up the blank pages he fed into his Underwood.

What it taught him, he said—all the hurt and the pain and the anger and the humiliation—was to sit at his typer and fight back. First, he had to fight for the time to write, but sooner or later he knew the tide would turn for him. The money was starting to roll in, mostly from men's magazines from Germany and from Martin's allowance.

He laughed at the idea of fame; those who caused him the most pain and taunted him with their stupidity could find themselves immortalized in one of his stories or poems, framed forever in their rage or pettiness or cruelty. That was what Bukowski was after. It was not about money or fame; it was about craft and excellence and getting back at the world that mocked him and shunned him and made him into the hard, drunken, street fighter he was, "sorted, stamped, and delivered by the United States Post Office. What else?"

I asked him to take me through an average day. He thought about that for a moment, then he took another hit on his cigarette and plunged in:

"Okay. I started at 6:18. It was supposed to be an eight-hour day but it never was. They'd say, 'Route so and so, you're required to work one hour overtime.' Then you'd gird yourself for that. Then they'd say, 'You're required to work two hours overtime.' 'You're required to work *three* hours overtime. There will be no exceptions.' It happened about like that every night. It was an eleven-hour night. It used to be twelve, but they cut it to eleven. When you were a sub, they'd have your days off on the board. They were way ahead. They'd give you four days off in a row. You'd get up to the four days and they would cancel three of them. You were cheap labor, you see."

"So that's what you share with your readers? That's what you know that John Updike doesn't?"

"I don't know about John Updike," he said. "I just know about myself."

He wanted his readers to feel what he did. He was writing for the guy who was "punching another man's time clock." He said he was writing for the guy at the bottom of the toilet bowl, like Celine and Hamsun. They lived in the real world too, working in factories, cutting up fish—all the nasty jobs. He told me that I was lucky to have worked in a box factory on Long Island; that I got my hands cut up picking strawberries and I still had the scars. Some day, he said, he would write a book about all the crazy jobs he'd taken just to stay alive. He said he knew *Post Office* was not a great book, but he'd write more novels and they'd be better. They'd be the real thing, the real Bukowski.

Several months later, *Post Office* was published, and we were on our way to Santa Anita for a day at the races. Driving downtown from Hollywood, Bukowski suddenly and unexpectedly pulled up into the lot at the Terminal Annex. He told me he needed to mail some letters to Germany. "It won't take a minute." He parked his blue VW in the front lot, not where the employees parked, and I followed him in for a look around.

"I collect stamps," I said. That made him laugh, but it was true.

Bukowski hadn't been to Terminal Annex for quite some time. Before we got in the door a friend spotted him.

"Hey, look. It's Hank. How ya makin' it, Hank?"

Bukowski shook his hand and smiled. "Surviving," he said.

"Boy, that book is really a hit around here. You sure got that fucker Stein real good."

Bukowski smiled and then they all started coming out from the back.

"Hey, Hank." He waved sheepishly. "You made it, man. You made it out of this place."

He got his letters mailed to Germany and we headed out to the track.

"See? Just like I said. Those poor fuckers are still stuck in shit." He waved his head as though he'd just avoided decapitation.

I thought we were done with the post office, but he asked me to put my machine on. He had a few more things to say. About the post office.

"I left a lot out of *Post Office*," he said. "Now I'll tell you the rest."

First he wanted to talk about Christmas. "That was the worst," he said. "There were no days off. The place was packed with extra help. You couldn't breathe. Mail was everywhere. Everything went to hell."

He told me he got to hate Christmas.

"The idea of it still makes me sick. The Christmas cards were so large they wouldn't fit in the case. The work went on forever. It was like slavery. Those guys in there . . . What else do you want to know?"

I asked about theft; how did the government keep track?

He just shook his head. "Parts of this are in the novel," he told me.

"They had these plants. They'd assign you to a seat and they'd be behind a large pole. You'd go around and sit down and there'd be these big fat envelopes. There'd be money in 'em and bonds. Only a damned fool would reach in there. But you were tempted. They'd watch you. They had runways in the walls, and they had these peep holes to look out at you. They had guys in the walls." He laughed.

"Come on, Bukowski."

"No. Really. Just to tease them (it was such an obvious setup) I'd look around and pick one up and I put it down. They'd say, 'He's biting. He's biting.' I just teased them a little, then I went and saw the supervisor and I said, 'Hey, I'm not workin' that plant tray. Give me another tray.' He'd say, 'Whadda ya mean? Whadda ya mean?' 'All these open letters, bonds, money sticking out. I'm not touching them.' So he said all right and he gave me another tray."

The thought of it still made him dizzy. "Mail fraud is a federal crime," he said. "If they couldn't kill you by working you to death, they'd find a way to put you in stir." He told me they caught one of his friends stealing money from a plant tray. "But they made a deal with him. They just let him quit. You'll see him sometimes out at the track."

At Hollywood Park, when he was putting down a bet on the first race, his friend Spenser showed up. I asked him if that was the one. He said no. "But I got him hooked on the horses and now he's down about five thousand dollars." He told me Spenser still worked nights at the Terminal Annex.

Spenser was a cultured black man who spoke softly and patted Bukowski on the arm. "He used to go with me on the bus," he told me, "and he'd let me read my form in peace. That's what I like about him best. He's quiet . . . He's a cool guy. He never jives me."

On the way home, after winning three hundred and twenty dollars at the track, Bukowski continued to talk about the post office. He still wasn't finished.

He told me his last year there was the best and the worst. He got dizzy spells and he drank more and more. He was writing his "Notes of A Dirty Old Man" column for *Open City* and much of what he wrote was about the post office.

One night, driving home after work, his blinkers didn't work. He recalled trying to make a left turn onto Fountain Avenue and not being able to move his left hand up to signal out the window.

"I stuck three little fingers out. It was as far as I could get. It was so ridiculous. I couldn't lift my left hand. I said, 'They're killing me, those dirty shits.' I couldn't even put my arm out the window. So what else?"

I was about out of questions. I asked if he ever had a chance to advance up the post office food chain. He choked with laughter. He remembered one night coming in dressed in a silk shirt and tie, "Just for the hell of it," he said. "They put me on the loading dock. That's the way they were. They didn't want you to emerge from the cellar. But I got them back."

As Bukowski got close to the end of "punching another man's time clock" his articles in *Open City* were mostly about the things that caused him pain, mostly about the post office.

"I got my kicks," he told me. "Everybody knew. When I'd go up the escalator and I'd be starting work, I'd have a cigarette dangling from my mouth and they'd say, 'There's that guy who writes the column for *Open City*. He writes about the post office.' They were very much on me. They thought I knew everything. I didn't know shit. But the supervisors were a little bit scared because I had use of THE WORD. I could fight back. Other supervisors would come around. They'd be in hot water. They'd tell me their stories. It got quite interesting. And that's about all I know about the post office."

Sharks & Vegetables

"The vegetables were steamed and cooked and sliced on a slant: slender string beans, melons, tomatoes and parsley, radishes and orange slices and limes; Bukowski in the land of Gourmet Magazine and loving it . . ."

A short time after Bukowski left his Hollywood apartment for a house in San Pedro, he gave me a call. First he asked if my car was running. That's always a major concern in Los Angeles, where distances are great and mass transit is a misnomer. I told him my car was running.

"Good," he said. "Can you come down on Saturday?" He said he had a little problem that wouldn't go away; he'd explain it when I got there. I told him I'd come.

"After twelve." I knew the drill. He started to give me instructions. "Take the Harbor Freeway to the end and look for Bandini."

"Bandini? You mean like Fante's Arturo?"

"The same. Probably where he got it from. The VW's in the drive," he said. "We're halfway up the hill. Look for the nunnery."

I thought he was kidding. Then he gave me his phone number and asked about Steve Richmond. I told him Steve was still planning to blow up a Cadillac dealership. He laughed.

"How's Linda?" I wondered.

"She's great. She loves it up here. She'll be cooking dinner. Shark. Remember, don't come before noon."

That Saturday I drove down to San Pedro and got lost in the hills, driving the wrong way on Bandini. I arrived at 1:00 p.m. and Bukowski was out on the front stoop waiting. He looked worried. "Where you been, Ben?"

"I got lost on Bandini." Bukowski laughed.

I parked my car in the street and looked at the house from the rear. It was a two-story bungalow, built squarely and solidly into the slant of the hill. Bushes and trees almost covered the house. The lawn was neatly trimmed and there were flowers in the front yard. Buk opened the door and yelled, "Hey, look who finally made it."

"We thought you'd get lost, Ben," Linda yelled from the kitchen. She was cutting up lemons. Butch the cat from Carlton Way scampered by. He had a bandage over one eye. I stopped to brush his fur, but after a moment sniffing my shoes, he scampered out of the house and into the garden.

"How's Butch like San Pedro?" I asked.

"He misses those Hollywood pussies." We followed Butch out into the garden and Buk showed me his Tournefortia tree. "I miss them, too," he said. "Let me show you the house."

First we looked at the downstairs bedroom. "This is Marina's room when she's around." She must have been in high school by then. Venice High. Then we walked through the living room with its sliding glass doors that opened onto the garden. Linda came in with a glass of white wine for Buk and a glass of Cabernet for me. "Ben loves red wine," said Bukowski. "It's his politics."

"He's a communist?"

"Anarchist."

I told them the anarchist colors were black, but Cabernet is a very dark red. Bukowski turned off the last round of a boring fight from Mexico and we sat down in front of his unlit fireplace. "So," I asked, "what's this all about Charles?"

He laughed at that. No one ever called him Charles. "What's so important you give up a day at the races on a Saturday afternoon?"

"It's the fucking movie business. Taylor Hackford wants to turn *Post Office* into a movie set during the Vietnam War."

"Oh," I said. I'd never met Taylor Hackford and I was bored to death with Vietnam. I'd told Bukowski "Some of our best writers wrote their worst books about Vietnam." He agreed. He saw the Vietnam War as a trap for writers, a place to dump out all their moral guilt and frustrations, a short dead end for writers with a sense of humor. I told him I didn't see what good I could do him; I'd never met Taylor Hackford and I hadn't fought in Vietnam. Or any other war.

"Never mind," he said. Only Bukowski could say that word with an inflection half between irony and idiocy. He made me laugh. "Just drink your wine, Ben. That'll do the trick. First we're going down to Pedro to do a little shopping."

Linda drove. I climbed in the back seat of his little VW with the Iron Cross hanging from the rearview mirror and started to eat my knees. Bukowski sat beside Linda sipping his wine. I asked if he'd been back to Hollywood recently. He said, "Yes, saw Sam the Whorehouse man. He asked me for five bucks. I gave him the usual: 'I was just about to ask you for the same.' He didn't even know I'd moved." He laughed and Linda parked the VW in a lot alongside one of San Pedro's piers. The air was fresh and smelled of salt.

"So you like the new house?"

"It's okay. What keeps me going is my typer and my time at the track."

"What about me?" Linda did her mock little girl.

"And Linda Lee's food."

"Thanks a lot." We walked out on the docks into a large fish market. "Wait till I show you the view from my workroom at the top of the house." Linda was sizing up two large pieces of shark. She let Buk sniff them for approval, and after he nodded she handed one to the fishmonger who weighed it, wrapped it in white paper, taped it shut, and wrote out the price with a big black marker. Bukowski carried it back to the car. "This is the best place in all of L.A. to buy shark," he said proudly. "Right in the harbor."

Then we walked across the street to an open vegetable market where Linda bought potatoes, three kinds of beans, radishes, carrots, celery, broccoli, two kinds of lettuce, parsley, lemons, oranges, and a funny kind of brown lump that looked like ginger. "See," said Bukowski, "I don't need Hollywood. I can write about vegetables."

Surrounded by all that nutritious food, Linda was in her element.

As we drove back up the hill to his new house, I asked Bukowski what he thought of San Pedro. He said he liked the look of it. It was working class, real people, houses that looked like houses not architecture, no phony Hollywood types.

"You mean whores, pimps, and drug dealers?"

"Not that Hollywood," he said. "Taylor Hackford's Hollywood." Then he told me for the fifth time how Hackford had been president of his class at USC, how he had perfect teeth and no belly, and his shirts were always pressed. "That Hollywood." As Linda parked the car, Bukowski and I carried in the food. He showed me the fridge. It was stuffed with vegetables, vitamins, fruits and juices. No beer. No chops. No peanut butter. He pointed to a space between the living room and the dining room. Built-in bookcases.

"All my books," he said. "Have a look."

"Where's *It Catches My Heart*?"

He laughed. "You know who stole it." I knew who. Three large shelves of Bukowski in Dutch, German, French, Spanish, Swedish, Japanese, Korean, and Serbian. Not a single name but Bukowski. As we sat on the couch to pour out our wine, Linda started up in the kitchen. It was after three. The former owner of the Dew Drop Inn was up to her elbows in vegetables.

"So what are you doin' kid?"

"Writing."

"What else?"

I told him I was between books. He liked that. He hated to talk about anyone else's work. Then he started in on his latest novel. *Women*. He gave me a chapter to read. It made me laugh. That was all he needed.

"So what's all this stuff about Taylor Hackford?"

"He's coming for dinner to talk about *Post Office*. He bought the rights."

"What does that have to do with me?"

"You just drink your wine and do what you always do when you have too much. That's all I need from you."

"Just the four of us?"

"No. He's bringing his wife, Lynne, and his kid. He has a weird name."

"You mean like Taylor?" I asked. Bukowski laughed.

"They're coming at six."

I began to worry. "If I get that drunk I'll never make it home on the freeway."

"If you get that drunk, you'll never make it down the hill. You're sleeping here tonight. In Marina's room. It's all arranged. Right Linda?"

"Right, Charles." She'd been listening all along.

By the time Taylor Hackford, his wife Lynne Littman, and his son Rio got there, I was so drunk I could not stand up to greet them. Both Bukowski and Linda were smiling. The Fool for the evening was in place, and I would do their bidding. Hackford looked just like Bukowski had described him: his shirt was pressed, his teeth were white, he was a little shorter than I'd suspected, but he had no belly and his shoes were polished. He was about thirty-five years old. He smiled and held out his hand. I tried to get up. Linda brought me more red wine.

His wife, Lynne Littman, looked more serious; I could see in her eyes that something was riding on this dinner. Rio was perhaps ten; he looked like one of those bright, bored kids who should have stayed home with his friends.

Since I couldn't get up, Bukowski sat next to me on the couch as Hackford and his wife settled down in separate chairs. The kid went off to look at the garden or torture Butch the cat. I knew what was coming. Literary talk. Hackford plunged right in. He'd just been up the coast to Carmel, and he'd stopped to look at Tor House, the house Robinson Jeffers built out of stone when Carmel was still a village.

He asked Bukowski if he'd ever seen it. Bukowski said no.

I told him when I was there I looked in the yard and it had a basketball hoop. "The place is overrun with bad writers and rotten painters and Jeffers is lucky he's dead," I said. Bukowski agreed. He just shook his head. He laughed because I was doing the talking for him and I was doing just fine. Hackford smiled, but his wife Lynne looked worried. Who was this wild card, this joker who smelled like a tasting room at Napa and had wild hair and ill-matching clothes? She didn't say anything, but I sensed a degree of panic.

The wheels were in motion. Next came dinner.

Seated at his dinner table heaped with fruit juices and vegetables of every sort, I could only laugh at this remarkable transformation—the Bukowski I knew, the Bukowski of Carlton Way and DeLongpre, the struggling Bukowski who worked at the post office, ate chops and Hoagies, and fatty foods like baked potatoes smothered in butter was now up in the hills of San Pedro hiding behind salads. Now here we all were up in the hills of San Pedro, hiding behind our salads. I pushed mine away, calling it "rabbit food," but the others ate theirs, picking through the lettuce to find rare treats like artichokes and kiwi fruit. Taylor and his wife dug in with gusto, all that greenery but no meat, no fat, just shark marinated in something rare. Gone were the six-packs, the bleached white bread, the lamb chops, the Mother's Cookies. Everything was vegetables. Wasn't it Mary McCarthy who wrote a novel about a young man in Paris who took his plant for a walk?

It was a transfiguration! The vegetables were steamed and cooked and sliced on a slant: slender string beans, melons, tomatoes and parsley, radishes and orange slices and limes; Bukowski in the land of *Gourmet Magazine* and loving it, as Butch the cat ran by looking completely lost. Where were the mice? It reminded me of the story Bukowski told about his namesake, the real Charles Bukowski who'd lived in Indiana and showed at his father's funeral. Uncle Charles.

"He was a real drunk," Bukowski told me, "but he gave up drinking on his wife's orders. It must have been really good pussy."

Well, Bukowski hadn't given up drinking, just switched from beer to expensive white wine (German), but here he was with a napkin on his lap, picking at cucumbers and peas, dressed in a fresh ironed shirt and new white pants with a belt.

Coffee was served, but Linda made it known she preferred tea. I kept wondering how long this connubial bliss would last.

"Relationships rarely make it past three years," Bukowski always said. "At their best they might last six, but after that look out."

There was no dessert.

After the food came the conversation. First there was praise for the shark. Shark was all the rage that year in Hollywood; it was the fish of choice. I could only speculate why. Then the conversation took a Russian turn. First Chekhov, then Ivan Bunin. Before long we were all hurling Russian names at each other. Tolstoi, Dostoevsky, Gorky, and Stanislavski. I threw in Kropotkin, the Russian prince who'd become an anarchist. "Ba KUN in," shouted Bukowski.

"You know Bakunin?" Hackford asked in wonder.

I must have mentioned him once in one of my drunken letters, and Bukowski answered by sending me a postcard that read Mikhael Bakunin, 1814-1876. When I thought about it later, I had to admit what Bukowski wrote was rather profound. To him that's all there was to Bakunin's life, a name and the dates of his birth and death.

Then the two women stared at each other as though we were going to get down to business. The business of sharks and vegetables. The film business.

That's what I thought, but Taylor Hackford was pretty new in that business. He was known for only one film, a documentary on Bukowski. He'd lost his job at KCET after a revolt of the Palace Guard, and now he was searching for the Yellow Brick Road that would later lead him to *Officer and a Gentleman* and Helen Mirren, but those days were a long way off.

Bukowski would be his meal ticket, but there was hair in the soup. The original Bukowski documentary shot in Los Angeles and San Francisco had been cut by KCET or Public Television or both, from one hour to a half-hour, and much of Bukowski's colorful language had been trimmed. Promises had been made, and in Bukowski's view they had not been kept. A documentary for Public Television was one thing, but the real film world was something else. Bukowski despised the film world. He viewed the industry as a group of demented moguls whose sole purpose in life was to destroy writers. He saw John Fante as their major victim.

All the time, Hackford was trying to be cautious, but every step he took was the wrong one. He started off talking about Henry Miller, another Bukowski minefield. Hackford said he had a friend who knew Miller, a very young guy who Miller took a liking to. His young friend said Miller knew about Bukowski. It was old, familiar ground. Hackford wanted Bukowski to visit Henry Miller. He said his friend had shot a film on Miller using only his bathroom. Bukowski spoke about a letter he'd received from Miller a few years back advising Bukowski to give up drinking. Bukowski held up his glass. "More wine, darling!"

Then there was the book of Miller's letters I'd reviewed recently for the *L.A. Times*. I mentioned Miller's anti-Semitism.

"He hated the Nazis," said Hackford defensively.

"I love the Nazis and I love the Jews," said Bukowski. We were now back in our original seats by the fireplace. I looked at the two women again. Linda was lighting the fire. Rio helped. Bukowski always told me if you want to know what's going on with writers, look at their wives. I looked at their eyes. Their eyes were both hard and their mouths were set. The flames came up with a burst, and Linda chortled, "Look at the gorgeous fire."

But no one could top Bukowski's remark, "I love the Nazis and I love the Jews."

It just hung there in the air like stale smoke. It was his house, I thought. He could say what he wanted in his own house. Pride of ownership! No landlord could come pounding on the wall and tell him to shut up.

Within a few minutes everyone got up and went to the bathroom. When we returned, Hackford tried to put the discussion back on track. "You got two balconies, Bukowski," he said.

"Yeah. In Hollywood I had too many roaches and here I have too many balconies."

As the wine continued to flow, I got a better look at Taylor Hackford's wife, Lynne. She was putting the pieces together quietly, slowly, and from what she'd heard so far, the film *Post Office* seemed to be fading back into "development" from whence it came. I started in about Miller again. I mentioned what I'd said in the review.

"Ben is a very cynical liberal living in the seventies," said Hackford. It was another tactical blunder.

Liberal, for Charles Bukowski, meant rich, guilty hypocrites talking about poverty or unemployment or the wars they kept their sons from fighting. Anarchists Bukowski respected because they had muscle, they fought in the streets and beat up cops—but liberals went along with sitting on couches at dinner parties; all they did was talk.

And then I got it. Hackford wanted to turn *Post Office* into an antiwar film. That's what was bugging Bukowski. Another cliché. I'd known Bukowski for fifteen years, and one thing he wasn't was a cliché!

Hackford began looking desperate. Bukowski smiled, lit up a Bede cigarette and began to talk about his house. He was proud of his house. He told Hackford he'd been up on his roof looking for Butch "with the wrapped head," when he put his foot right through the ceiling. Now there was a leak upstairs that had to be fixed. "The whole place, after we moved in, has been one crisis after another," he said.

"You know what?" Hackford rejoined, looking for an opening to bring back his project, "That's what happens when you own your own house."

He asked me if I owned a house. "Never have, never will. Property is theft. Proudhon."

Another dead end. Hackford was becoming desperate. His wife was silent. Linda brought out wine and cheese. "You know," said Hackford, "if you walk to the end of the park down there," he pointed toward the south, "that's where it dropped about twenty feet after the earthquake."

"That's where they filmed parts of *Chinatown*," said Linda. "Robert Towne."

"He's great," said Hackford, finally thinking he'd found the opening that would lead to a slam hand.

Hackford now had the ball: "The little hamburger place that sells beer, by the way, is *in Chinatown*. When they walk up from the barrio over the cliff, that's in San Pedro just beyond Point Ferman and the diner across the street, the Pacific Dining Car, is the place."

Hackford suggested they go there for a beer. Another mistake.

"No more beer," said Bukowski.

Hackford was shocked. "What's wrong with beer?" he asked.

"Terrible," said Linda. "Worst thing for the kidneys."

"I don't like what it does to my gut," Bukowski added.

"Of all the alcohols," said Linda, "wine is best."

So there it was, the conquest of Bukowski. Not only was he up there on the roof looking for Butch, he was eating all his vegetables; he'd given up cigars for a sad little Indian smoke that looked like a paper feather; and he'd given up beer, Pabst Blue Ribbon in a bottle, and all the rest.

So much had changed. I was about to say something when Butch the cat showed up. He'd been out on the prowl, but he didn't look happy. He jumped on Bukowski's lap, looking around at the others with disdain.

"So," I said, "Bukowski thinks *Post Office* should be like he wrote it. Nothing to do with Vietnam. That's a trap."

Hackford agreed. No Vietnam. He shook his head. What had happened? He hadn't gotten anywhere with Bukowski on the film and Rio was falling asleep. His wife Lynne figured it out. This was a house of demons. Bukowski and Linda and myself all were demons. She could see that *Post Office* would never be a movie. Not Taylor Hackford's movie. She composed herself and got up from the couch. The liberal couch. Then she woke up Rio and Hackford rose. He said to Bukowski, "I'll call you." It was the Hollywood kiss of death, that line.

Then we all shook hands and we watched Hackford and company drive down the hill past the nunnery, headed for the city. It was dark and the night was filled with stars. Real stars from the heavens, not Hollywood stars.

"Thanks, Ben," Bukowski said as we turned back toward the door. "You did it."

"I didn't do anything."

"No, you did. He'll never make a movie out of *Post Office*. Not in my lifetime. Now let's go upstairs. Let me show you where I work."

We walked up to a little room at the top of the house. There was his table and a new typewriter, not the Underwood Linda King had

destroyed. The table was the same one he worked on in Hollywood. His battered paperback *Mirriam Webster* was the only book in the room along with the stack of neatly typed pages that would soon become *Women*. "Take a look!"

From the window I could see the whole harbor of San Pedro spread out before me.

"You go to bed now. I've got to work. Don't wake me in the morning unless you sleep till noon. Linda will give up a towel."

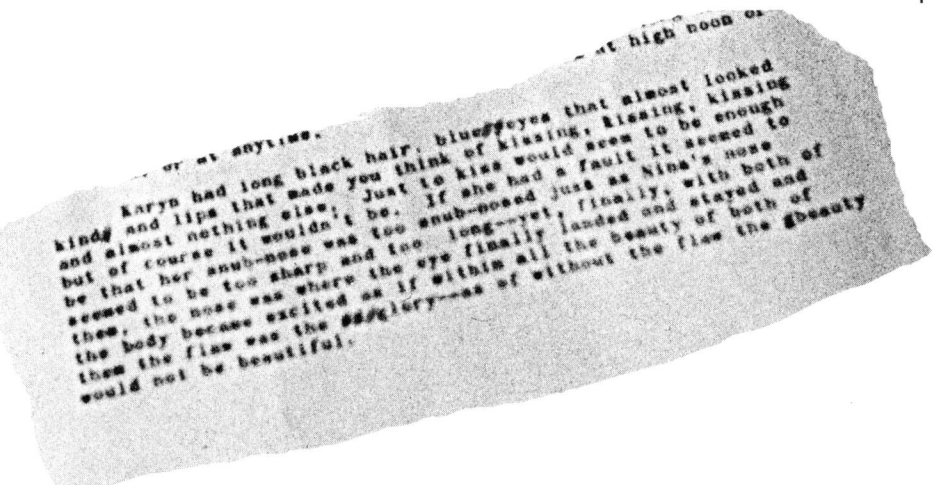

I said good night and went to sleep in Marina's bed. I could hear Bukowski pounding away on his typer late into the night. That was what it was all about, writing, not movies.

In the morning I got up at ten, drank a cup of coffee Linda made, and drove down the hill back to the Harbor Freeway, back to Beverly Hills. I was happy Bukowski had found shelter. I liked his house that stood in the slant of the hill near a nunnery. Linda was good to him. She was nurturing.

Both he and Butch were sleeping when I drove off.

How to Write a Short Story

> "I asked him how he got started with the short story. He told me when he was in his twenties he was turning out five stories a week. 'They were lyrical. They were rambling. The plot and content were secondary. It was a vomiting up, an effusion of feeling.'"

Charles Bukowski was a warrior and he used words as a weapon; he loved literary squabbles. Verbal warfare was his métier and his typer blazed more brightly when he was on the attack, but only when the names were changed to protect him from lawsuits. When lawyers got involved, Charles Bukowski, a celebrated tightwad, withdrew, viewing an attack on his bank account as life-threatening.

In the late 1970s, as his star began to rise and his bank accounts swelled, Bukowski sat up in the highest room in his house in San Pedro and looked out on the harbor at night with all its marine lights and loading cranes and docked ships, aiming his typer like a 50-caliber machine gun down on all the enemies of his life: the women who'd betrayed him; the critics and scholars who'd dismissed him as a "gutter poet"; the poets who envied his success; the bosses who'd fired him; the friends who'd sold him out for a $200 magazine article; the editors who'd mocked his work; the editors who owed him money; and every member of his family who ever gave him a minute's grief. Bukowski was at the top of his game, and the game was King of the Mountain; now it was time for revenge. As long as he changed the names.

But in July of 1976, Bukowski was still stuck in Hollywood, sharing conversation with Sam the Whorehouse man, and I was having my own problems. I'd named names in print, and if I wasn't hounded by lawyers I was attacked by what Bukowski called "the lit/crit shitters."

One of them was Clayton Eshleman, editor of such solipsistic poetry journals as *Caterpillar and Sulfur*. On July 20, 1976, Eshleman attacked me in print, taking me to task for a review I wrote about John Ashbery's poetry volume *Self-Portrait in a Convex Mirror*.

I said of Ashbery's work:

> It is a kind of private meditation that is best kept private, but Ashbery wants it both ways. He wants our praise and he wants to be left alone to his sensitive genius, such as it is.

> It is time to openly flail such art. A few prestigious poets will praise it (in return for future praise), a few woeful fossils of magazines like *Poetry* will find it "vibrant" or "refreshingly expressive," a large enough number of libraries will dump it out on a dusty shelf after the *New York Times Book Review* has done its best to push it along, but ultimately the work is hollow, hopelessly cut off from the real world, wrapped in conceits. Sadly, Ashbery has written his own little epitaph: "His case inspires interest but little sympathy; it is smaller than at first appeared."

A few weeks later Clayton Eshleman struck back. In a letter to the *Times Book Review* titled "The Cult Lint," he attacked the review and a poem by Lawrence Ferlinghetti published in the *L.A. Times* a few weeks earlier. Eshleman wrote:

> Ben Pleasants' review of John Ashbery's *Self-Portrait in a Convex Mirror* (*Book Review*, July 13) reads like a follow-up on the Ferlinghetti poem that appeared in the *Book Review* several weeks previously. Both the Ferlinghetti poem and the Pleasants review mock serious poetry by asserting that unless poetry is written for "the people" there is something ridiculous about it . . . Pleasants' "voice" is that of a little man (in the Reichian sense), outside of the central evolving image of poetry in our time, and bitter about it . . . Both the Ferlinghetti poem and the Pleasants' reviews appear in the *Book Review* because there is no serious reviewing policy . . . It is a continual shame, an aspect of failure in Los Angeles for poetry to ever be taken seriously, that *Book Review* backs such pot shots.

When Bukowski read the review and Eshleman's response, he was delighted: literary warfare in Los Angeles at last! It was like the old *Kenyon Review* days from the 1940s. The thought of those old Marxists who'd attacked Jeffers and Pound and John Crowe Ransom made his eyes fill with rage.

Lawrence Ferlinghetti

But what he told me surprised me. He said I'd finally gotten to where I wanted to be; I'd made the establishment so mad they wanted me gone. He said that was really enough; that I'd done my job reviewing poets no one else reviewed and now it was time to move on. He told me to write more poetry and begin writing fiction. He said it was time for me to grow up and listen to my own voice. "Write some short stories. I'll help you send 'em out."

He'd just received a large check from *Hustler* and he wanted to celebrate. So he drove his little blue Volks over to Barney's Beanery for drinks. Strictly on Bukowski! We'd been there several times, on Santa Monica in West Hollywood. The food was terrible, but the drinks were large and cold. The customers were working-class types who spat on the floor, smoked while they drank, and sprinkled "cunt," "fuck," and "cocksucker" into every line of conversation they spoke. Bukowski's kind of people.

He always stopped and pointed out the sign in front: Founded in 1920. "Same as me," said Bukowski. "Andernach, 1920."

He liked the other sign even better—the sign over the bar: NO QUEERS ALLOWED. He'd shout it out like a bad little boy in the first grade who'd just pulled the panties off a crying six-year-old girl. And just in case you didn't get the point, he'd quote Steve Richmond's poem "Let the fags have San Francisco." He wanted me to know where he stood.

It was the perfect hangout for members of the Meat Poetry School. But I never got it, the macho stuff. I still liked F. Scott Fitzgerald and Hart Crane; I read Pablo Neruda and H.D. and Galway Kinnell and Emily Dickinson and Charles Tidler and Marge Piercy. Bukowski yawned at the thought of them, except Tidler. "Charles Tidler is the greatest poet in Canada," he said to a packed reading in Vancouver. And he meant it. But he was happy for me; that letter from Eshleman was like a medal from Kaiser Wilhelm.

"You drew blood this time," he said over a pitcher of dark beer. He told me I should put it to work for myself in stories. Like him. He told me what he was getting from *Hustler* was real good money, a lot better than The Sparrow or the *Free Press*, even if it wasn't steady.

He said I should write about the women I knew, especially the teachers and nurses who were living on the edge, caught between ecstasy and hypocrisy: their sexual habits, their drug usage. He was especially fond of a story I told him about a woman I'd worked with in a drug hospital who slept with all the principles on both sides of a labor dispute and, by using her body as a weapon, broke the strike. I told him I disapproved of what she'd done. He said I was hopeless. He called me his "Beverly Hills Anarchist Boswell." By then I was supposedly writing his biography; but whenever he sent me to interview a friend it always ended the same way—either he owed them money or he'd smashed up all their furniture or he'd peed on their sofa, or he slept with the wife or girlfriend.

He thought all people on the West Side lived off their parents' wealth, spent their evenings in nightclubs, and lived in fear of two things: venereal disease and drug overdose. He held Steve Richmond up as the prototype of West Side lifestyle: a rent collector who lived off his father's millions.

He said if I couldn't write about women who'd fucked me over, I should write about what I knew: newspaper people, the inside stuff; how much they drank; who fucked them over; their troubles with money and ego and drugs; their suicides. Did I know any? I said I did. I told him the Gary Mayfield story, but he said that was too easy; it was already in print. I reminded him of the Ramon Navarro story he'd written, about his murder up on Laurel Canyon. He told me he was hard up for a column that week, and besides the story had caused him legal problems.

He asked me to tell him the real stuff at the *L.A. Times*. We were on our third pitcher of beer and our second bloody steak. Meat School Poets; only I wasn't one of them.

I said I once met Otis Chandler in the elevator and he was carrying a fine leather case. Everyone else stood there not making a sound, but I asked Otis Chandler what was in the case and he told me a hunting rifle. He was shooting wild sheep on Catalina Island. I asked if he'd open the case. He did right there in the elevator, or maybe it was the lobby. I said it was like a kid playing with his toys.

He asked if I hated Otis Chandler. I told him he was the best publisher the *Times* ever had. Bukowski was disappointed. He wanted an Otis Chandler scandal. I told him he ran over an eighty-year-old lady and they knocked it right off the news. He told me that wasn't sexy enough. It had to be a blonde in a tight skirt; but I could start with the old lady and add the blonde. That was the joy of fiction. I was beginning to get it. After all that beer I was starting to feel the hunger.

He said I should take on the big boys, that I was stubborn enough to survive in a rich man's world, stubborn enough to draw blood. That was true.

So I told him what I knew. I told him I'd worked as a copy boy at twenty-six just to get my nails into the concrete enough so the *L.A. Times* would publish my stuff. I told him I liked being called an anarchist. He told me he liked the fact that I could keep up with him, bottle for bottle, on an all-night bender; that I laughed at myself; that

I let life hit me in the mouth and could still see the sadness without giving up. I liked what he said. I still do.

Bukowski was very careful with writers' truths, but every once in a while he'd hit me in the face with one, using the Bukowski Zen stick.

He said a real writer should have kids. We both had daughters about the same age. He'd met my daughter once in the living room of my Beverly Hills apartment, while he spent most of the afternoon looking up my wife's shorts. My daughter was ten at the time and she seemed afraid of him.

I'd seen his daughter, Marina, several times when she was little, playing with crayons and paper on his beer-soaked carpet. He told me over and over that whatever money he made from his writing would go to Marina. Money didn't matter much to him, he said, as long as he had a place to write and publishers who'd print him and enough money for beer and smokes. He told me having a daughter gave him a special edge; it allowed him to see through the eyes of a child. He thought poets who lived for their work alone—for art, and had no children—were cut off from the real world, the world of love and work and murder and sweat.

He said that poets were sad creatures, but they could be funny. He mentioned a dozen we both knew, all with no children. He ended with Steve Richmond. He told me he was so tired of the small presses. He laughed at all the stuff John Martin had asked him to do so he could sell out his "Collector's Copies" for Black Sparrow.

Larry Flynt, on the other hand, asked only for the typed manuscripts, pure and simple. "There's a guy who understands women." He told me it was time to "fuck off poetry, write prose. Write stories. Unless you can curse the gods like Jeffers. Or me."

"But how?" I asked. "How do you break through?"

He thought back to when he was a kid of twenty, sitting on a park bench, running away from World War Two. He told me he'd been reading *Kenyon Review* and *Sewanee*, which he pronounced as it was spelled, not as it's sung in the song "Way Down Upon . . ." And he was surprised it was the same word. So we talked about critics. The New Critics. He said that the poetry he read on that park bench in Texas was stilted and dead, without any feeling, so different from Jeffers who always thrilled him; but the critical articles were bristling with anger, frustration, and hatred.

"These guys were so neatly bitchy in such a high intellectual, vicious way. The way they used the language in those critical articles was on a far higher level than all their creative work." He told me to forget about Eshleman, to laugh off the viciousness of a minor leaguer. "It doesn't count for anything."

Bukowski told me that poets have only that little bit of turf to quarrel about. "Nobody reads them. They read each other. They hate me because my poetry sells; because I connect with the real world and guys like Eshleman and Ashbery connect with no one." He told me they were born dead and could only exist through viciousness. "Just cool off and get the fuck off the poetry train. Write straight fiction. Write a play. Anything but poetry." I had another beer and considered his words. I felt better already. That was the third time Bukowski told me to read John Fante. Fante would help me find the way just as he'd lit up Bukowski.

Bukowski showed me a story he'd just written and sent out to *Hustler*. "These guys publish real stuff. Send them something. And they pay real money." On the table was a check for $1,200. And then we got down to writing short stories, holding the line, hammering it home.

I asked him how he got started with the short story. He told me when he was in his twenties he was turning out five stories a week. "They were lyrical. They were rambling. The plot and content were secondary. It was a vomiting up, an effusion of feeling." The rejection slips told him he should write poetry. "I didn't think much of poetry. I thought I was really cutting loose with this new form, like a Mahler symphony."

When he started writing stories in 1941, he told me he was looking for something; looking for a mentor, so he headed east on his way to Florida to find Ernest Hemingway. "I made it to Miami and then I ran out of money," he said. He got stuck with the same dead-end jobs he always had and continued batting out stories until he hocked his typewriter in Philadelphia and couldn't afford to get it back.

I asked if he'd read John Fante by then. He told me he'd read him when he was nineteen or twenty, but Fante's method of vivid writing and short chapters was hard for him to imitate.

Only when he ran into D.H. Lawrence's "The Prussian Officer" did he get it. "It's about ultimate human cruelty," he told me. He recalled his earliest stories, the ones he'd hand-printed and sent out, always about the same thing: "People mentally fucked up and unhappy, not knowing what to do, how to get out of bed, how to get a job, how not to get a job, how to get through another day."

He recalled working at a job at Coronado Parts Warehouse on Flower and 17th Street. "The job was easy and the boss was not too bad." He went home and wrote "Twenty Tanks From Kasseldown," which was accepted for publication by Black Sun Press in 1946. Henry Miller was the prose editor, but Bukowski didn't like the story. He was learning. Then he wrote a story for a small magazine titled "Matrix." It was about a baseball player who'd been playing baseball "for quite a while. One day he's standing in the outfield. He's been doing some thinking. The baseball came to him and he just didn't want to catch it. He just stood there. He didn't care. I think it was a pretty good story," he told me, "but I think I could write it better now."

I asked if he'd like it republished. He said no. He was still learning then. He didn't quite have it. Not the way Fante did. Drinking and working tired him out. "I don't think I had so much energy in those days. I didn't put as much into each story. I just pushed them out. I didn't keep carbons. I'm a little bit calmer now. It gives me a chance to put more feeling . . . I don't want to say false feeling, that can happen, too." He knew he was getting there. He put in the time, but the stories weren't jumping off the page.

He recalled writing another story called "The Itch To Scribble." But he told me he still didn't have it. He said he was learning how not to write a short story. What he needed was to learn about THE FEMALE.

He was between women at the time and laughing a lot about his busted relationships. He told me how Lisa Williams tried to hold onto him by taking pills, by trying to overdose. "I had to reach down her throat and she had these false teeth. I pulled out the teeth." He was laughing. The blood, the pills, the vomit, the false teeth. "You need those smoking hot cunts that drive you crazy, that keep you up all night drinking and screaming at the moon. That's when you learn . . . but first let me tell you how *not* to write a short story."

He talked about all the early work that had disappeared into the trash. "They were full of complaints. I wanted too much too fast, and I was weeping in the wind. The unrecognized artist shit. 'THE WORLD SHOULD KNOW THAT I HAVE THIS GIFT.'"

We drove to his place on Carlton Way.

He asked what I was working on. I told him about a story I was writing about Vietnam. He turned up his nose. It was after 2:00 a.m. We drank more beer and there was a knock on the door. It was Cupcakes and her friend, Georgia. Cupcakes needed some money.

Cupcakes, Bukowski told me, had been Miss Pussycat Theatre a few years back. She was the kind of woman who drove him crazy and moved him to his typer. Georgia was the ugliest woman I ever met. Cupcakes grabbed a twenty, then split with Georgia. Bukowski joked they were headed to the Time Motel. He liked the name. He said his neighbor, Sam the Whorehouse Man, worked there at night. They were all in his stories, he told me. That was the way it worked. You needed materials you could work with, even if they looked like Georgia and Sam and Neeli Cherry (later Cherkovski), with that tic of his that twisted his head around whenever he got flustered. Like the people in Celine; but they had to be fictionalized.

Cupcakes went off, wobbling on her high heels, smoking a cigarette. Bukowski waved at her through the window. "See, that's what you need. A woman like that."

"How about Jane?"

"Jane was worse." He told me about Jane. About Jane and Baldy and about Jane and all the other guys he'd caught her with. He asked me if I ever caught my wife in bed with another man. I told him one day I came home early from work, and she was lying in the bed stark naked when she should have been at work, but I never found the guy. Maybe there was none. Maybe she just came home sick. Bukowski laughed. "Sure," he said. "There was a guy, and maybe he fell out the window and broke his back." He remembered the apartment on Doheny. It was on the second floor. He told me I should use that, but make it ten times worse; first drink some beer and then get it all down like a blues singer crying about his lost love, but make it funny; that was the thing.

"Use pain," he said. "Let it all in." He told me when he was struggling writing stories it just got worse and worse. He had to stop. He had to take in all the pain and let it settle like grounds in bitter coffee. He said one day he got up and threw all his stories away, settling down to a ten-year drunk. He really didn't care then whether he lived or died. He said he lived on a candy bar a day. I'd heard that story many times; how he'd hocked his typer in Philly and started over with his stories.

He told me it was women who make men write. He knew that woman, Camilla, had really put her hooks in John Fante. He told me to look for a woman who was really hot but not too smart, like Cupcakes. I said I had my eye on a few. He wanted to know who. I mentioned Kate Braverman, one of the most beautiful, talented, and exciting women I'd met.

Bukowski was aware of her. He'd read her work, but he told me she was too smart, and she was Jewish. Jewish women always put him off. He told me a woman like Kate Braverman could really make a man crazy, but he thought she'd pack it all away in her own poetry and fiction. I argued it was possible for two people to take away materials from one experience. He told me I'd be better off writing about my wife. "Just write real stuff."

I decided to try out his suggestions. I gave up writing poetry reviews. I walked across town and got myself a job at the *Free Press* as special arts editor. I checked out Braverman, followed her around for a while and began reading poetry at the Alley Cat. And I wrote a few stories.

A few months after my drinking with Bukowski, Kate Braverman called me. She asked if I'd do a reading with her at the George Sand Book Store in Westwood. We'd read in tandem, just the two of us. She suggested we read all our Europe poems. When the reading was over I spoke with the owner, Charlotte Gusay. She had a question for me: Did I know Clayton Eshleman? I laughed and told her no, I'd never met him. She had a letter to show me written by Clayton. It was about Charles Bukowski. Charlotte had written Eshleman to ask about Charles Bukowski. Would he be a good reader? Eshleman thought not. Bukowski was unpredictable, he said. He could be violent. He was boorish and crude. Eshleman neglected to mention that Bukowski was getting from $500 to $1,000 up front for each reading and the rooms were always packed.

I was amused. Bukowski and Eshleman had the same publisher. I asked Charlotte if I could photocopy the letter. I told her I was Bukowski's authorized biographer. That was true at that time. She gave me the letter. I called Bukowski and read what Eshleman had written. I thought it would give him a laugh. It didn't. He was angry. He wanted a copy of the letter. Over and over he'd told me he was the locomotive pulling the Black Sparrow train. "I have to deal with these fucking poets cutting my balls off behind my back." I took him a copy of the letter and handed it over personally. He bought me three pitchers of beer.

A few weeks later Bukowski was brimming over with joy. He told me Eshleman had been John Martin's house guest for the weekend. "Martin asked him when he got there if he'd been saying anything about me. Cursing me out. Eshleman denied it. Then he asked him again at dinner." Bukowski was smiling. He loved stories like this.

"John asked him the same question a few more times. 'Have you been saying anything bad about Bukowski?' Clayton said, 'No.' He loved Bukowski. Bukowski was great. And then he showed him the letter to Charlotte Gusay, owner of the George Sand Book Store."

By this time Bukowski's voice was animated. He told me Eshleman just stood there stunned. He didn't know what to say. He was caught in a flat-footed lie. Bukowski laughed his evil laugh. Ah Ha Ha Ha Ha Ha. He'd finally caught one of his backstabbers with his pants down. He reminded me about the letter Eshleman had written to the *Times*, "The Cult Lint."

"See," he said, "what did I tell you?"

A short time later I heard from Charlotte. She wasn't too pleased, but she did see the humor in the situation. Eshleman had called her. He was furious. She'd given him my number. Then Eshleman called me. He could hardly contain his rage. Why did I give his letter to Bukowski? I told him I didn't. I gave him a copy. He could read between the lines. All those poetry wars were still going on in Eshleman's little head, but for me events were merely comical. I laughed in his face and reminded him about his attack on Ferlinghetti. He was irate and he wanted his letter back.

I'd returned from France a week early; my wife was with a new boyfriend on the Tiburon peninsula off S.F. My daughter was at home and gave me the number in Tiburon. Shortly after, my wife filed for divorce. At first I was angry and then I was glad.

I told Bukowski the latest about my wife. "Now you have a novel," he told me.

I told him I'd rather write short stories. He said to "beware of overabundance; too many lines. The unsaid things can be much more powerful than the said." He told me not to feel sorry for myself. I said I just felt sorry for my daughter; she was in the middle.

Since I had him on a subject he never talked about, I asked WHO Bukowski wrote for. He told me "D.H. Lawrence said 'Art for my sake.' Let's just say I'm getting the poison out. It helps me survive."

But we were both still laughing about Clayton Eshleman.

It still makes me smile when I think of the expression Eshleman must have had on his face when John Martin read that letter.

As for Kate Braverman, she went on to write four fine novels and several volumes of poetry. I did an interview with her for the *L.A. Times* about poetry, of course, when she was thinking about having a baby. I met the guy. His name was Rubin something. They never married, but she had a lovely daughter. I was glad for her. She was still very beautiful, but as Bukowski told me, she was too smart for me.

Hustler published my first commercial story in their July 1978 issue: "Even the Kings in Their Winter Palaces," fiction about a Vietnamese father who carried the head of his dead son from Quang Tri to Hue. Bukowski thought it was a good story and it all turned out okay.

Portfolio I Leaf One

My Blue Sweater

Your blue sweater that you left
with me for the winter
when my husband came back from Algiers
when I put it on had your smell
the smell of you when we last made love
in Grenoble
for nine hours and you never came
and I came 400 times
till the neighbors banged on the walls.

Your blue sweater
I'd wear on the balcony in the spring
when the sun came back
without panties on
or anything — just your blue sweater
and the smell of you as you stayed
on me sooooo long. That husband's gone.

Your blue sweater —
sometimes I used to put it on in the summer when I sweat—
"I'll never wash the smell out," I told myself
and that friend of yours Ted would come by
and eat me like an ice cream cone
his head under your blue sweater
as I looked out from my balcony
knowing you'll never return.

Still — your blue sweater
alllowed me finally to move on
to a new man — a doctor
who collects mushrooms in the Vercour.
I let him wash out all your smell
when he moved in
and the blue dye ran
into my underwear
and bedsheets
and your blue sweater shrank —

But there are nights when my husband's on call
and alone with my thoughts
I put it on again and feel the hole
in the elbow
where you once were
in your blue sweater.

Photograph by Marcy Mendelson   *Poem by Ben Pleasants*

CODA

There were two events in my life that changed my view about writing forever. One was my longtime friendship with Charles Bukowski that stretched over the entire landscape of Southern California and still fills my mind with amusing, outrageous and uncensored lived life. The other was the short and warm relationship I had with John Fante, mostly at his home on Point Dume in the presence of his wife.

In the late Seventies and early Eighties I was writing profiles for the *Los Angles Times* on writers I thought were overlooked by the provincial critics of New York City. I convinced my editor, Art Seidenbaum, to take a new look at John Fante's work through the eyes of his greatest fan, Charles Bukowski. That must have been in the end of 1977, when I wrote Bukowski a letter (December 13, 1977) suggesting "the idea of issuing a John Fante Reader." Fante was an obsession with Bukowski and I had caught the disease.

A few months before, after discussing Fante on tape and the phone, Bukowski wrote me a letter defining the role Fante's novel *Ask the Dust* had played on his writing. It was dated October 4, 1977. I was suggesting we campaign to get Fante's work republished.

"I never said it was important to rescue Fante," he wrote back." I only know of the effect he had on me as a writer."

On December 18, 1978 I began a series of interviews with Fante and his wife. When I told Bukowski Fante was blind and legless, that he lived mostly in his mind, Bukowski was even more reticent "to bother him." Still, he wanted to know everything about John Fante. Could I find out who Camilla was? What was his relationship to H.L. Mencken? What was his house like? Did he have a family? Were there any unpublished works?

Finally, on December 10, 1979, while conducting an hour long interview at the Fante house in Malibu, I brought up Bukowski's name. I had spoken to Lawrence Ferlinghetti about republishing *Ask the Dust*. Fante was worried about hospital bills and I thought City Lights might pay him more money than Black Sparrow, but I was in over my head. I knew nothing about agents and book publishers and advances and world rights, but I was trying. I should have left it all to the professionals.

Fante trusted me. No one was doing anything for him anyway. My profile on Fante's life and work had run in the *LA Times Book Review* earlier that year (July 8, 1979) and it had caused a stir. I had written

John Fante and Ben Pleasants, 1979.

to several writers about Fante's condition and many of them, like Budd Schulberg, wrote back suggestions.

It was one of the happiest times of my life. I was doing what every critic dreams of: resurrecting a neglected masterpiece! It was then I mentioned Charles Bukowski to John Fante and his wife. I told them Bukowski was a figure known around the world, though he was not yet famous in America. I said Bukowski was John Fante's biggest fan.

His favorite novel was *Ask the Dust*. What I said is down on tape. Here's a snippet:

"I asked Bukowski, after I read *Ask the Dust* . . . will you do an introduction?

His name is very hot right now and . . . it would get (*Ask the Dust*) immediately into France and Germany. He (Bukowski) said he would love to do it."

Fante and his wife thought that was a fine idea, but they had never heard of Bukowski. I had to spell his name. Fante wondered why Bukowski was ignored in America. I mentioned his Nazi past. I told Fante "That's just a pure case of a group of people sitting down and saying we don't want this guy to be . . . read. The Bukowski book Ferlinghetti published at City Lights has sold more than a quarter of a million." It was not the whole story, but I didn't have the heart to tell Fante that his biggest fan had told me "I love the Jews and I love the Nazis." Maybe I'll tell him when I'm dead.

Next time I came, I brought John Fante a copy of *Factotum*. Joyce, his wife, read him parts of it. Fante thought it was a fine book, worthy of Hamsun.

That was the beginning. I mentioned Bukowski's speculation on what had become of his hero, John Fante.

"I understand he went Hollywood, and it's hard for me to know why he did it. He seemed to have so much, but maybe he just got tired. Maybe he wanted to drive a new car. Maybe he fell in love with a whore who stripped his spiritual chances. I don't know."

"That's pretty close," John Fante replied.

There was a huge silence. HOLLYWOOD, the forbidden subject, was on the table. It was like mentioning brain cancer. I had opened up a wound. Had Hollywood destroyed John Fante, as Bukowski suggested? I had no idea. I hadn't said a word, but the damage was done.

When I next met Bukowski, I suggested that John Fante had gone to Hollywood to feed his family. He was no Knut Hamsun, no Celine, no Charles Bukowski. He had four kids and a wife he loved.

But I was on shaky ground.

Then there was my push with City Lights. I had already written to St. Martin's Press and they had turned me down flat. The friend I had there had recently lost his job. A New York publisher *did* pay advances, but I mentioned that City Lights was paying Bukowski 75% of royalties on *Erections*. That's what Bukowski told me.

Joyce Fante liked the looks of *Factotum* in the Black Sparrow Edition. She asked what kind of advance John Martin would pay? I said probably nothing. When Ferlinghetti got the photocopy of *Ask the Dust*, he wrote me back to say he could see what Bukowski liked in the Fante novel, but it wasn't his kind of book. Not for City Lights and the Beat Generation. I understood.

Black Sparrow picked up Fante and the rest is history. Me too.

I had played my part and it was over. When John Fante died in May of 1983, Bukowski and I moved on. By 1984, Bukowski had become a sensation. He was saluted by *Rolling Stone* and The Rolling Stones. He was on his way to immortality.

It saddened me to see the way Bukowski savaged his childhood friends in *Ham on Rye*, and beat up on the women who cared about him in *Women*, but writers will be writers and Bukowski, to my mind, was fast becoming the Prussian Officer.

In the Eighties Bukowski and I both took dangerous chances: he savaged Hollywood and I defended the idea of a Palestinian State. I had known Alex Odeh when I was at Shriners Hospital. Alex was helping injured Arab children get medical care in America through the Shriners, who are an international philanthropic organization. Odeh was also the founder of the Arab-American Anti-Discrimination Committee. I told Bukowski what I was doing and he was amused. He reminded me he had been an "appointed Muslim" while he worked at the L.A. Post Office and he added that politics is a lot more dangerous than literature. But I persisted.

After a hopeless struggle with the *L.A. Times Book Review* who would do NOTHING on Palestinian rights, I spoke with my old friend Digby Diehl, then book editor at the *L.A. Herald Examiner*. Digby gave me the chance to review Noam Chomsky's book, *The Fateful Triangle*, a powerful work on Israel, the U.S., and the Palestinians. It was published in the summer of 1984. According to Christopher Hitchens in his book of essays *Prepared for the Worst*, my review was one of only two published in major presses in the entire U.S. Hitchens wrote:

"In Los Angles Chomsky has an admirer who is also a local book reviewer. He prevails after a struggle." I sent the review on to Bukowski with copies of Chomsky's letters. In the first one, dated April 15, 1984, Chomsky wrote:

"I'll be curious to see if you can get the book reviewed in the *L.A. Times.* I doubt it." In the second, date July 16, 1984, Noam Chomsky thanked me for the review in the *Herald,* adding:

"I'm writing to Mr. Diehl, thanking him for his efforts, which surely took considerable courage."

Chomsky went on to say: "For the record, this is the first review in the U.S. press, to my knowledge, apart from the *Boston Globe*, where, I was informed, a review appeared over the objections of the book review editor after direct intervention of the editor-in-chief, whom I had known from the peace movement days . . ." Bukowski responded over the phone. He said he was impressed. I told him I was amazed that a book by a such distinguished American writer as Chomsky on a subject so important as the Middle East, could be shot down by special interests who acted as censors!

"The safe Creeleys," Bukowski laughed. "You don't back down, Ben. Even when it costs you."

"You either," I said. "You were a good teacher."

That was true, Nazi or not. By 1984 Charles Bukowski had reached a world audience without the help of a single major American publication, unless you include *Hustler*.

And he was right about politics being dangerous. On October 11, 1985, Alex Odeh was murdered by a pipe bomb while opening the door to his office in Santa Ana, California. I never worked for the *L.A. Times* again.

Bukowski and I rarely saw each other after that. When he asked me to attend the opening of his movie *Barfly* in 1987, I told him I'd show if I could find a date.

"Same old Ben," he said. He knew I wouldn't make it.

"Hollywood," was all I could add.

"Yeah, Ben. It killed John Fante and it will kill us all."

I knew what he meant. I said I was still working on my Bukowski book. He told me to write what I wanted and I did! Enough said.

Books by SUN DOG PRESS

Steve Richmond, *Santa Monica Poems*

Steve Richmond, *Hitler Painted Roses*
(Foreword by Charles Bukowski and afterword by Mike Daily)

Steve Richmond, *Spinning Off Bukowski*

Neeli Cherkovski, *Elegy for Bob Kaufman*

Randall Garrison, *Lust in America*

Billy Childish, *Notebooks of a Naked Youth*

Dan Fante, *Chump Change*

Robert Steven Rhine, *My Brain Escapes Me*

Fernanda Pivano, *Charles Bukowski: Laughing With the Gods*

Howard Bone with Daniel Waldron, *Side Show: My Life with Geeks, Freaks & Vagabonds in the Carny Trade*

Jean-François Duval, *Bukowski and the Beats*

Dan Fante, *A gin-pissing-raw-meat-dual-carburetor-V8-son-of-a-bitch from Los Angeles*

David Calonne, Editor, *Charles Bukowski, Sunlight Here I Am: Interviews and Encounters, 1963-1993*